D0941468

Accelerating Development

The Necessity and the Means

McGRAW-HILL SERIES IN INTERNATIONAL DEVELOPMENT

Advisory Board

E. Gordon Alderfer
Murray D. Bryce
Milton J. Esman
John M. Weir

Alderfer · *Local Government in Developing Countries*
Benjamin · *Higher Education in the American Republics*
Brannen and Hodgson · *Overseas Management*
Bryce · *Industrial Development: A Guide for Accelerating Economic Growth*
Bryce · *Policies and Methods for Industrial Development*
Currie · *Accelerating Development: The Necessity and the Means*
Davenport · *Financing the Small Manufacturer in Developing Countries*
David · *International Resources in Clinical Psychology*
David · *International Trends in Mental Health*
Dunn · *International Handbook of Advertising*
Eicher and Witt · *Agriculture in Economic Development*
Ettinger · *International Handbook of Management*
Fryer · *World Economic Development*
Harbison and Myers · *Education, Manpower, and Economic Growth: Strategies of Human Resource Development*
Harbison and Myers · *Manpower and Education: Country Studies in Economic Development*
Meier · *Developmental Planning*
Montgomery and Siffin · *Approaches to Development: Politics, Administration and Change*
Powelson · *Latin America: Today's Economic and Social Revolution*
Reidy · *Strategy for the Americas*
Reimann and Wigglesworth · *The Challenge of International Finance*
Singer · *International Development: Growth and Change*
Staley and Morse · *Modern Small Industry for Developing Countries*
Thut and Adams · *Educational Patterns in Contemporary Societies*
Walinsky · *The Planning and Execution of Economic Development: A Nontechnical Guide for Policy Makers and Administrators*

Accelerating Development

The Necessity and the Means

Lauchlin Currie, Ph.D.

Professor, National University of Colombia
Director, Foundation for the Progress of Colombia

McGraw-Hill Book Company
New York London Sydney Toronto

ACCELERATING DEVELOPMENT:
THE NECESSITY AND THE MEANS

 Library of Congress Catalog Card Number 65-21573

14921

To Jacob Viner

A Great Economist and Teacher

The difficulty lies not in the new ideas,
but in escaping from the old ones
which ramify, for those brought up as
most of us have been, into every corner
of our minds.

—J. M. Keynes

Preface

ANOTHER BOOK on development? The only excuse for adding to the outpouring of the past fifteen years is that the problem unfortunately still awaits solution. Despite the borrowing of some $30 billion, it cannot yet be claimed that any of the underdeveloped countries has gained assured control of the economic environment in terms of acceptable levels of well-being of the masses, in terms of a sufficient fall in the birthrate, or in terms of insight into the functioning or malfunctioning of the economic system.

The solution proposed here draws heavily on various episodes in the history of developed countries—the fall in the birthrate experienced by all developed countries with a rise in well-being and education, the remedies now generally accepted for mass unemployment, the astounding latent productive possibilities brought to light by the efforts to meet wartime goals, the continuing and accumulative effect of investment in the reconstruction of Western Europe after World War II.

These and other lessons are applied to underdeveloped countries in the selection of economic and social goals, in the diagnosis of the problem, and in the attack suggested. In the present war on the development front, the enemy is the poverty of the masses that has its roots in many causes, chief among them being massive unemployment, though disguised, and growing inequality. This poverty, largely rural, in turn gives rise to a self-perpetuating sequence of ignorance, excessively high birthrates, continuing disguised unemployment, and poverty again.

To break this vicious circle once and for all and to replace it by a beneficent sequence require a massive concentration of effort for which the most relevant precedents can be found in World War II and the Marshall Plan. Hence the name of the attack proposed herein—The Breakthrough Plan.

A prerequisite for a breakthrough on the development front is a thoroughgoing change in the approach to the problem on the part of the United States government and the various international agencies. They are now fighting and losing a tremendous war in a lackadaisical and absent-minded fashion, not even knowing who the enemy is, being distracted by a host of feints on many fronts, and committing their reserves in a piecemeal fashion. Meanwhile the enemy grows more numerous daily. There are no general staff, no clearly defined objectives, no coordination, and no strategy other than an indiscriminate sprinkling of good works.

The international agencies have lived so long with the problem that they have themselves become apathetic and appear to have lost a sense of urgency or a conviction that time is fast running out and millions of people are being condemned unnecessarily to live in misery.

Still another prerequisite is a little economic statesmanship in the international trade field. It is almost a truism of elementary economics that it is impossible for all countries to increase exports and decrease imports at one and the same time and, indeed, disastrous to try. Nevertheless, this is what governments of developed countries are actually trying to do. Apparently economic statesmanship still stops at the frontier.

It is true that economics in the United States does not seem to be so important as it was thirty years ago, for many of the most urgent problems appear to be having a solution. But economists should be concerned with people in general rather than only with Americans or British. Actually, in terms of mass and growing poverty and misery, economists are confronted with the greatest challenge and responsibility in the history of our subject. The suffering and the unemployment in the depths of the Great Depression were nothing as compared with the magnitude and difficulty of the problems facing two-thirds of the people today. These problems cannot be swept under a rug and forgotten. Last year 63 million people were added to the world's population, most of them in poor families in poor countries.

So I would venture to suggest that while economics was never so important as now, the economists are not giving a clear lead to public opinion and to the governments of developed countries, to say nothing of the harassed and infinitely less well-equipped governments of underdeveloped countries.

I have tried to write for both professional economists and laymen, a venture which is always difficult and hazardous. The nonprofessional, in particular, may not always appreciate the novelty of the points of view expressed or the somewhat controversial nature of my treatment. Therefore I would strongly urge such readers to couple a reading of this book with that of a more conventional approach, of which there are many. This juxtaposition will naturally be done in more advanced courses on development. Perhaps the most controversial theme of all is that of agrarian policy, which is central to the argument of the book and which cannot be straddled. This is an issue on which emotions run high and on which all people concerned with development must sooner or later take their stand on either one of diametrically opposed sides. The decision will in turn determine attitudes on a number of other matters.

In 1953, after directing five economic and public administration studies in Colombia, I retired to indulge in a long ungratified desire to raise purebred Holstein cattle. Although I built up the highest yielding herd in the country and enjoyed the work, Dr. Virgilio Barco, then Minister of Public Works, persuaded me in 1959 to do just one more study as director of the Robert Nathan Mission. This was a mission organized to study the problems that would emerge following the opening of one of the last railroads to be built in the world, the Atlantic Railroad, which had resulted from an earlier recommendation of mine. It was a fateful decision, as once again I became interested in economic problems and deeply concerned over trends that had developed since I was last active in the field. A series of studies followed for the Foundation for the Progress of Colombia, intermixed with conferences and seminars, and finally resulted in the present work. I hope Dr. Barco has had no occasion to regret the outcome of his persuasive powers.

The other person who must bear some particular responsibility for this work is Dr. Alberto Lleras Camargo, President of Colombia from 1958 to 1962. It was his offers of the directorship of the National Planning Office in 1960 and of membership on the Planning Council in 1961—both of which I had to decline because of other commitments—that started me thinking again of national development problems.

In 1961 President Lleras authorized Dr. Barco, who was on his way to represent Colombia at the Court of St. James, and me to proceed to Washington for the purpose of trying out the basic ideas of what I then called Operation Colombia on a group of distinguished economists, including, among others, Gerhard Colm, E. M. Bernstein, Robert Nathan, Walter Salant, and Emile Despres. I am grateful for their friendly and constructive comments which encouraged me to continue.

Since sensitivity to criticism is characteristic of people of developing countries and since what I have written will undoubtedly sound critical to them and particularly to Colombians, let me hasten to add that I have been a citizen of a developing country—Colombia—since 1958, which I trust gives me the right to say "we." Moreover, I hope I have been critical only for the purpose of being constructive.

Albert Berry and Murray D. Bryce read the first draft of the manuscript and made helpful criticisms and suggestions.

My secretaries Señoras Celia de Cardoso and Alicia de Tellez labored long and painstakingly on this work and on the many studies on which it is based. Continually meeting deadlines can be exhausting, I know.

Finally, I must thank all those in Colombia—too many to mention individually by name—who by their support encouraged me to think more boldly than I otherwise would have dared on the necessity and the means of accelerating development.

Lauchlin Currie

Contents

PART ONE

A General Statement

CHAPTER 1

Introduction

In the past fifteen years, development economics has become a new and exciting field of study. Many institutes and advanced schools have been founded; all developing countries are deluged with missions and specialists of all kinds; books, articles, and reports appear daily; and there is probably not a day in the year when a meeting or convention of development experts is not in progress somewhere.

And yet, with all this intense interest and activity, the results have been disappointing. In capitalist economies, the spectacular upsurges have taken place in Western Europe and Japan. Progress in most developing countries has been discouragingly slow and has barely counterbalanced the population explosion. The first enthusiasm for development in Latin America is in danger of petering out in recriminations, with the Northern economists blaming the disappointing results on local cultural lags and deficiencies, and the articulate groups in developing countries pointing to worsening terms of trade and inadequate financial assistance. Perhaps the time has come for a little healthy soul-searching.

It is possible to study the problem of development from various aspects. The first is to consider how and why growth begins. The second, which has occupied the economic historians, is to explain the degree of growth that has occurred—a historical and analytical exercise. A third, which has interested many writers, is to search for a consistent pattern of growth that will fit many diverse cases. In this third approach, it is probably hoped that one of the many growth models will in turn lead to *the* theory of growth. A fourth procedure is to inquire why growth has not proceeded more rapidly—that is, to carry out what I refer to here as the diagnosis of the problem. The fifth—and the main preoccupation of this book—is to consider how to accelerate the rate of growth or, as I prefer to put it, how to go about deliberately and consciously raising the degree of well-being.

All are defensible ways of treating the theme, and yet it is not difficult to see that a broad gulf separates the first three approaches from the last two. The first three are best treated with detachment: the less one's emotions are involved, the better the probable result. The last two almost necessarily are motivated by value judgments, and the more strongly one feels, the more inventive he is likely to be and the less he is likely to be daunted by obstacles. I do not believe this means that one must in any way abjure a scientific attitude in dealing with the last two approaches. It does mean, however, that one is trying to utilize his knowledge of economics and related fields in the solution of the problem of enhancing human welfare. In this sense the last two approaches are pragmatic instead of detached or historical. One is concerned not so much to explain as to show how something may be achieved.

For some reason I have never been able to understand, the first three approaches are regarded by many economists as being more "scientific" and hence of a higher category of merit than the last two. In reality, diagnosing a current problem correctly would seem to be a more difficult and challenging task than analyzing a problem in the past when most of the relevant data are missing. Suggesting ways and means to improve the functioning of the economic system always seems to arouse the most intense opposition on the part of an economist's academic colleagues. While few economists would care to defend the existing system in all its details, they tend to react like laymen instead of objective scientists when changes are proposed. Perhaps the justification of this attitude can be found in the probability that most proposed changes would impair rather than improve the functioning of the system. But it remains true that the functioning *can* be improved, and presumably economists are the ones who are best qualified to propose changes to this end.

This book has as its background not only my experience in wrestling with the overall mass unemployment problems that confronted the New Deal from 1934 to 1940, but also my studies of national, regional, agricultural, and industrial problems in Colombia. These culminated in an outline submitted to the Colombian government in 1961 designed to provide a crash program for accelerating development. The moment could not have been worse chosen. Technicians of ECLA (the United Nations Economic Commission for Latin America) had just produced their program for Colombia, and it had been adopted by the government. In addition, the Alliance for Progress was being launched, agrarian reform legislation was in passage, and Colombia had joined LAFTA (the Latin American Free Trade Association). In the rosy excitement of that year, with its accompanying thunderous oratory and screaming headlines, my suggestions appeared not only inept but totally uncalled for. Even further study along those lines was not believed necessary. But now that the bloom has departed from all these roses, there may be more willingness to consider alternatives.

The discussion in this book is directed primarily toward economic planning. It is designed to narrow the widening gap between the "pure" theorists working on theoretical problems related to growth and development and the programmers working on specific national programs in quantitative terms. I have used familiar concepts—disguised unemployment, factor immobility, imperfect competition, and so on—and have incorporated certain direct types of controls not customarily regarded as suitable instruments of programming, in order to work out a rational and consistent plan of accelerated development for a group of countries possessing certain characteristics. Whatever novelty the plan has lies in the combination of its elements. It therefore runs the risk of being dismissed by the growth theorist as lacking originality and by the programmers as being too advanced or extreme to be practicable. I can only take this risk and plead that a change in emphasis is necessary.

The convictions which have shaped my approach can be briefly indicated:

1. I am doubtful that there is such a thing as development economics. I am inclined to believe that there is only economics and that what we call development economics is the application of economic theory to particular problems. Excellently trained Northern economists often assume that many of the themes they are concerned with do not apply to developing countries—that, for example, land tenancy reform would be ridiculous in the United States but quite proper and desirable for developing countries, that an incomes policy[1] is necessary for advanced economies but not for developing ones, and so on. According to my view, it is not the theory but the environment that is in many respects different. Dealing with the problems of developing areas is basically a process of applying our regular tools of analysis to special cases.

Neither is this a theory of growth. It is directed toward two problems: the necessity and the possible means of accelerating development—or, better, of quickly achieving a higher level of well-being in a group of countries in a certain stage of development. It follows that I also question the utility of attempting to develop a "theory" of growth, although I do this in full awareness that some of the best minds in economics have been engaged in the task for the past fifteen years.

2. I do not believe that there is a ready-made program which can be applied indiscriminately to a variety of countries with a variety of cultural, social, and economic conditions. Each country poses peculiar problems, and these problems compel a program tailor-made for the country. While this book was greatly influenced by Colombian conditions, so that there may appear to be an inconsistency with the previous sentence, I believe the general approach can be applied, with suitable modifications for each country, to a certain group of nonsocialist, intermediate developing countries which have the following characteristics: an infrastructure of

[1] I.e., a policy based on the idea that the state has a vital interest in the process of income determination of the various factors of production.

transport and public services; an industrial base and an entrepreneurial class; a large portion of their people in agriculture; resources which, if efficiently exploited, would permit a high standard of living; and sufficient actual or potential exports to finance a period of accelerated development. In this hemisphere, countries that might fall into this category include Mexico, Colombia, Peru, Chile, Brazil, and, to a lesser degree, Argentina (with a smaller proportion in agriculture) and Venezuela (with very large revenues from oil).[2] The same approach might be applicable to many other countries, but this could be determined only by detailed studies that I have not been in a position to make.

3. My interest is definitely pragmatic. I am concerned not with the question of how growth begins, which is the preoccupation of that excellent and stimulating book, *Theory of Social Change* by Everett Hagen, but rather with the problem of how to make the transition from an under-developed or developing to a developed country. In achieving this transition, the Art of Getting Things Done is as difficult as, or more difficult than, the art of planning. It requires practical knowledge of motivations and capabilities and a fine judgment of feasibilities. One must be an idealistic politician as well as a scientific practitioner of economics—admittedly an unusual blend of qualities.

In my observation of a single country, it is only the man or mission with money to lend or give that has much chance of accomplishing something, and this only as a part of the conditions of the loan or gift. I do not deny that one may encounter genuine reform governments, such as that of Muñoz Marin in Puerto Rico, but these cases appear to be rare. Missions that have only advice to offer are usually completely disregarded. It may also be noted that the spectacular advances in Western Germany, Italy, and Japan owed nothing to foreign advice.

Throughout the past decade, the International Bank has been in the strongest position to influence policies in developing countries. By and large, however, it has restricted its influence to establishing conditions for specific loans, such as insisting on better-prepared projects or on rises in tariffs of power or transport companies. Its tremendous potentialities for guiding national policies have gone unused. This may or may not have been a good thing, depending on one's estimate of how that guidance might have been exerted. In any case, the natural consequence was that the operations staff of the bank developed at the expense of the economics staff. An economics staff was an ornament that a wealthy institution natu-

[2] There may be some question whether Venezuela should be listed as an under-developed country, since it has enjoyed an exceptionally rapid rate of growth and the standard of living is relatively high. Yet there is great inequality, and the country is confronted with many of the problems commonly associated with developing countries.

rally had to have, but was not to be taken too seriously. Therefore, until recently, at least, the bank actually was not interested in or well equipped to play a decisive role in national programming.

Similarly, other American and international agencies have in general not attracted or held outstanding economists in the field of national planning, and certainly not in the numbers required to gain profound insights into the nature of the individual countries' problems. And the large number of economists attracted to the foundations, institutes, and schools for advanced study in development problems have probably devoted too much of their time to searching for generalized statements in a field which is still relatively new and where the problems are essentially specialized. Whatever the explanation, few Latin American economies have received prolonged analysis by outstanding economists who also understand something of the Art of Getting Things Done.

4. To deal pragmatically with the problem of development, it is absolutely essential to understand and take into account the impact of cultural forces on economic development and programming. Disregard of cultural realities has been a pervasive factor in the failure of United States policy to have a greater impact on development, and this regard has led to much needless recrimination and ill will. There are frequently different ways of attaining the same objective, and the one should be chosen that is most in accord with the customs or culture of the country. The Colombians, for example, are prone to compromise, to avoid conflicts on principles, and to improvise in economic matters. All this may be irritating and frustrating to a Northern economist; nevertheless it forms part of the milieu in which he must work, if his work is to be fruitful. The need to adapt to cultural forces accounts for various features of the present approach that Northern economists might consider unnecessarily complicated or excessively restrictive of individual freedom of action.

5. Generally, to achieve a desired effect, there must be a concentration of effort. The diffusion of effort by a host of international agencies in a small, relatively unimportant country like Colombia has been unbelievable. If one tried to wage a war with such diffusion of responsibility and dispersion of effort, the result would be calamitous. The result in Colombia has naturally been disappointing. Good intentions, teams, committees, and lots of money are still not effective substitutes for straight thinking and individual responsibility.

6. The words "development" and "growth" are too well entrenched to be replaced, and yet they suffer from vagueness and ambiguity. I am inclined to let the distinction between developed and developing countries turn on the degree to which the countries appear, in the happy phrase of W. Arthur Lewis, to be in control of their economic environment.

An essential element of such control is the attainment of a modest rate of population growth not by an excessive death rate, but by a relatively low birthrate. By this test, neither Mexico nor Venezuela can be said to have attained sure control of their economic environment. Jacob Viner points out that the benefits of the industrial revolution of the eighteenth and nineteenth centuries began to be felt by the masses only after 1870, when their own birthrate began to fall.[3]

I believe our main concern as economists should be the abolition or amelioration of dire poverty, which in turn means that our goals and criteria of success should relate to the well-being of the poorest sections of the community. Only in this way can control of environment be attained, with its assurance of self-generating development. As is apparent by now, I am quite frankly an advocate, although I hope my advocacy is a disciplined one. In other words, I heartily subscribe to Joan Robinson's definition of economics as "a branch of ethics striving to become a science."[4]

7. There is the regrettable fuzziness of the words "planning," "policy formulation," and "programming." The tendency is for programming to become strictly quantitative. This, in turn, has led to emphasis on quantitative relationships to the neglect of theory and qualitative considerations. The process can be seen clearly in an excellent book, *Programming Techniques,* written by a group of experts for the United Nations and published in 1960. While making many important observations on planning, this work has a tendency to reduce planning to programming—as when, in discussing the imponderables that enter into the judgment of individual projects, it says, "If they are therefore to be included as elements in programming, they should be assigned some estimated values; otherwise, they cannot form part of the programming models which are worked out in quantitative terms."[5] While the authors were referring to projects, their remarks apply equally to qualitative considerations in general. I shall argue that while programming is essential, over and above it must be planning—the choice of objectives, the diagnosis of problems, and the strategy of the attack on the problems to achieve the objectives. However, I shall continue to use the words "plan" and "program" interchangeably, because it appears hopeless to try to redefine their meanings at this late date.

8. Finally, the policy program suggested here has some aspects of a crash program. It has appeared to me that conditions have been deteriorat-

[3] "The United States as a Welfare State," in Edgar Edwards (ed.), *The Nation's Economic Objectives,* The University of Chicago Press for Rice University, Chicago, 1964, p. 154.

[4] *Economic Philosophy,* Aldine Publishing Co., Chicago, 1962.

[5] *Programming Techniques for Economic Development,* E/C.N., 11/535, 1960, p. 34.

ing in large sectors of Latin American economies and that drastic measures are called for to reverse trends.

Rightly or wrongly (rightly, I think), the Americans believe they have vital interests at stake in accelerating development and lessening inequality in developing countries, and they believe this so strongly that they are prepared to give and loan sizable amounts of money in pursuing these objectives. Nevertheless, it is curious that they have made no real effort to diagnose the situation in each country or to study the problem of how the maximum result can be achieved with the very limited sums available. Possibly the explanation is to be found in the extreme sensitivity in the United States to charges of imperialism. In any case, we are presented with the strange spectacle of a country embarking on a large and costly spending program which is not based on any specific economic program other than delegated powers to spend and a general indiscriminate sprinkling of grants and loans for a variety of unrelated projects scattered among many countries.

With his usual perspicacity, Viner wrote:

> Aid, moreover, is not and will not be granted with the sole consideration of supporting or promoting growth. It will be given to countries whose growth rate exceeds ours, and it will be given to countries which are not enjoying any per capita growth at all. It will be given as a reward for merit and effort and also in the hope of bringing merit and effort into existence. It will be given to friend and to foe, for strategic reasons and political reasons, in submission to blackmail and as bribe, and out of sheer humanity without any other genuine reason.[6]

This indiscriminate spending (one can hardly call it a program) is intermingled with Peace Corps activities, disposal of surplus goods, technical assistance from various bodies, and loans from the International Bank, Interamerican Bank, Export-Import Bank, the IMF (International Monetary Fund), the IFC (International Finance Corporation), European countries, and private groups. Meanwhile, borrowing capacity is being used up, debt-paying capacity remains generally unchanged, inequality is increasing, and even the rate of growth in gross product exceeds by very little the rate of population growth.

These are some of the convictions that underlie my approach to development. On specific points, both in the diagnosis and in the remedy, I may have been too influenced by my Colombian background. If so, I hope that economists in other countries will give attention to the main thesis and apply the modifications necessary for their different conditions.

I have made no attempt to cover the vast literature on development and growth. Certain authors and books have been singled out for comment

[6] Jacob Viner, "Economic Foreign Policy on the New Frontier," *Foreign Affairs*, July, 1961, p. 14 of an offprint.

not necessarily because of their contributions or importance but because I happened to be familiar with them and because they illustrate different points of view or appear pertinent to the argument. If I have failed to give credit to writers who have earlier made the same points I make, I can only apologize and assure them that such omissions were inadvertent.

Part One, which I hope is more or less applicable to a group of countries, is concerned with the necessity and means of acceleration. Part Two is an attempt, for expository purposes, to apply the approach to a single country—Colombia. While it appeared desirable to separate the general treatment from the specific application, this procedure unavoidably entails some overlapping. I can only hope that if a reader is interested in the general approach, he may wish to see how it might apply to a representative country of the group.

Although I have tried to write this book simply so that it can be read by the intelligent layman, there is actually a good deal of theory involved, and some elements of it have novel aspects. Therefore, I must warn the general reader that he will encounter quite difficult and controversial arguments. The important and difficult thing at this moment is to try to reach agreement on the basic problems. Later, actual programming to implement planning will be the easiest part of the task.

A Note on Saving-Investment Terminology

In certain cases, terms used by economists have acquired specialized connotations different from the same terms in popular use. Since this is particularly true of Keynesian terminology, I shall make a heroic attempt to present the main features of this terminology in the following paragraphs.

All the costs of production appear, after double accounting is eliminated, as somebody's income. The total of all the individual sums representing the value added by all the factors of production is equal to the gross value of all the goods and services produced, after the inclusion of government salaries and adjustment for the net foreign balance. Gross production can be divided, even if arbitrarily, into the value of goods produced and sold to final consumers in a period ("consumption") and those not so sold ("investment"). But the value of goods produced and not so sold to final consumers is equal to that part of income that is not spent on consumption, or is "saved." Hence, by definition, national investment is automatically and always equal to national saving. In this terminology,

Gross National Income = Gross National Product
= Consumption + Investment + Government Expenditures on goods and services

Saving = Income − Consumption
= Value of goods produced but not sold to consumers
= Investment, or Capital Formation

This has become standard terminology since the publication of J. M. Keynes' *General Theory of Employment* in 1936. The extension of the concepts of saving and investment to government accounts has complicated the original simplicity of the Keynesian concepts. R. F. Harrod in 1939 and E. D. Domar in 1946 added the concepts of the relation of incremental investment to additional output in a real sense, as well as the relation between the accumulated stock of capital and output or income. Hence the terminology was adapted for the treatment of development problems.

Throughout this book the above terms will be used in their Keynesian sense. I do not think this will occasion much difficulty for the general reader except in Chapter 9.

CHAPTER 2

The Objectives of a Development Plan

THE OBJECTIVE OF a national economic program is frequently assumed to be self-evident but, as I hope to show here, it is by no means so. In fact, an absence of careful thinking in working out the diagnosis and setting explicit goals is probably the basic reason for the inadequacy of many programs.

The Punta del Este Document (Alliance for Progress) is open to the criticism of setting too many goals, confusing means and ends, and containing a diagnosis so general as to be of little value. Of course, it was not intended to be a program but rather a general statement of aspirations and possible measures. It is explicit, however, in stating that at least one goal should be the attainment of a minimum growth in per capita gross product of 2½ percent per annum.

A rare phenomenon has arisen in recent years with the passage of the economist's rather abstract and technical terms into popular usage. Anybody with any pretension to economic sophistication now talks glibly of the gross national product, national income, income and consumption per capita, and investment and saving (in the economist's sense). Elections are being fought in terms of percentage points in the growth of the GNP. Weighty editorials are written comparing one country's performance favorably or unfavorably with others in this respect. The newer jargon of input-output analysis, capital-output ratios, and macro- and microeconomics has not yet reached the layman, but we may be confident that it soon will.

From one point of view, this is all to the good, because it focuses attention on highly important concepts and probably makes it easier for the laymen to understand the economist, and for the economist to exert more influence on policy. At the same time, however, it places more responsibility on the economist, and it becomes his duty to caution the layman on the misuse and limitations of these concepts and statistical data, as well as to point out their usefulness in certain connections.

The GNP is, in theory, the value of all the goods and services produced in a year in a country. Since all this value accrues to people as income, it also is the gross national income. All government expenditures on goods and services (but not "transfer" expenditures) are included in production and income. Adjustment is made for foreign transactions. The gross value of all goods produced and services performed is a simple concept and an important one. The difficulties and dangers arise in the attempt to measure this value—and in its identification with economic welfare or well-being, the basic concern of economics.[1]

Regarding measurement, one has only to recall the extreme poorness of data in developing countries, especially on agricultural production, to appreciate the very approximate nature of data on large segments of the economy. The estimate of the value of the production of the self-employed is generally what economists call an educated guess. Again, little reliable information is available on contraband foreign trade and fluctuations in its volume.

Another approximation is involved in moving from value in money terms to the concept of real or physical production, and from there to real production and consumption per capita. The first step is accomplished by "deflating" a rise in the value of total production by the rise in prices. But this introduces the problem of what price index to use as a deflator. Ideally the price index should be one of all goods and services, weighted by their relative value importance in the total. But the relative importance of any category changes. Hence, over a period of years, any constant price index becomes more and more inappropriate as a deflator to obtain *real* changes in the value of production. On the other hand, the use of a constantly adjusted index would give a better basis for comparisons from year to year, but would not be an accurate deflator over a longer period. Oskar Morgenstern has rendered an outstanding service in pointing out the pitfalls in handling statistical data even in highly developed economies, especially for such aggregates as the GNP.[2]

In short, the inadequacy of the basic data, and the technical difficulties inherent in converting changes in values to changes in real terms, make it dangerous to endow figures of GNP in developing countries with too great accuracy and significance. Frequently, changes in methodology in calculating the GNP result in very substantial revisions in past series. In these circumstances, one should not read too much into changes of a few percentage points in the GNP.

An even worse abuse of the figures is made in international comparisons,

[1] For a brief discussion of some of the conceptual difficulties, see Thomas F. Dernburg and Duncan M. McDougall, *Macro-Economics,* McGraw-Hill Book Company, New York, 1960, pp. 34–49.

[2] *On the Accuracy of Economic Observations,* Princeton University Press, Princeton, N.J., 1963.

which are violently affected by more or less arbitrary changes in the rates of exchange and by the varying composition of different standards of living. It is a moot question whether such comparisons may not be more misleading than helpful.

In cold countries, the tremendous annual expenditure just to keep warm enters into and increases the production and incomes per capita. No offset, of course, is made for this in comparisons with incomes of countries that do not need to make such expenditures.

However, it is in the implicit or unconscious identification of changes in national product per capita with changes in average well-being that the greatest danger lies. A rise in national income per capita is, under certain conditions, perfectly compatible with a decline in national well-being.[3] An average may conceal grave and increasing inequalities. The figures themselves make no judgments. A very large sum unwisely spent is accorded the same investment value as an equal sum wisely spent. An increase in the income of the few wealthy people or of the urban workers may more than compensate for a decline in the income of the many rural people, but who can doubt that in such circumstances there has been a decline in average national well-being?

In his excellent book *The Theory of Economic Growth*,[4] W. Arthur Lewis expressly rejects any identity of growth with well-being: "It is possible that output may be growing, and yet that the mass of the people may be becoming poorer" (p. 2). While one may admire the frank and uncompromising nature of this declaration, it does seem that Lewis involves himself thereby in a certain difficulty. In an appendix, "Is Economic Growth Desirable?" the question is answered affirmatively: "The case for economic growth is that it gives man greater control over his environment . . . it enables him to have greater leisure . . . more services . . . and frees women from being beasts of burden" (pp. 421–422). All this seems to be a justification of economic growth in terms of well-being and makes more puzzling the earlier exclusion of equality or inequality from the theme of growth.

Well-being is an illusive concept defying precise measurement, and economists have never been happy in dealing with it, even though it used to be considered the subject matter of their science. The textbooks in economics generally point out the dangers of identifying well-being with increasing income, and they acknowledge that the conditions under which work is carried on—leisure, diversions, health, and education—are all im-

[3] "If [a country's] population has undergone substantial increase, the numbers of those living at the margin of subsistence or below, illiterate, diseased, undernourished, may have grown steadily consistently with a rise in the average income of the population as a whole." Jacob Viner, *International Trade and Economic Development,* The Free Press of Glencoe, New York, 1950, p. 127.

[4] George Allen & Unwin, Ltd., London, 1955.

portant factors in a state of well-being or standard of living. (More and more, however, the latter term is identified with money or "real" income.) But these elementary observations are thereafter generally forgotten. Even individuals are inclined to lay too much stress on relative money incomes as contrasted with these other factors.

The concept of marginal utility—the additional satisfaction afforded by an additional increment of income—rarely appears or is used only in advanced texts, and yet it is of the utmost importance. Within what an older American economist, Simon Patten, called a "pain economy" (read "underdeveloped economy") a slight addition in income, whether it be in goods, health, or education, may yield infinitely more satisfaction than a large addition in an already wealthy community. Similarly, within a developing society, a small gain for the masses will yield much more satisfaction or well-being than a large gain for the better-to-do classes.

The gross and per capita national product concepts take no account of these considerations. Such relative neglect is probably explained, but not excused, by the intangible character of concepts like marginal utility and well-being and the difficulty of dealing with them in quantitative terms. Economists have tended to salve their consciences by assuming that, while it is not precise or proportional, there is *some* direct relation between income and welfare. They let it go at that, thereafter concentrating on things that can be measured and dealt with in quantitative terms. Thus what should be the basic concern of economists—people and their welfare—has tended to be pushed into the background.[5] To mention the subject of human misery and suffering in the rarefied atmosphere of the quantitative economists is to run the risk of committing a social *faux pas,* or to be regarded suspiciously as a demagogue or worse. Even the term "economics" itself is in danger of being replaced by the terms "macroeconomics" and "microeconomics." In the well-known textbook *Macro-Economics* by Dernburg and McDougall, the word "welfare" does not appear in the index, so it is getting difficult to say what the field which a few years ago was called "economics" is now actually concerned with.

Another term that is being abused is "investment," or capital formation. This, traditionally, has the connotation of an allocation of resources made to secure a higher money or physical return. In order to use Keynesian concepts quantitatively, it has been extended to public expenditures, where "investment" may include army and police establishments, jails, roads, schools, and so on, and "consumption" may include such things as expenditures on maintaining public order.[6] Most of these things are probably

[5] "The method by which the egalitarian element . . . was sterilized was mainly by slipping from *utility* to physical output as the object to be maximized." Joan Robinson, *Economic Philosophy,* Aldine Publishing Co., Chicago, 1962, p. 55.

[6] In the category of capital formation Simon Kuznets includes weapons and military construction (a large figure in the United States), but not expenditures on

desirable or necessary, but they may not add to physical output per capita. Construction of homes—which are really durable consumer goods—is treated as an investment which gives an actual or imputed money income. Money "invested" in a car, however, is generally called consumption.

The extensions of suburbia, and of roads to link suburbia to the urban centers, are all listed as "investments" yielding returns. The terrific costs of individual transit, loss of time, and deterioration of zones between the centers and suburbia do not lend themselves readily to measurement and so are not offset against the "returns" yielded by transit and homes in the suburbs. Also, the constant rises in urban land values enter into rents and hence national income, although this is a reflection of shortage rather than abundance.

There is another source of confusion in the use of the term "investment." It has the older connotation of an expenditure made to obtain a future return. In the Keynesian sense, however, it is that part of the national product that corresponds to saving. An increase in investment has a multiplying effect on the gross national product, *in money terms,* through the propensity to save and the multiplier, though it may have no effect on the national product in *real* terms. The return on the total stock of capital, deflated, has been added to the original Keynesian concepts to permit use of a capital stock–national product ratio in real terms, though this has not in practice done away with the confusion arising from the same term being used in other senses. There is still another use of the word "investment" by laymen which would include the purchase of existing property. The economic implications of the latter use are vastly different from the absorption of labor and materials in the construction of a capital good. The varying connotations of this term have resulted in much confused thinking.

In short, the complaint against the global income concepts is not against their proper use, but against their misuse or overuse. As long as they do not serve as a substitute for straight thinking about the end purpose of economic activity, they have their place. But both economists and opinion-forming groups should always keep in mind the basic limitations of these concepts in dealing with welfare economics. Otherwise, we are in grave danger of permitting the passion for measurement and quantifying to influence and distort our thinking on the nature of welfare.

Few wriers have even discussed the question of objectives or have accepted the objective of growth as measured by gross or per capita national production as something obvious. Henry Bruton places the issue squarely. "Per capita income is chosen as the main measure of growth for two simple reasons: One, almost all writers direct attention to this variable;

---

army pay. *Capital Formation and Economic Growth: A Conference,* Princeton University Press, Princeton, N.J., 1956, p. 20.

two, despite some obvious weaknesses in its use, there does not seem to be a practical alternative."[7]

It is central to the argument of this book that not only are there practical alternatives but that these alternatives are superior. Again, it is a matter of emphasis and interest. If our interest lies in the construction of models of growth or in the elaboration of a theory of growth, we will naturally adopt per capita income as a convenient measuring rod. If our interest, on the other hand, is in abolishing poverty quickly or raising the level of well-being of the lower 30 or 50 percent of the population as quickly as possible, we will find average per capita income unsatisfactory and other measures, such as nonagricultural employment, housing, per capita consumption, and so on, more significant.

A rate of growth in the GNP as an objective of a program for a developing country has the additional disadvantages that it is unknown until it becomes history and that it does not correspond to anything which is in one's experience or which can fire the imagination. It is in reality an end product of a host of variables that make the rate of growth very difficult to program for with any precision. Even in the United States, where excellent statistical data and refined techniques have made it possible to estimate the GNP currently, the preoccupation of the government has been with more specific objectives, such as a reduction in the number of the unemployed, improvement in the balance of payments, resolution of the agricultural problem, housing, transport, social security, and so on.

In recent wars the economic objective became that of producing as large a volume of military supplies as possible with the fewest possible workers, while maintaining tolerable minimum standards for the civilian population. Because of the concentration of effort and the subordination of all objectives to that of production, spectacular results were obtained through intensive use of equipment and nonmilitary human resources. It would seem that much of value for development purposes could be learned from a study of wartime economics.[8]

Governments in most economically developed countries have laid much stress on the reduction of inequality through social security on the one hand and progressive taxation and strict tax collection enforcement on the other. Success in achieving these objectives may not affect average per capita income—indeed, may even lower it—but certainly raises average well-being.

Again, if a country that has already achieved a high and widely diffused

[7] "Contemporary Theorizing on Economic Growth," in Bruton Hoselitz et al. (eds.), *Theories of Economic Growth,* The Free Press of Glencoe, New York, 1960, p. 241. However, he cites Adolph Lowe in Moses Abramovitz (ed.), *Capital Formation and Economic Growth,* Princeton University Press, Princeton, N.J., 1956, pp. 581–635, as an exception.

[8] This point is discussed at some length in Chap. 7.

production of goods and services chooses to enjoy the fruits of further gains in productivity in the form of less work and more play, the growth in per capita income might fall to zero, and "growth" would stop. By identifying growth with welfare, we would in this case arrive at a ridiculous conclusion. Actually, the developed countries have made a choice of more leisure at the expense of production per capita. The economist has not the slightest right to say that the choice is irrational or the economy is stagnating because his objective of growth does not include a five- or four-day week or universal prolonged education (except as a means of increasing production per capita!).

The emphasis on material things rather than things of the spirit has become a leading issue in the wealthiest countries. But it is in services that the rate of return is generally lowest. In recent years, the entire increase in employment in the United States was in services. It may well be that the highest rates of growth as measured by per capita output are only possible in less well-off societies and that the more emphasis is placed on education (as an end in itself), music, travel, and the arts as contrasted with things and gadgets, the lower must be the rate of growth as defined by the quantitative economists. This, again, does not make sense. Another factor that may be found to have a profound influence in the rate of growth of output is the degree of shifting from low- to higher-paid occupations. But in this case, there would be a closer correlation to an increase in well-being.

Because so many objectives have been pursued at the same time, there have naturally occurred contradications and inconsistencies, and compromises have naturally been necessary. A large rise in educational expenditures in a poor country may decrease the growth in production per capita in the short run and increase it in the long run. An increase in agricultural investment and productivity may worsen the condition of large segments of the population and heighten inequality, and so forth.

Two technical papers were presented to the Punta del Este Conference that drafted the Alliance for Progress Declaration—one submitted by the Organization of American States (OAS) and one by the State Department of the United States. Not only do they illustrate the difficulty of saying anything very meaningful in a short paper that applies to nineteen different economies, but they show the confusion that prevails in the matter of objectives. For example, stable prices and changes in land tenancy were listed as objectives in themselves rather than a presumed means to broader objectives. However, both papers listed first (it is not clear whether this was also first in priority) the attainment of a rate of growth of 2½ percent per capita per annum in gross product.

In the case of countries that have a rate of population growth approaching 3 percent, this would call for a rate of increase in the GNP of 5½ percent—a high rate considering the structure of the economies of most developing countries and the generally prevailing difficulties of increasing their exports. The usual means relied upon to achieve this goal will be discussed below. It may be mentioned here, however, that they are generally so remote and hypothetical in their probable effect that there is danger that the "objective" will become valuable solely for propaganda. In other words, to all intents and purposes there will be *no* overriding objective. In its place a number of public entities will follow a number of separate, uncoordinated, and even contradictory programs in pursuit of limited objectives. Thus a developing country that officially can point to an objective of a rate of growth in the gross product per capita of 2.5 percent may actually be drifting along without any comprehensive and coordinated program and without a rigidly enforced system of priorities. The results will probably be disappointing despite a relatively large volume of foreign assistance.

A 4 percent rate of growth in the GNP would be a high absolute rate calling for a great deal of construction and public service activity. Yet where the population is increasing at a 3 percent rate, little increase in even average per capita consumption would result from all this activity, although the effort would give rise to constant headlines and no doubt impress foreign visitors. This struggle to supply the needs of a rapidly growing population probably explains the existence of highly favorable economic reports on countries that in reality, and in terms of per capita consumption or progress toward greater equality, are stagnating.

There appear to be two possible solutions. One is to make a great effort to subordinate all other objectives to the 2½ percent formula by drawing up a truly consistent program that is calculated to (*a*) increase investment from domestic and foreign sources and (*b*) increase the return from new and existing investment along conventional lines by screening projects and establishing and enforcing priorities. For reasons stated above, it is doubtful whether this alternative could be enforced and, if enforced, whether the results would be satisfactory. It would quickly be discovered that countries valued other objectives.

Raymond Frost points out that equal per capita growth rates conceal a "rather grim statistical trick . . . an equal 1½ percent rate of growth would mean $33 per annum for Americans, compared with about 90 cents for Indians . . . the absolute difference between the wealth of the two nations becomes inexorably wider."[9]

A second alternative would be to seek objectives which are more comprehensible, at least to the general public, and design a program to attain them, regardless of the effect on the GNP. If the two or three overriding objectives are chosen wisely, it is probable that the GNP will even rise more rapidly than otherwise. This, however, could be something for the

[9] *The Backward Society,* St Martin's Press, Inc., New York, 1961, pp. 13–14.

statisticians to ascertain later. The adoption of this alternative would provide a means of resolving the problem that especially perplexed the Americans who took part in framing the objectives of the Alliance for Progress: how to reconcile the "economic" objective of achieving a certain rate of growth in the GNP with the "social" objective of achieving a better distribution of income.

The apparent conflict of objectives would not arise if priority were given to a program designed to assure the elements of a minimum tolerable standard of living for, say, the poorer half of the population in terms of the basic necessities of food, clothing, housing, health, primary education, miscellaneous goods, and amusements[10] through (1) the creation of additional job opportunities with sufficiently remunerative income, (2) the provision of certain services by the state, and (3) the strict enforcement of moderately progressive income and inheritance taxes on individuals. Naturally such an objective could not be rigidly enforced; class differences in the standard of living would persist. However, it would provide a criterion, now lacking, by means of which proposals, programs, and policies could be appraised, and it would provide at least an argument against the adoption of policies that would tend to widen existing differences in the standard of living. It would shift the emphasis to employment and consumption.

The choice of objectives immediately influences the diagnosis of the problem and the nature of the program. The objective of a rate of growth in the GNP, as we have seen, tends to subordinate human values to arithmetic. It gives rise to an apparent conflict between economic and social goals; it tends to foster an indifference to inequality or growing inequality, since these conditions may lead to greater saving and investment; and it encourages an equal indifference to the pattern of demand and the types of investment, so long as the latter are "productive." If the value of output per worker is high, this is considered good per se. Thus the manufacture of motor scooters may be favored over handmade furniture, and heavy or what are occasionally called "basic" industries over traditional "light" consumer goods activities. Consumption loses its place as the goal of production, and production and investment themselves become almost the final goals of economic activity. The ideal becomes to cut down on consumption in order to increase investment and production.[11] In this

[10] This objective is close to that of Jacob Viner, though he stated it in a defensive way: "Were I to insist, however, that the reduction of mass poverty be made a crucial test of the realization of economic development, I would be separating myself from the whole body of literature in this field." *Op. cit.*, p. 127. Actually, he did insist on this test in various writings. The latter part of his statement is, I hope, less true today.

[11] "The social tensions of these times have led more than once to the employment of an excessive proportion of these resources [savings] to increase present consumption or to realize social investment of immediate welfare, to the prejudice of

topsy-turvy world, the old idea that investment is a cost which entails sacrifice and which should be kept as low as possible to achieve a given result is no longer respectable.

It nowadays rarely happens that investments in roads or land reclamation projects, for example, are treated as necessary evils, to be done as cheaply as may be consistent with their purpose. Instead they are considered good in themselves. This attitude, of course, applies particularly in the public sector, where projects are turned over to engineers (or thought up by them) without the cost limitations generally imposed by the private investor. It is usually enough to say that a road will "open up" a part of the country or that a land project will permit so many additional acres to be "put into cultivation" for such projects to receive a favorable reception.

Since "investment" traditionally was made to secure a future return, and since the main instrument relied upon by many economists to secure a growth in the production per capita is increased investment, there is apparent a tendency to justify public spending by calling it investment. This is another semantic device to reconcile the conflict which is believed to exist between economic and social goals. If expenditures on schools, hospitals, and even jails and barracks can be called "investment," they cease to become "uneconomic" and become both economically and socially desirable. The expenditures in the Colombian budget are now classified under the headings of "operating," e.g., for the salary of a schoolteacher, and "investment," e.g., for a school. The ideal appears to be to reduce personnel expenditures (often referred to as merely maintaining bureaucrats) and increase investment. Such is the power of semantics.

Fortunately, it was decided to call expenditures on housing "investment" instead of "spending on consumer goods." Doubtless a decision now to change this custom, with a consequent tremendous decline in "investment" and increase in consumption financed by "installment credit," would cause consternation. It is, of course, well understood that home financing encourages saving whereas installment credit encourages one to be extravagant and live beyond one's income. It is fortunate indeed that this semantic hurdle does not stand in the way of the acceptance of my proposed national objective for developing countries, since the attainment of a minimum standard of consumption would require large expenditures on decent housing. On the other hand, housing for poor people often comes perilously close to being classified as for "social" purposes.

---

economic investments for future welfare, thought not very distant. To yield to this pressure would inevitably defeat the attainment of the social objective of raising persistently and strongly the standard of living of the masses." Raul Prebisch, "Towards a Dynamic of Latin American Development," reprinted by Banco Nacional de Comercio Exterior, Mexico, 1963, p. 8. For other references see Chap. 8.

In most developing countries, the poorer segment of the population lives in the rural areas and small towns. Consequently, the emphasis of a national program based on the attainment of a minimum standard of consumption or well-being would be largely concerned with the welfare of this segment, *though not necessarily concerned with improving its welfare where it now happens to be and engaged in what it is now doing.* In the following chapters, an attempt will be made to give specific content to this alternative objective of national economic planning.

For those who still think that the well-being of the poorer segment is too vague to be a national objective, I will anticipate my argument by saying here that it can be expressed in *x* number of additional nonagricultural jobs a year to absorb the addition to the labor force and reduce the actual and disguised unemployment. The achievement of this overriding goal, in turn, calls for other specific objectives.

The usefulness of this objective, the possibility of achieving it, and the nature of the program that would be appropriate depend in part on the diagnosis of the economic situation and potentialities in each developing country. As the OAS working paper at the Punta del Este Conference properly remarked, "Each nation needs a strategy appropriate to its own environment." Nevertheless, I believe that certain generalizations can be made on objectives, diagnoses, and programs to achieve accelerated development that would apply to a sufficient number of developing[12] countries, especially in Latin America, to make such generalizations worthwhile. This will be attempted in the following chapters.

[12] It is difficult to give much precision to the term "underdevelopment" (formerly "backward" or "poverty stricken" and now being replaced by "developing"). As used in the present work, it refers loosely to a group of Latin American countries that offer the possibility of achieving a much higher standard of living for their people, rather than to those countries that have hardly started to develop economically or to others where the population is already pressing on resources, and where a breakthrough probably requires an even more heroic effort than is here suggested.

CHAPTER 3

The Diagnosis of Underdevelopment: A First Approximation

As there is no single cause for being a developing country, there is no diagnosis that would apply to all, and the search for one is probably fruitless. That which comes nearest is a condition of low productivity, but this almost amounts to stating the problem in other words and is hardly a diagnosis. Moreover, it omits the important concept of equality or inequality of incomes. The objective of this chapter is to provide an explanation of conditions that could apply to a certain group of countries. These countries still possess abundant resources in relation to population. They have an entrepreneurial class and an industrial base, an infrastructure of transport and public services, and actual or potential exports adequate to support further industrialization; and yet they are characterized by a relatively slow growth in income and consumption and by great inequality in the distribution of these and a high rate of growth in population.

Even for this relatively small group of countries, so many explanations are offered that it is difficult to gain perspective and separate the primary causes from the derivative ones. As a first approach to the problem, I have found it helpful to think of the different situation of my forebears when they settled in a rocky, forested part of Nova Scotia two hundred years ago. The Indians were hostile, the growing season was about three months of the year, and the winter was abnormally long. Add to these unfavorable conditions the facts that they brought with them few capital goods and little technical knowledge, and that there were no programs of foreign loans or technical assistance and little foreign trade, and the problem appears almost insuperable. And yet in a generation or so, they created for themselves a high standard of living in terms of food, clothing, shelter, health, and education. It is instructive to study this example and those of French Canada and Ontario because conditions in these areas were much less favorable than in New England. In the light of our problems today, the achievement appears almost unbelievable.

In accounting for it, four factors appear to be of major importance. The first was an abundance of natural resources in relation to the population. The second might be called a cultural inheritance of work and foresight—the awareness, from prehistoric times, that you prepared for the winter or you died—which dominated economic activity. The third was a basic equality in income. The fourth was the existence of an economy simple and understandable in its structure and functioning.

The initial capital was small—a few implements and utensils, seeds, and domestic animals. Thereafter, the growth of capital, mostly buildings, boats, and livestock, resulted from the combination of work, foresight, and natural resources. The simplicity of the economy and the equality of income made it easy for all to grasp the relation between work, income, and consumption, between "investment" and future returns. The work may not have been very productive in comparison with the possibilities of today, but it was for oneself and not for the lord of the manor. One could rather easily weigh the benefits of specialization—of exchanging the product of one's labor for that of another—against the less efficient but possibly more advantageous utilization of resources that would otherwise be idle or less productively used. (An example would be the choice between cutting wood and exchanging it for boots, or making the boots yourself less efficiently during the long winter.) On the other hand, things like guns and gunpowder obviously had to be gained by trade, and things had to be made and grown that the merchants of Halifax would accept. As in the present developing countries, the birthrate was high. One big difference was the simplicity and inexpensiveness of the infrastructure, and the healthfulness compensated in part for the costs imposed by the long winter.

We may now return to our original question. Why, with all the benefits of science and invention, and with great aid and investment programs, are the developing countries, even in the relatively favored group we are here studying, finding it so difficult to achieve the minimum standards won by the early settlers in Canada? In Mexico, Colombia, Peru, Brazil, and other countries, millions and millions of country people are on a bare subsistence basis, practically outside the money economy, with a standard of living in basic essentials lower than that we have just been considering.

In terms of the four major factors mentioned earlier, the natural resources of the countries under discussion are certainly sufficient for a decent minimum standard of living. It is true that the large size of a population in itself necessitates expenditures (wells and privies, for example, are not acceptable in cities), but up to a certain point, largeness permits economies of scale. Moreover, as we have seen from our example, large stocks of accumulated or imported capital are not necessary for the attainment of a decent minimum standard. A great portion of the elements of such a standard can be created internally (housing, food, clothing, furniture and miscellaneous goods, beer, and tobacco, health, and education), though if advantage is to be taken of modern techniques, import requirements of specialized machinery must be larger. Even here, it may pay to use country resources less efficiently (say by protecting an industry) if the alternative is nonutilization of such resources.[1]

It is in the other three factors that significant differences appear—the little work that is actually done, the complexity of the economy with concomitant lack of understanding of its functioning, and the gross and widening inequality.

Where half the population is engaged in growing food and fibers for the other half, despite the coexistence of mechanized, technical farming, one may be sure that the work of the bulk of the rural people is of such little economic value that we would be justified in calling them unemployed, at least in an economic sense. Where their condition differs from the Canadian subsistence farmers described above is in diet, housing, health, and education. To stay alive without work is not difficult in a tropical or semitropical country. On the other hand, the incidence of intestinal parasites and amoebas is very high, and these lower not only initiative but resistance to other diseases.

A combination of factors brings about wide and growing inequality. A very small minority has a monopoly of education and skills, and these people intermarry and exercise great influence. Poor public administration, inadequate tax enforcement, and chronic inflation conspire to make these wealthy property holders still wealthier. This group in turn has attempted to make its peace with the organized urban workers by providing relatively high fringe benefits in the labor laws and by granting frequent wage advances and extralegal benefits which are not difficult to pass along to the consumer. Thus there are two types of inequality: the traditional one between the propertied classes and the workers, and the newer one between the organized workers on the one hand and the self-employed and casual laborers—mostly rural people—on the other.

The importance of the distribution of income in developing countries is not always fully appreciated. It is difficult to cite statistics on this inequality. However, Carl S. Shoup et al.[2] estimated that in Venezuela the 43 percent of the population that is rural earned 10 percent of the income and that members of independent professions averaged 80,000 Bs (around

[1] Compare our boot-making example above. This argument is strongly presented by Sidney Dell in *Trade Blocs and Common Markets,* Constable & Co., Ltd., London, 1963, pp. 162–163.

[2] *The Fiscal System of Venezuela,* The Johns Hopkins Press, Baltimore, 1959.

US$24,000) and petroleum workers 20,000 Bs (US$6,000), as contrasted with an average of 900 Bs. (US$270) earned by agriculturalists (Shoup, pp. 24–26). The authors conclude: "Given the very low income and inheritance taxes in Venezuela, these inequalities in ownership can be perpetuated and perhaps even intensified, in a way that is hardly possible in countries with much more severe taxation" (p. 32). Milton Taylor et al.[3] arrived at a similar conclusion in Colombia for the distribution of income within the labor force. For 1961 it was estimated that the lowest quartile of the labor force received 5 percent of the income while the upper quartile received 65 percent.

Gross inequality is usually deplored because it offends one's concepts of social justice. Occasionally it is defended as encouraging saving. It is doubtless true that much of the saving is done by the wealthy, especially in a country with an inadequately enforced progressive income tax system. But it is also true in the countries under discussion that great inequality in income leads to great inequality in consumption. Well-to-do Latin Americans do travel a lot, and their children are educated abroad for at least part of the time. Their houses are usually luxurious, and they all have one or two cars and the full complement of other consumer durable goods. They have an abundance of servants. The socially expensive pattern of suburban living and individual driving to work, and the consequent necessity of devoting more and more of the scanty national savings to urban roads, is already apparent. In short, the pattern of effective demand is strongly affected, or one might say distorted, by wide and growing inequality in income. A good part of the labor of the community is for a new lord of the manor. His effective demand leads to the diversion of investment to dacron plants, while millions may have scanty clothing of native cotton; to the import or local assembly of cars, while public buses are unbelievably overcrowded. Hundreds of thousands with very poor housing are engaged in constructing costly homes for a relative few. If any thought is given to this, it is defended as providing work. The "money veil" prevents its full significance from being grasped.

Inequality of income has other harmful effects. In the absence of quantitative restrictions on foreign exchange, it leads to excessive imports of luxury goods (in relation to available exchange resources), to heavy personal expenditures abroad, to the export of capital as a measure of caution or prudence, and to a large business in contraband.[4] On balance, it would

[3] *Fiscal Survey of Colombia,* published for the Joint Tax Program by the Johns Hopkins Press, Baltimore, 1965, p. 2. This excellent study arrived too late for me to use it as extensively as I otherwise would have liked to do.

[4] An interesting argument made by William McGreevey in an as yet unpublished Ph.D. thesis, Massachusetts Institute of Technology, 1965, "The Development of Colombia," is that for a long period in Colombian history the growing of tobacco, a plantation crop, led to great inequality, luxury consumption abroad, and little

appear that developing countries pay a heavy and generally unrecognized price for the savings of the wealthy.

The second form of inequality—that between the organized city worker and the self-employed countryman—likewise has its effect on the pattern of demand, though of course to much less degree. This type of inequality is harmful more in dampening down the rate of growth in demand for goods of mass consumption and in preventing the benefits of growing efficiency in manufacturing from being shared in any way by the self-employed rural portion of the population.

In developed countries, the contribution to continuing unemployment made by "wage inflation" resulting from strongly organized unions in industries that do not have much difficulty in passing along increases in costs has long been recognized, and the concept has recently been extended to other incomes. It has not been generally appreciated[5] that this phenomenon has its counterpart in developing countries. There it slows up industrialization and obstructs mobility of labor by causing demand, production, and employment opportunities to be less than they otherwise would be.[6]

This type of inequality has some curious results in encouraging overmechanization in industry and undermechanization in agriculture. For example, at a certain point in the rise of white-collar workers' salaries, it will "pay" to install costly imported office machinery. If earnings had risen more in line with the overall growth in productivity, it would not have paid, and the exchange resources could have been spent on other things. The displacement of workers by machines often makes little sense from an overall national point of view if human resources are inadequately utilized. The machine may merely add to the disguised unemployment. Similarly, the low rural earnings delay the point when it pays to use

---

accompanying industrial development, and that toward the end of the nineteenth century the introduction of coffee, a small man's crop, ushered in the transition to development. Whether or not this actually was the explanation, it is a logically defensible point of view despite the fact that a plantation crop could theoretically give rise to more savings than a small-peasant-holding crop. The point might be made of pre-Civil War cultivation in the United States in both the South and the North.

[5] But see R. S. Eckaus, "The Factor Proportions Problem in Underdeveloped Areas," *American Economic Review*, 1955, pp. 539–565. Also Jan Tinbergen, *The Design of Development*, Johns Hopkins Press, Baltimore, 1958, discussed below in Chap. 9. The existence of a much higher level of wages in industry in developing countries was recognized by Gunnar Myrdal, but instead of examining the implications for the growth of effective demand, he cited this as a justification for even higher customs protection. *Economic Theory and Underdeveloped Regions*, University Paperbacks ed., Methuen & Co., Ltd., London, 1957, p. 95.

[6] It may be objected that by widening the spread between incomes, wage inflation encourages mobility. True, it does make mobility more desirable, but it does not create more jobs, and country people cannot offer their labor at a cheaper rate in organized industries.

more and better machinery. Thus this type of inequality also distorts the pattern of demand and the allocation of investment resources.

Another consequence of intense poverty combined with great inequality can be readily seen in the bitterness and resentment involved in wage negotiations and labor relations. Demands have little to do with the value of the work performed or prevailing incomes of the disguised unemployed. Negotiations are conducted by the union leaders in terms of "equity" or "justice" (the poor versus the rich), and the basis of comparison is the highest wages paid (in Venezuela and Colombia, by the foreign oil companies). Foreign companies are special targets because they are foreign, they are fearful of their public relations, and their foreign personnel live so obviously at a far higher standard of living than the workers.

Where it is possible to meet union demands by rises in prices, this is done. In other cases, it may prove possible to contract the work out to small operators who can disregard the Labor Code and resist any attempts at unionization. In the case of a foreign firm in Colombia needing a supply of cut logs, it was found that the cost of acquiring them by purchase from smaller operators was one-fifth the cost of direct cutting by the company. The explanation lay almost entirely in wage rates and fringe benefits. In fields where the system of contracting can be employed, it is very difficult for companies guaranteeing steady employment at much higher levels of remuneration to compete. The small contractor, frequently working with his men, apparently escapes the resentment directed at large employers. By and large, however, industrialization results in larger units, unionization, and less opportunity for subcontracting, so that the areas of wage or cost inflation may be expected to grow as industrialization proceeds.

The persistence of small artisan shops, particularly in the metalworking and woodworking trades, has often been deplored by foreign writers. Such shops are, however, a natural consequence of wage inflation in the organized and presumably more "technical" companies in these fields. It has been alleged that small contractors exploit their men. But they can hardly be blamed for the low standard of living set by the disguised unemployed, and in reality their activities are helping to raise the general standard of living more than those that secure a relatively high wage for the few at the expense of more unemployment for the many.

In the kind of economies described here, one must constantly be on one's guard against an implicit and unwarranted assumption that the factors of production are fully employed in accordance with a pattern of demand and an allocation of resources that make sense, viewed as a rational and well-functioning economic organism. It is surprising how much of our reasoning must be modified when this assumption does not hold.

As has been frequently noted, it is a characteristic of the type of underdeveloped countries under discussion that they combine simple subsistence economies with highly complicated money economies. In a pure subsistence economy with basic equality and abundant resources, the knowledge of how the economy functions is easy to acquire but is really not very necessary. In the hybrid economies, the functioning is complex and yet vitally important to understand. The combination of impatience, readiness to resort to direct action, and hasty intervention constantly creates problems that economists in developed countries rarely have to take cognizance of, at least to the same degree.

For many years there has been little understanding of the problems created by monoexportations, by the fewness of industrial units, and by highly complicated provisions of the labor laws. It is common to raise wages by decree or to engage in inflationary actions and at the same time freeze prices; to push up income tax rates and yet grant more exemptions "to encourage industrialization." There is abundant faith that credit expansion restricted to "productive" uses cannot be inflationary; the concepts of a relatively small volume of national saving and the consequent necessity of the establishment of strict priorities are completely absent; public "investment" in any amount is "good"; borrowing abroad for any purpose on any terms is permissible and indeed desirable. Sometimes import licenses are refused because of the existence of excess capacity; at other times they are granted to encourage competition. There is almost no understanding of the incidence of taxation. Big, costly, more roundabout and time-consuming works frequently are favored over a multitude of small investments yielding quick and high returns.

The consequence of widespread economic illiteracy in an already complicated economy is inevitably the adoption of mistaken policies. Neither the traditional forces of competition, freely moving price systems, and factor mobility work satisfactorily, nor does the system of improvised intervention. Policies are uncritically taken over from developed countries without study of whether the conditions in the developing country differ in kind and degree. Extravagantly generous social security benefits for a few and nothing but charity for the many is an example. The application of agricultural support prices when there are no adequate statistical data or administrative machinery is another. The payment for mistaken policies and ill-conceived intervention must be a slower rate of growth than would otherwise be attainable.

It is difficult to disentangle cultural factors from lack of economic understanding. However, there appears to be some basis for characterizing the culture of the group of countries under discussion as being more individualistic than that of most developed countries. In these developing areas, people's dedication to causes outside the welfare of their family group is mostly restricted to the religious. People do not readily distinguish true reforms from blatant demagoguery, palliatives from basic solutions. Ideas are things to play with, not live by. Old-style oratory, with the trembling voice and flailing arms, still flourishes. The term "economist" is used lightly—it can and often does apply to engineers, newspaper writers, lawyers, and people who had had only undergraduate training in economics. Consequently, the views of economists are accorded little respect. The handful of foreign-trained academic economists is perhaps naturally tempted to take refuge in a remote world of analytic geometry, calculus, algebra, linear programming, and, of course, macroeconomics, that has little to do with welfare. As a result, their influence on policy has been slight.

In recent years, swarms of foreign missions—the modern missionaries with their diverse prescriptions for economic salvation—have been added to the babel of voices and counsels. Despite some recent efforts at coordination, the diverse foreign lending agencies go their own ways. Debt is piled up without reference to an overall program or to debt-saving capacity.

How, in this atmosphere, can a careful diagnosis and a coordinated, comprehensive national economic plan based on that diagnosis be developed to achieve certain goals? If such a program is worked out, how can effective, and above all persistent, execution be ensured? These questions would have been irrelevant in my case of the early settlers. They are of paramount importance and difficulty in the developing countries of today. The combination of economic illiteracy and various cultural characteristics in complex economies must be included in the answer to the question "Why is the standard of living so low for so many people in countries with great natural advantages?"

Still another element is the rapid rate of growth in population which, when projected, raises truly frightening prospects. Unfortunately, this question has been discussed too often in terms of food and hunger rather than of a decent general standard of living. While undoubtedly hunger and dietary deficiencies exist in the type of countries in question, these result more from ignorance and faulty distribution of buying power than from population pressing on natural resources. The more serious problem is the drag on development imposed by a 3 percent annual growth rate in population in an already poor country. A large proportion of savings, investment, and imports must be devoted to meeting the needs of the *additional* people rather than to raising the productivity and the standard of living of the *existing* population. This can be clearly seen in the case of municipal services of water, sewers, electricity, streets, and so on. It would also apply to the necessary additional equipment to make the basic consumer goods for the additional population, although a compensating factor, up to a point, would be the attainment of greater economies of scale.

A sudden cessation of population growth would, of course, create certain problems of adjustment in demand within various industries, especially agriculture. However, deficiencies are so great that a pause in the population growth would afford an invaluable breathing spell. For the time being, the real problem caused by population growth lies in the drag it imposes on a rise in the standard of living in items other than foodstuffs. This drag makes it more difficult to break the vicious circle of poverty—poor health—ignorance—high birthrate—poverty.[7] John Sheahan points out that a rapid rate of increase in the working force makes the automatic allocation of labor resources easier.[8] This suggests that in the hypothetical case of no growth, greater deliberate efforts would be called for to secure an actual change in occupations.

The explanation for a country being underdeveloped and experiencing an excessively slow rate of development with the gains very unevenly distributed is obviously complex. However, for countries with the conditions we have assumed, it will be argued that the basic causes are lack of economic understanding and various cultural characteristics.[9] These in turn lead to gross inequality with harmful effects not only on well-being but on development itself. They foster imperfect competition, lack of mobility and a faulty working of the price system, an excessive rate of population growth, faulty utilization and allocation of physical resources, and shocking underutilization of human resources. In other words, the problem is man-made and can be resolved. This may sound like tautology; I do not believe it is. One sometimes gets the impression that there are things outside the developing countries' control—such as the worsening terms of trade, or the population explosion in conjunction with too limited resources—that make the problem of accelerating development unsolvable for the countries concerned. It is worthwhile, therefore, to insist that for many countries the problem is at least *capable* of solution, though it is extraordinarily difficult.

But, while lack of economic understanding and various cultural patterns may be the reasons why the problem of development has not been solved by some potentially rich countries, these factors are only the most fundamental parts of the problem. I have touched on some other parts (inequality, for example) in this chapter. The following chapter will discuss others, though I shall repeatedly return to the subject of inequality of incomes, wealth, and opportunity.

[7] This supremely important vicious circle is accorded more extensive treatment in chap. 6.

[8] *Promotion and Control of Industry in Post War France,* Harvard University Press, Cambridge, Mass., 1963, p. 13.

[9] It is interesting that another writer profoundly influenced by his experience in Colombia, Albert O. Hirschman, stresses an analogous point: "Our diagnosis is simply that countries fail to take advantage of their development potential because, for reasons largely related to their image of change, they find it difficult to take the decisions needed for development in the required number and at the required speed." *The Strategy of Economic Development,* Yale University Press., New Haven, Conn., 1958, p. 25.

CHAPTER 4

The Diagnosis of Underdevelopment in More Detail

The Agrarian Problem

Northern economists are prone to understand by the agrarian problem in developed countries something entirely distinct from the problem in developing countries. In the first group, there is coming to be general agreement that the problem shows itself in overproduction, surpluses, production controls, farm price and income supports, dumping in international markets, and protection of home markets—in short, in excessive resources devoted to one form of economic activity. The root causes are found in a great acceleration of agricultural technification and mechanization, especially since the Second World War. The increase in agricultural physical productivity has outstripped that of many industries.

Thus in almost all advanced capitalist countries, we are treated to the economically ludicrous spectacle of the adoption of measures to accelerate productivity in agriculture still further, while at the same time other policies are adopted to deprive consumers of the benefits of this productivity in the form of lower prices. But this pursuit of apparently contradictory policies is not as ludicrous as it first appears, because in conditions of inelastic demand, price and income adjustments can bring in their train great individual suffering. Insofar as the present policies may be said to have a rationale, it is that the number of excess farmers is relatively small, and the cost of keeping up their incomes by producing unsalable goods, or by not producing, is at least financially bearable as an income equalization policy. Further, the number of farmers will continue to decline, both absolutely and relatively, so that in time the problem will be solved and we will have the benefits of the growth in physical productivity without too much agricultural production.

The flaw in this rationale is that if the policy of income equalization is really successful, the incentive to move out of agriculture is greatly diminished. One faces the possibility of indefinitely holding back production and supporting people in an activity which is not economically justified. It is as though the state deliberately created and sustained some characteristics of monopoly in agriculture. Later I will discuss the grave effect of these policies on developing countries. Here, however, the point of discussing the agrarian problem in developed countries is to insist that *it likewise applies to many developing countries.*

Easy generalizations about hunger, dietary deficiencies, great landed estates and peons, etc., have led some Northern economists to believe that the nature of the agrarian problem is completely different in developing countries. In these countries, the economists believe, the problem is not inadequate agricultural incomes but inadequate agricultural production, an entirely different thing. There is an implication that production is inadequate because of the inexcusable perversity, laziness, or indifference of the great landed proprietors, spending half their time as playboys in France. Therefore it seems that the remedy is to expropriate these idle lands, settle peasants on them, and in this way increase both agricultural incomes and agricultural production. Everybody gains and nobody loses except, justly, the Bad Wolves.

This version of the agrarian problem in Latin America has gained wide credence in economic professional circles and undoubtedly influenced the thinking leading to the Alliance for Progress program.[1] It has its roots in the glorification of the Free Land of the American West, in the Mexican Land Revolution, in the alleged Peruvian "Forty Families," in the publications of FAO (the Food and Agriculture Organization of the United Nations) emphasizing hunger and inadequate food production. When there is no longer any need to study the soundness of an economic explanation because it is accepted as self-evident, a hearing for any other explanation is extraordinarily difficult to obtain.

Instead of making an assertion to the contrary, therefore, let us first *suppose* that the nature of the agrarian problem is essentially the same in many developing countries as in all developed ones. Production is too high in terms of effective demand; agricultural incomes are too low; there is competition between the mechanized and efficient farmer on the one hand and the marginal farmer on marginal land and in uneconomic-sized holdings on the other; support prices and even dumping are necessary. In short, there is too much land under cultivation, there are too many people dedicated to agriculture, and their average income is too low.

[1] See Paul Prebisch, "Towards a Dynamic of Latin American Development," reprinted by Banco Nacional de Comercio Exterior, Mexico, 1963, and Gunnar Myrdal, *Economic Theory and Underdeveloped Regions,* Methuen & Co., Ltd., London, 1957, p. 81.

If this hypothesis should happen to apply, as I hope to show later that it does in at least one developing country which I believe is representative of a group, something like a revolution in our thinking is called for. If, for example, the agrarian problem is essentially the same in developing countries as in developed ones, then it makes little sense to try to get back to the ideal of the Quarter Section for All, to pour more resources and manpower into agriculture, to mechanize and technify, and to extend support prices and equalization payments *for half the population.* Since price support and income equalization payments to apply to half the population are obviously out of the question, the consequence of increasing agricultural production faster than the growth in effective demand can only be generalized and intensified poverty. Either most people will retreat to subsistence farming, or there will be a wholesale migration to cities. In the absence of a job program, such a migration would merely transfer the unemployed to different sites.

In other words, if the hypothesis is correct, then the agrarian problem is different from its counterpart in developed countries only in its magnitude, in the frightening numbers of people involved, and in the different nature of the solutions the politicians can adopt (i.e., support prices and income equalization payments are out of the question in developing countries). If the United States government, Western European countries, and various international agencies really think it important to aid the development of the type of countries under discussion, surely they should devote a little study to the nature of the agrarian problem rather than assuming that production is too low.

If, for example, it should be found that hunger or poor diet had their roots in gross inequality and a faulty distribution of buying power, that the dietary deficiencies were concentrated mostly among rural people themselves, and that the cause did not lie in deficient overall agricultural production relative to effective demand, a fresh start might be made in determining the source of lack of buying power. The first unsophisticated reaction would doubtless be to propose an extension of subsistence farming, only better. Those hardy perennials, "the diversification of agriculture" and the idea of growing things for the farmers' own use, would be resurrected. But thereafter, it would not be too much to expect that a few better-trained or more thoughtful persons would begin to ask themselves whether a considerably generalized increase in agricultural production on the part of 30 to 60 percent of the people can possibly be a desirable solution. And at that point, analogies from developed economies would begin to come to mind.

It is doubtless theoretically possible for 50 percent of the people to withdraw from specialization and interchange and to provide for their own needs, as in early Canada and New England; but in the tropics the health, the knowledge, and the ambition are lacking. People want things they cannot produce even if they have to steal them. Anyway, a way of life that made sense two centuries ago does not make sense today when people *know* there are tractors and easy and efficient ways of producing things. Subsistence homesteading, usually proposed by city people and intellectuals, only expresses their wish to hide and forget the problem, like sweeping dirt under a rug.

Raymond Frost cites the excessive parcellation of land in the Far East as the greatest single obstacle to technification and mechanization.[2] Yet this policy is being deliberately adopted by Latin American countries with the blessing and urging of the United States, because it is easier than finding ways to utilize labor not needed in agriculture.

Those who still picture the agriculture of developing areas as all primitive would do well to examine a few copies of a magazine published in Kansas in Spanish and called *Agricultura de las Americas.* Apparently, equipment manufacturers find it worthwhile to advertise their latest products extensively throughout Latin America. The technical revolution is definitely on the way, and only misguided policies, shortage of exchange, and the desperate competition of colonial-type farmers can slow it.

Some Implications of the Agrarian Problem

If we assume that in many developing economies the agricultural technical revolution is under way and that relatively few farmers on relatively little land can now or will shortly be able to supply all the needs at a price that will pay, what are the implications for small farmers and for the economy as a whole?

Turning to developed economies again, we can see that the technical advances will permit relatively lower prices if they are proceeding at a rate faster than other items in the price index, and that, given the relative inelasticity of demand for foodstuffs, cotton, and wool, the advances will permit progressively less and less human and material resources, relative to the total available, to be devoted to agriculture. Insofar as these phenomena do not occur or are prevented from occurring, the benefits from agricultural technification are questionable. When technical advances take place in industry, the immediate and visible impact is worker displacement and unemployment. The initial impact in agriculture is not so visible. A colonial-type farmer may remain "employed," in the conventional sense that all farmers are listed as employed. In an economic sense, however, his work may become of such little value that he is virtually unemployed. He joins that unmeasurable category of "disguised unemployment." This concept is very useful, as it helps us to see the implications of technification in agriculture, the nature of the problems, and by analogy, the response of economic forces if they were functioning as we would like them to function.

[2] *The Backward Society,* St Martin's Press, Inc., New York, 1961, p. 109.

As solutions to the problem of this unemployment which embraces more and more of the population, we have already discarded the alternatives of promoting self-help or subsistence farming and of making *all* farmers into commercial-type, efficient agriculturalists. Likewise, the solution of support prices, dumping, and heightened protectionism, a solution of very questionable wisdom for rich, developed economies, is a counsel of despair for developing economies. For the 20 to 30 percent of the population to support the 40 to 50 percent in disguised unemployment is unthinkable as a permanent policy. The only alternative left to us, therefore, is that of the traditional response of the economic forces that functioned in this field more or less efficiently up to the 1930s in the United States and up to the Second World War in Europe: the flow of resources out of depressed fields into expanding fields. Factor mobility has never been a smoothly functioning, frictionless mechanism. While throughout this period human wants were to all intents and purposes unlimited and the validity of Say's Law[3] held *under certain conditions*, still the machinery for converting potential wants into effective demand, of setting idle men to work to satisfy felt wants, broke down repeatedly in cyclical terms and always needed a good deal of time to work out.

Throughout the nineteenth century and up to the 1920s, factor mobility appears in retrospect to have functioned relatively smoothly. This comfortable view arises in part from "broad historical perspective." It probably did not appear that way to the New Englander forced to abandon the land he had cleared at vast expense in labor terms. The lure of new land in the Midwest eased the pain, but it can never be pleasant to abandon a heavy capital investment and the fruit of one's very hard toil. The mechanism broke down badly in the case of the rural South devoted to cotton culture, where an enclave of depressed labor persisted for one hundred and fifty years. The South's case is very instructive, and I shall return to it later.

If we except part of the South and take a long view, the movement of agricultural labor out of agriculture and into urban occupations more or less kept pace with increasing agricultural productivity on the one hand and growth in demand on the other. Some favored farmers made a good living through this long period, but there was constant pressure on the marginal farmers, who always constituted a large group. The migration was probably composed mostly of young people.

The mechanism broke down in the Great Depression. Then in the 1950s, both technological change and the forces impeding mobility accelerated at such a rate that, politically, first the United States and later other countries could not face the consequences of the free play of natural economic forces.

[3] This law says simply that production creates not only the supply of goods but also the demand for them.

Governments quite deliberately sacrificed some of the benefits of increasing agricultural efficiency because of certain resulting human costs.

If governments had imposed no obstacles to movement out of agriculture, it seems unquestionable that most of the industry would have suffered a severe and prolonged depression, not only with a fall in incomes to levels far below those of urban workers, but also with declines in land values and in rural properties. The reasons why this would have happened are various. First, there are the natural tendencies of people, especially as they get older and less venturesome, to try to hang on to what they have, to continue doing what they know how to do, and to find it harder to learn new skills and adjust to new environments. The great strength of these tendencies can be clearly seen not only in the cotton South before the Second World War, but also in southern Italy until very recently and in the so-called depressed areas which have persisted for long periods in many countries. Possibly the great exception was the wholesale migration of the Irish in the mid-nineteenth century, but it took a famine to spark this. Thereafter the existence of numerous relatives in the United States facilitated a continuing migration.

Migration away from an activity because of depressed conditions has been aptly called migration in response to a "push," whereas if outside opportunities cause people to migrate, it is called migration in response to a "pull."[4] Doubtless all migration or mobility is motivated by both factors in varying degrees, but it will be argued here, following Street, that to prevent undesirable and long-continued inequalities today in developing countries, the pull factor is infinitely more desirable and more effective than the push, on which most reliance has been placed in the past.[5]

One reason for the ineffectiveness of the push factor lies in the cumulative or vicious-circle aspect of poverty. Poverty often begets not only more children but also disease and ill health, ignorance, lowered productivity, and still greater poverty. An inverse selective process takes place, with the young, able, ambitious workers leaving. The group that remains becomes even more sunk in the slough, from which it is difficult to extricate them even if anybody cares to try. It is at this point that the healthy, wealthy, and wise grow censorious and accuse the poverty-stricken of being drunken, immoral, and generally no good, whereas what they are really witnessing is an extreme consequence of the working out of natural economic forces. The economic machine, being both brainless and soulless, continues doggedly with the same response long after the situation requires an entirely

[4] James Street, *The New Revolution in the Cotton Economy,* The University of North Carolina Press, Chapel Hill, N.C., 1957, p. 177

[5] Where conditions are really desperate, people may flee to the cities in an effort to escape starvation. This appears to be the principal factor in a study of migrants in Bombay reported by J. C. Sandesara, *International Development Review,* June, 1964, p. 12.

different remedy. What is required may be direct intervention and a completely different calibration of the machine.

We come here to a finding of fundamental importance. Once the elements of agricultural technification have been mastered and there are no support prices and dumping, the growth of agricultural output depends, within rather narrow limits, on the growth of effective demand, *regardless of the resources poured into agriculture.* The adjustment mechanism becomes not prices and elasticity of demand, but a retirement of marginal land from cultivation and a retirement of marginal farmers into subsistence farming. Urban job openings may not even be adequate for the additions to the labor force. In such conditions, the more land reclamation, irrigation, and drainage projects, etc., the more will people elsewhere be driven out of farming for the market. On the other hand, the faster the growth in effective demand, as shown by a very slight rise in farm profitability, the more rapidly will the supply increase.

Thus, by neglecting the demand side and focusing on the supply, not only do developing countries waste resources and increase inequality, suffering, and poverty, but *there is no greater growth in supply than there would have been in the absence of the additional investment.* (This statement applies not to the immediate harvest but to the following harvests.)

The same general conclusion holds for developed countries, except that instead of farmers being driven into subsistence farming, the state is forced into import restrictions, production controls, support prices, and deficiency payments. The facts of the slow growth in effective demand for unprocessed foodstuffs and the continuing technical advances throughout the developed world lead inexorably to the conclusion that "the heart of an agricultural industry reorganized on modern lines . . . is a reduction in the number of farmers,"[6] or again, "in terms of modern farm technology the present high man-land ratios in all countries—even the United States and Canada—are anachronisms."[7]

Coppock recommends that most governments should adopt as a target an annual decline of 4 percent in the number of people engaged in agriculture, or a decrease by over a third in a decade (p. 211). He does not anticipate that effective demand for foodstuffs will increase in the developing countries by more than 1.5 percent per annum: livestock 2 percent; crops other than cereals 1 percent; cereals a minus rate of growth (p. 135). A reduction of 4 percent per annum, applied to Colombia, would mean a net reduction of over 800,000 workers in agriculture in ten years to a national percentage of 25 percent of the gainfully employed.

John Sheahan, in discussing the relation of agriculture to industry in France, remarks:

[6] John O. Coppock, *North Atlantic Policy: The Agricultural Gap,* Twentieth Century Fund, New York, 1963, p. 207.

[7] *Ibid.,* p. 209.

> The 1950's have shown considerable improvement in the balance between agriculture and the rest of the economy. Between 1949 and 1958, income produced in agriculture rose only 4 percent while net national income in constant prices increased 52 percent. Emigration of labor from agriculture permitted income per capita within the sector to increase 24 percent, as against a rise of 46 percent outside the sector. Discontent within agriculture is understandable in the circumstances, but the process at work is fundamentally an accelerated transition toward a production structure consistent with a higher-income economy.[8]

To read what economists are saying to each other in developed countries and then to turn to what the technical assistance agencies are saying to one group of developing countries is, to say the least, a startling experience.

The Population Problem

The possibilities of geometrical progression in population are truly frightening, especially when the *rate* of progression is increasing with declining infant mortality. It no longer has to be argued that although we have the ability to feed many more people, there is a point in every economy where the ability to provide a constant rise in the standard of living will be checked by excessive population growth rates. We have here one of the key elements in the vicious circle of perpetuating or self-generating poverty in developing countries. Not only is the relation between people and natural resources becoming daily less favorable, but the task of supplying each additional child with the same man-made resources and with adequate education takes on a nightmarish or treadmill character. The relation between working population and dependents remains unfavorable.

I do not propose to go into this problem at length here except to stress that any humane solution has as its necessary basis the establishment of a desire by parents for a higher standard of well-being for themselves and their children. For those at the bottom of the heap—subsistence farmers in underdeveloped countries—we arrive at such a level of poverty, ignorance, and demoralization that any voluntary limitation of births appears to be out of the question. First a tremendous effort is necessary to raise the economic condition of such people to a level where they themselves can grasp the necessity and desirability of limiting their families. There exists little satisfactory statistical evidence on what this level is, but it seems to be somewhere around the status of a commercial-type farmer or that of a

[8] *Promotion and Control of Industry in Post War France,* Harvard University Press, Cambridge, Mass., 1963, p. 24. The figures cited by Sheahan were taken from J. Klatzmann, "L'Évolution des revenus agricoles," *Institut national de la statistique et des études économiques: études et conjonctures,* December, 1959, pp. 1067–1076.

steadily employed urban worker, and it does not appear to be compatible with the continuance of subsistence farming.[9]

A most authoritative study on factors influencing the birthrate in a developed country is that by Richard and Nancy Ruggles.[10] They found that the three high-fertility groups in the United States from 1890 to 1940 were the farmers, the foreign-born, and the urban native-born of lower education. "The rapidly falling birth rate since 1900 has been due in large part to the gradual attrition of these groups, and to a lesser extent to falling fertility within the groups themselves" (p. 155). They found a strong inverse relationship between both birthrates and the wife's and husband's education up to the level of four years of high school (p. 156). The decline of births within the farmer group has little relevance for developing countries, because in the judgment of the authors, it was associated with longer education and with farm mechanization, which did away with any economic advantages of large families (p. 159). The data did not permit an appraisal of the religious factor, but evidently it was not strong enough to affect the factor of socioeconomic status.

This study strongly suggests that there is little hope of a falling birthrate in developing countries as long as a large percentage of the population is in the ranks of the rural poor.

This same conclusion was arrived at by Albert Berry in a review of the available data on Colombia, "although the manipulation of the data was a little crude and hasty, this does not invalidate the hypothesis that the movement of the population toward urban areas, with their higher educational levels and wealth (which depends on substantial changes in the occupational structure), will result in a reduction in the birth rate."[11]

On the other hand, Lloyd G. Reynolds, in a highly important article,[12] points out that despite the spectacular growth in per capita GNP in Puerto Rico from 1950 to 1961, the rate of natural increase in population remained close to 2½ percent. Perhaps the answer can be found, as in similar cases in Mexico and Venezuela, in the continued low living standards in the rural regions, the gap between rural and urban incomes having risen markedly in Puerto Rico in this period. Another hypothesis is that the period was too short to reflect the impact on cultural attitudes of the sudden rise in economic levels. The point is so important that the population behavior

[9] The much higher rate of population growth in Colombia and Brazil than in Argentina might be cited in support of this position.

[10] *Demographic and Economic Change in Developed Countries: A Conference,* National Bureau of Economic Research, Princeton University Press, Princeton, N.J., 1960, pp. 155–193.

[11] Albert Berry, *Breve Estudio de los Determinantes del Crecimiento de la Población en Colombia,* Center for Studies in Economic Development, University of Los Andes, Bogotá, 1965.

[12] Lloyd G. Reynolds, "Wages and Employment in a Labor Surplus Economy," *American Economic Review,* March, 1965, pp. 19–39.

of these three countries merits careful study, with appropriate statistical techniques to separate the continuing rural groups, the young urban groups recently arrived from the country, and the long resident urban groups of differing economic levels. If the population problem in developing countries is found to be centered in the poor, as the Ruggles found for the United States, and especially in the rural poor, this would call for a radical change in economic objectives.

Imperfect Competition and Mobility

It seems preferable to treat the pull factor in labor mobility under the topic of imperfect competition which, though it touches upon only certain aspects of the problem, is so important and so generally ignored that it merits special emphasis here. Various writers have pointed out the handicap under which a developing country with a small internal market labors in establishing industries that can attain economies of scale and compete with established optimum-sized industries abroad. At this point, I am concerned with other aspects of the problem.

For many years it has been increasingly recognized that in modern industry, classical concepts of competition must be modified. In the case of great investments, it is increasingly disastrous and repugnant to the owners to compete in price, and new rules of the game have been evolved. Sporadic attempts to reverse this trend by *enforcing* competition and by breaking up trusts have been largely ineffective. Insofar as the state persists in them, it is probably because of a feeling that excessive conglomerations of capital control in few hands are "unhealthy" to a democratic regime.

In discussing the problems of development, various writers have pointed out the significance of smallness of unit sizes, but few have stressed (1) the imperfect competition aspects, (2) the effect imperfect competition has on earnings of capital and organized labor, and (3) the further effect these have on equality of income, the pattern of demand, and the allocation of resources. Even in such a traditionally competitive field as cotton textiles, the economies of scale possible in the dyeing and finishing plants in conjunction with the small existing markets favor the emergence of a few units. Such units may be either unable or reluctant to resist the demands of strong unions which are supported by generous labor codes and governments that are usually at least "politically" sympathetic to organized labor. (The bulk of the labor force—the self-employed—are not wage earners but slip into other categories of the "countryman" and the "artisans," to whom the codes do not apply.)

The result of all this is to create a small elite class of workers with incomes and standards much above the average. They, and the management, may absorb all the gains of increasing productivity and more, and the prices of goods where technological progress is more rapid may rise parallel with services where there have been no increases in productivity. However, we are not here concerned with questions of equity but of development. The previous section pointed out that the only feasible and economically defensible solution of the problems (and opportunities) that come in the train of agricultural technological progress is the movement of labor into nonagricultural activities. Such a movement would be greatly facilitated by the existence of urban jobs, or at least by a rapid growth in urban production, since this both directly and indirectly creates job opportunities. Growth in urban production would be favored by a low price–high production attitude on the part of industry and trade-union leaders. Yet what actually exists is the opposite. Thus the character of industrialization may place obstacles in the way of people shifting from less to more remunerative work. Sometimes the extent to which a strong union may secure benefits for its members far in excess of all surrounding workers is fantastic, especially a union dealing with foreign-owned companies. An example is the drilling and refinery ends of the petroleum industry. The industrialists are probably not more eager than their counterparts in developed countries to protect themselves from the rigors of competition, but conditions enable them to be more successful. Fortunately, there are other urban activities where work and job competition still hold.

Just as we have seen that the agrarian problem is basically the same problem in all countries where there is not a problem of inadequate resources relative to population, so it now appears that cost-push inflation and imperfect competition play similar roles in developed and developing countries. The coexistence in the United States of the highest wage levels in the world and a steady unemployment level of 5 to 6 percent of the working force is in part explicable in terms of job changing, but in part also by lack of job opportunities *at the going wage scale*. The inflation which is followed rather than preceded by monetary expansion is another symptom of the same phenomenon. An economic dilemma of our time—how to get full employment with price stability—has proved most difficult of solution.

The problem, however, is infinitely more serious in developing countries because the need for mobility and industrial expansion is so much greater.[13] With the exception of the small excess of workers who are in agriculture and in a few depressed areas, there is no longer need of mass migration in developed countries. The flow of the army of annual new recruits to different types of economic activity is sufficient to maintain relative equality in earnings.

In developing countries, however, mass movements of existing workers are necessary to reduce inequality and to raise the *whole* level of incomes

[13] On the other hand, Murray D. Bryce has pointed out to me that the necessary adjustments to the advance of automation can create a problem in developed countries comparable in difficulty and magnitude and similar in nature to the one discussed here.

and welfare considerably. Hence man-made barriers imposed at the beginning rather than well along in the historical process of industrialization have profound and alarming implications. Here, then, we find within the ranks of labor itself one of the root causes of the persistence of both low average productivity and extreme inequality in earnings and living standards. In reality, the solidarity of the working class and its identity of interests do not exist. In their place is an uneasy alliance between the bosses and the strongly organized unions, directed against the rest of the world.

As remarked before, industry fortunately does not include all nonagricultural workers. In a developing country possibly five to six times as many workers may be found in services, commerce, construction, and transport, which so far are much less organized and generally exist in smaller, and hence more competitive, units. However, to many of these, the Labor Codes do apply.

As in the historical process in the United States, the changes in the distribution of the working force seem to arise largely from the distribution of the additions to the working force. In some developing countries, military, police, and domestic services are means by which at a single jump young people may be transplanted from purely rural surroundings to the largest cities. Otherwise, without elementary education, special training, or references from previous jobs, they would find it extraordinarily difficult to make the shift, and for older people it would be doubly so.

The steady movement of young people out of low-paying into higher-paying activities would doubtless be sufficient if the progress in agriculture and the growth in demand were comparable to those experienced in the United States throughout much of its history. The difficulty (and, as always, opportunity) is that developing countries do not retrace the process of technological history. They take over the very latest equipment, the latest developed strains and varieties, the latest techniques. True, the technology they take over does not always give as good results as the same technology in developed countries. But the leap upward in physical productivity over that yielded by the ox or the hoe is spectacular. Therefore, the traditional means by which the labor force is distributed to assure equality in returns is barred or impeded by the early emergence of monopoly elements in industry and labor organization. A country relying on the traditional processes is completely unable to cope with the magnitude of the problem or to take advantage of the opportunity.

It appears highly probable that in many countries something like 60 to 70 percent of the labor force could be released from the countryside in a relatively few years if there were an accelerated conversion to modern agriculture, which would be done *if it paid*. Occasionally a mistake is made in setting the price of a government price-controlled agricultural commodity "too high." The response in area planted and production to such "mistakes" has been notable. It seems clear that the forces slowing up mechanization and technification are not ignorance or inertia, as so many foreign missions seem to believe, or even lack of foreign exchange, since agriculture has generally high priority, but the hopeless competition offered to machines by the man with a hoe. The competition is doubly bad: it delays technification on the one hand and worsens the condition of the colonial-type farmer—the overwhelming majority—on the other. A silent and bitter drama is being played out in developing areas in these years. The protagonists, the governments, and the foreign spectators do not appear to have the slightest awareness of what is happening. Consequently, the babel of advice and the measures actually adopted are just as likely to intensify as to ameliorate the problem. Actually there seems to be a perverse bias, since most of the measures are designed to increase agricultural production but not to create jobs for surplus agricultural labor.

In retrospect (and to some of us at the time), the spectacle of the American people's complete inability to understand and mold their economic environment from 1930 to 1933 was one of the most tragic and senseless episodes of our time. It is, however, now being matched in many developing countries with the concomitant idle men and idle machines, bitterly felt wants and inability to utilize the actual resources to meet these wants. Professional economists have gained great insight into the workings of the economic machine since that long-past age of innocence of the 1920s and 1930s. Now they are bold to propose tax reductions to stimulate demand (apparently, however, Japan took the lead in this). But they still appear to feel that development economics is a special field in which their hard-won knowledge does not apply. They will blithely propose or support agrarian reform for developing countries, though they would not dream of recommending it for developed countries. They recognize that piling up agricultural surpluses is nonsense, but they do not see that condemning peasants to subsistence farming is far worse. It would be a salutory exercise to envisage for a moment the agrarian problem in developed countries if they had 50 percent of the gainfully employed producing agricultural goods efficiently.

Distortion of Pattern of Resource Use

I am here using the phrase "resource use" as embracing all the factors of production. The great and repugnant extremes of wealth and poverty, of health, education, and opportunity, so characteristic of developing countries, are a complex phenomenon.[14] Foreign writers are usually prone to attribute them to the callous selfishness and abuse of power on the part

[14] Charles P. Kindleberger assembled scattered data on the distribution of income which suggested not only that the top 10 percent of receivers in underdeveloped countries secured 35 to 45 percent of the national income, but also that the lower the per capita income, the greater the degree of inequality. *Economic Development,* McGraw-Hill Book Company, 1958, p. 8.

of the "Forty Families," "The Oligarchs," or the "Privileged Classes." The selfishness undoubtedly exists, but it is too facile an explanation. The roots go down more to honestly mistaken policies and institutional factors than to deliberate exploitation. Given the technical revolution in agriculture, a wrong diagnosis of the agrarian problem, the complete inability of the mechanism of the mobility of labor to cope with the necessary short-term adjustment requirements, the early emergence of organized labor and strong monopoly elements in industry, poor tax administration, and chronic inflation—and the inequality and distortion of production and consumption patterns follow as a matter of course. The difficulty, however, arises from the fact that the causes of these patterns are unknown or forgotten, and they acquire an aura of correctness or soundness in themselves which they do not merit from any rational or nonaccounting point of view.

Probably nowhere else in the world do the well-to-do make (unconsciously and relative to total resources) such a lavish use of the work of so many other people as in present-day developing countries. Whereas, in developed countries and in my example from earlier days, effective demand approximates felt demand more and more closely, in developing countries the gap seems to be widening. The well-to-do and the growing upper middle class can exert their demand for the best doctors, the best private teachers, luxurious homes, motor cars and other durable goods of all types, foreign travel, education for their children abroad, Scotch whisky (not national drinks), and diversions. From the point of view of industrial mass production, the difficulty is that there are so few people in these classes that their demand, in terms of physical units, is easily satisfied by relatively small plants. The bottom of the pyramid, on the other hand, can make few of its demands effective and is consequently a poor customer for the new products of industry.

Thus it can be seen that the small degree of industrialization, or rather the relatively small proportion of the gainfully employed in industry, is associated with the character and magnitude of the market. This in turn is explicable in terms of the gross inequality and its causes, which we have just been discussing. If half or more of the population economically do not exist, or are unemployed, and if only, say, 20 percent of the remainder can exert a really effective demand for goods, the market is considerably smaller than appears at first sight.[15] Say's Law does not really have a chance to operate effectively in such conditions. To be solicitous about adequate capital, bank credit, foreign investment, tax exemption for industrial expansion, and so forth appears from this aspect to be putting the cart before

[15] "The urban poor, the ejidal farmers and the small landowners—making up perhaps two-thirds or three-fourths of the country—may have to be regarded as simply outside the market for many modern day products." Raymond Vernon, *The Dilemma of Mexico's Development*, Harvard University Press, Cambridge, Mass., 1963, p. 184.

the horse. What is really needed is a strong growth in *effective* demand—the conversion of the potential into the actual demand.[16] We need to become greatly concerned with investment only when we reach a point where the bulk of industry, as in wartime, is working three shifts and literally cannot meet the demand. Even in this case it may be found that the investment bottleneck lies in a shortage of foreign exchange rather than of internal savings.

Thus we can add another vicious circle: small market—small degree of industrialization—small urban population—poverty-stricken rural population—small market. This is another aspect of the circle of gross inequality—small market for mass consumption products—heavy disguised unemployment—weakness of the pull element in the mobility of labor—growing inequality. All these elements act and react in an interrelated complex.

It is to be doubted whether the liberal granting of tax exemptions, especially as they apply to progressive individual income taxes, plays any role in economic development in these countries except as it permits the wealthy to save and/or spend a larger portion of their income and leads to more government borrowings of an inflationary nature. Tax exemptions to agriculturalists and cattlemen favor only the very wealthy. They may also lead to a somewhat larger production than otherwise, a lower price, and hence some benefit to urban consumers, but this benefit is partly offset by the increased distress of poorer farmers.

In industry, the main incentive to invest is the prospect of profits. After the investment is made, the incentive to produce is demand. Tax exemption is in the nature of a bonus, which may or may not be passed along to the consumer in lower prices than would otherwise have prevailed, or passed back to the workers in higher wages. The problematical advantages hardly justify the harm done to the progressive tax system. The departure from the principle of taxing according to ability to pay promotes the growing inequality of wealth and income.

Kenneth Kauffman[17] has reviewed this favorite device employed by many countries and has concluded that only in Puerto Rico, where the relation to the United States creates special conditions, do such exemptions appear to have been at all effective. For Mexico, he concludes that "the total of fiscal revenues sacrificed . . . has been greater than the total of investments covered by the exemptions." He continues, "Unless it can be convincingly demonstrated, which does not appear to be the case, that the exemptions are vitally necessary, underdeveloped countries would do well to resist the temptation to adopt legislation that weakens even more the equity of their tax systems and heightens the pronounced tendency toward inflationary finance on the part of their governments."

[16] The reader should keep in mind the type of developing countries under discussion.

[17] "Exenciones de Impuestos y Desarrollo Económico," *Arco,* Caracas, March, 1962, p. 92. My translation.

Another source of malallocation of resources arises from the ability to borrow at fixed interest rates in conditions of chronic inflation. This combination distorts all cost-benefit calculations and means that in time all but the very worst mistakes in investment are covered up. The possibility of securing long-term financing at relatively low fixed rates in inflation-ridden countries is generally available mostly to public or semipublic entities or to private investments that the state wishes to encourage. The sources of the funds are taxation, foreign borrowing, or borrowings that have their origin in central banks.

If the returns resulting from such investments go up along with returns and prices in general, and if the borrowings and interest remain fixed, a nominal profit may be shown where actually, in terms of money of constant purchasing power, a loss may have been incurred. Even in the case of foreign borrowings in dollars whose local currency value rises with devaluations, it may be the state and the taxpayers, rather than the actual borrowing entity, who pay the additions to the sums required for interest and repayments.

The danger of misallocation of resources is particularly acute in long-range agricultural projects such as irrigation or reforestation programs. Everyone can see the small and nominal local currency returns, but it is difficult for people to appreciate the losses incurred by the community arising from the malallocation of resources. In the case of investments in agriculture, actual profits by the immediate beneficiaries may be more than offset by losses of small farmers driven into bankruptcy by the new competition and forced into subsistence farming. In Colombia, in addition to large-scale land recovery projects so financed, foreign advisers and foreign and local financing agencies were responsible for a large supervised credit program which was designed to diversify production and was restricted to relatively well-to-do farmers in one state. Apparently, it is very difficult to envisage what this increased competition means to the farmers whom the program did not benefit and who had previously supplied the demand for these products. Since these programs were not accompanied by others designed to provide employment for displaced country people, more disguised unemployment probably resulted.

There is much talk of proper project evaluation. Rarely, however, can such evaluations take account of the indirect effects on other producers or of future changes in the purchasing power of money. Thus in most of the countries under discussion, there undoubtedly exists a widespread misallocation of scanty resources.

Again, too low rates for electric power may encourage extravagant use and misallocation of resources. Misallocation in the private sector arises mostly from a faulty distribution of national income. Errors in public "investment" or investment sponsored by public bodies may arise from faulty or inadequate calculations or from plain mistakes in policy. The conclusion would appear to be that it is desirable to seek a better real return on investment, considered in the widest social and economic context of the word, rather than to concentrate exclusively on increasing the nominal volume of investment.[18]

A further objection to inflation and the distortions that arise from it is to be found in the lag of tax returns, especially those based on property, since increases in yields depend on the slow process of reassessment. Costs, on the other hand, rise immediately, or if they do not rise, the quality of government service further deteriorates. This is part of the explanation of chronic deficiencies in public services.

Balance of Payments

There is no danger that this factor may be slighted. In fact, it is the subject of endless discussion and preoccupation. Nine times out of ten the explanation offered for a developing country's slow rate of growth is the worsening terms of trade for primary products and discrimination by developed economies against the products of developing areas. A popular formulation of the explanation is that "the countries on the periphery are being victimized by the center."

Myrdal, Prebisch, and recently Dell have insisted not on the advantages but on the dangers of trade between developed and developing countries. "That there is a tendency inherent in the free play of market forces to create regional inequalities, and that this tendency becomes the more dominant the poorer a country is, are two of the most important laws of economic underdevelopment and development under laissez faire."[19] Myrdal finds the explanation of his "laws" in the vicious-circle effect. Prebisch stresses the tendency toward worsening terms of trade for countries producing primary goods.

Viner, on the other hand, questions the existence of such laws or tendencies. Some countries which export primary products are enjoying a high and rising standard of living. Laws, at least scientific ones, are not supposed to have exceptions. Myrdal clearly goes too far when he says that "a quite normal result of unhampered trade between two countries, of which one is industrialized and the other underdeveloped, is the initiation of a cumulative process towards the impoverishment and stagnation of the latter."[20] It can hardly be claimed that the export of coffee from Colombia or Brazil and oil from Venezuela is responsible for their relatively lower standard of living. As far as the terms of trade are concerned, there does not appear to be any well-established tendency, though it is true that the demand for *most* primary products increases less rapidly than that for fabricated prod-

[18] For a further discussion of defective allocation of resources see pp. 200–202 in Part Two. It is probable that much of the treatment there applies in more or less degree to other developing countries as well as to Colombia.

[19] Myrdal, *Economic Theory and Underdeveloped Regions*, p. 34.

[20] *Ibid.*, p. 99.

ucts as a whole. On the other hand, as Viner points out, terms of trade mean little without reference to costs, and there is a tendency for the quality or productiveness of capital goods to increase relative to primary products. What can today be secured in exchange for a given volume of coffee or oil is much more productive than what could be secured twenty years ago.

Dell is on firmer ground in emphasizing the factor of unutilized resources, but as I shall argue below, there are other and more economic ways of utilizing the unemployed resources than by providing protection for any product. I believe Viner gives a more scientific diagnosis when he says that the perpetuation of poverty in a developing country is not due to its foreign trade but that "the real problem in poor countries is not agriculture as such, or the absence of manufactures as such, but poverty and backwardness, poor agriculture and poor manufacture."[21] He could have added two more factors, as he does elsewhere in the same volume: an excessive rate of population increase and failure to adopt proper internal policies. He concludes that "the remedy is to remove the basic causes of the poverty and backwardness." Myrdal's refutation is that "as his argument is narrowly static, Viner misses entirely the point that industrialism is intended to rectify an economy in imbalance and to give a dynamic momentum."[22]

The use of emotionally charged words should not lead us away from the central point that it is not the trade between developed and developing countries that is the villain of the piece, but rather the failure to resolve internal problems which the developed countries have already resolved. This is not to say that on occasion the infant-industry argument for protection, or underutilized-resources argument, or the argument for provision of special stimuli to exports is not valid.[23] But in most cases these are only a few of the weapons in our arsenal, and not the most important. Undue emphasis may, and undoubtedly has, distracted our attention from other and more effective weapons. It is particularly unfortunate that writers associated with the United Nations have given such emphasis to the "victimization" of developing by developed countries, because this provides indolent statesmen in developing countries with a respectable excuse for not espousing necessary but unpopular policies at home. The example of Japan in financing its amazing development by a massive shift of resources from rural to urban activities, and with little aid from foreign trade and loans, must not be forgotten.

I do not mean to deny that a real problem exists. But again, the unfavor-

[21] *International Trade and Economic Development*, The Free Press of Glencoe, New York, 1950, p. 52.

[22] Quoted in *ibid.*, p. 29.

[23] In a later paper, Viner concludes that free interregional trade may work toward factor price equalization but that the tendency may be offset by other forces working in the opposite direction. *Indian Economic Journal*, January, 1962, p. 288.

able balance of payments is too easy an explanation. As emphasized in the last section, there are generally few cases of internal productive capacity inadequate to meet the effective demand on a triple-, double-, or even single-shift basis. The lack of certain industries is more a reflection of the lack of sufficient internal demand to achieve the economies of scale than the result of a shortage of exchange. The relatively high cost of imported capital goods in terms of exports may add little to the final price of goods to the consumer relative to the surcharges arising from underutilization of equipment and high earnings by union workers and stockholders. In many cases, lack of sufficient exchange resources *could* impose a real barrier to accelerated development. But in the light of the factors discussed above, it is doubtful how far inadequacy of exchange resources can be cited as *the* explanation or even one of the most important explanations of the slow rate of development that has occurred. It is true that Venezuela, with exports of oil which are large in relation to a small population, has experienced a rate of growth surpassing the others; but the fruits have been very unevenly distributed and the country people do not appear to be much better off than in the other countries under study. Venezuela for some time approximated the case of a country exchanging an abundant and valuable natural resource for a great variety of imported goods. It would be unreasonable to claim that the absence of such an abundance per capita of imports is the general explanation for a slow rate of growth.

As Charles Kindleberger so ably brings out,[24] it is difficult and dangerous to generalize in this field. Raymond Mikesell has pointed out that some exporters of primary goods, such as New Zealand and Denmark, have done and are doing very well insofar as a very high standard of living is concerned.[25] Petroleum, of course, is a primary export of great value. At various times Colombia and Brazil have done well in coffee; at others the Argentine in beef and wheat. At such times, the rate of development (i.e., GNP per capita) speeded up a bit, but usually not in any spectacular way, and without fundamentally redressing the deep-seated ills. Mexico has a bonanza in tourist receipts and yet still has 50 percent of her people making a poor living on the land. For most countries (excepting some highly specialized economies) the great bulk of the product is produced at home, and well-being depends mostly on what is done there.

Though all this is true, it is likewise a fact that many developing countries have had increasing difficulty in recent years in selling their products abroad, and present trends are by no means reassuring. The smallness of the remaining agricultural population in the United States and Western Europe has made it fiscally bearable for the rest of the population to carry a heavy

[24] *Foreign Trade and the National Economy,* Yale University Press, New Haven, Conn., 1962, especially chap. 12, "The Impact of Trade on Growth."

[25] "International Commodity Stabilization Schemes and the Export Problems of Developing Countries," *American Economic Review,* May, 1963, p. 76.

load of subsidy payments, as would have been out of the question in the nineteenth century. Technological advances are daily making it more possible for this small minority of farmers to supply an increasing proportion of the agricultural requirements. The same technical advances are making it more and more possible for economically advanced countries to overcome whatever advantage developing countries possess in low wages. On some of the completely mechanized giant farms of California, it takes no more than ten man-hours—a day's work—to produce a bale of cotton. The full impact of this is not felt because of support prices and production controls, but the threat to other cotton-growing areas is obvious.

It is always possible for a single relatively small country, through exchange manipulation, barter deals, or other ways, to increase its sales abroad without invoking retaliation. What is not so sure in the present world climate is whether it is possible for *all* of them to do this on balance. The present worldwide drive for autarky may pass, but meanwhile it is difficult for newcomers to build up exports other than tourist services.[26] One of the greatest contributions the developed countries could make to the solution of the problem of the developing areas would be a generalized and rapid reduction of the agricultural work force in their countries and a readiness to extend the principles of the international division of labor to agricultural goods. Even without protection, support prices, and deficiency payments, the developed countries could probably retain a large part or most of their home markets, but they would greatly aid the countries that export foodstuffs.

It is a curious but true fact that the developed countries could probably make the greatest contribution to developing countries not by sacrificing income but by adopting policies *that most aided their own development and well-being*—expansionist policies on the one hand, and income and price policies on the other, to the end of promoting greater mobility of labor, a better pattern of resource use, larger imports of primary and simple manufactured goods, larger exports of more complex goods, more vacations abroad, and the abolition of poverty at home. It is the unnecessarily slow and uneven rate of growth that leads to restrictive policies which offset the benefits of "aid."

The solution proposed in Latin America is the formation of a free-trade zone which is not really designed to be a free-trade area but rather a preferential area. There are manifest difficulties, progress has been almost negligible, and the prognosis is not very favorable.

Some developing countries have a marked absolute advantage in one export (Colombia, coffee; Venezuela, oil). At the exchange rate at which it is possible and desirable to export this one product, it is usually not possible

[26] See the discussion in Sidney Dell, *Trade Blocs and Common Markets*, Constable & Co., Ltd., London, 1963, chap. 5.

to export anything else, and very costly protection must be provided to start industries and crops to substitute for imports. Instead of showing an appreciation of the nature of the problem, the Monetary Fund has exerted what influence it could against the practice of multiple exchange rates, even though this appears the most defensible or least objectionable way of diversifying exports for certain countries. Certainly it is not more harmful than granting protection to infant industries, which is generally condoned.

Another practice that the Monetary Fund disapproves is exchange licensing. Clearly, other things being equal, it would be better to control imports through customs tariffs, designed for either revenue or protection. But in some developing countries the inequality of income is so marked that imports free of quantitative restrictions would probably lead to an excess of luxury consumer goods or the purchase of exchange at the import rate for travel and capital remittances. Enormous sums are believed to have departed from Venezuela in particular in this manner. Admittedly, what is now lacking is a sound objective criterion, founded on a comprehensive plan, to license or ration available exchange. Given a shortage of exchange in terms of a soundly based plan, rationing may be on balance preferable to relying on the free play of market forces. The difficulty arises from both faulty planning and faulty administration.

Commentators in developed countries are inclined to be critical about the flight of capital, accusing the wealthy of being unpatriotic. This is no doubt regrettable, but it is difficult to blame individuals in view of the general lack of security and order that is characteristic of our type of developing countries, the vicious-circle effect of improvisations, and the legality and ease of transferring funds. Rather, it is governments that should be blamed for not making it more difficult and costly to transfer funds or for not creating a reassuring domestic atmosphere. In an analogous case, an individual would not be blamed for taking advantage of a legal loophole in the tax laws. Nevertheless, the existence of the loophole makes an inequity possible and impedes the efficient functioning of the economic system.

One alarming and unexpected result of the Alliance for Progress is that it has tended to reduce the pressure and slow down the search for means to increase exports. When exchange can be borrowed, why sweat to export? Any project that can secure foreign financing on any terms is a "good" project. The higher the total figure of the annual borrowing, the greater the pride and credit the government takes. So far as I have been able to discern, the limits to borrowing are those imposed by the multitude of lenders, by the internal inability to raise the necessary matching funds, and by the lack of suitable projects. Not even planning boards, where they exist, have been interested in the limits of debt-paying capacity, in the consequences of net debt repayment, or in whether the nature of the project or program makes borrowing advisable. Occasionally foreign private investment is opposed to borrowing, but this is usually traceable to the operation of national competitors.

Where the tax system is highly regressive, public foreign borrowing may contribute to inequality.[27] This is the case where the initial spending favors the wealthy class (contractors and importers) and the repayment leads to heavier tax collections than would otherwise be necessary. An offsetting factor may lie in the nature of the benefits yielded by the public investment.

Consequences of the Lack of an Urban Policy

Most developing countries try to combine excessively detailed types of regulation with large gobs of complete *laissez faire*. One example of the latter is the lack of a true urban policy, as distinct from city planning in a physical sense, which latter follows conventional lines. The consequences are increasingly undesirable. Rational planning, or molding the environment to make the best use of resources to enhance well-being, has abdicated to the twin dictators, land values and the private motorcar. Despite the examples of metropolitan New York, London, and Tokyo, Argentina and Mexico have permitted Buenos Aires and Mexico City to become overblown giants. All the horribly expensive and dreary phenomena of American urban development—towering congested centers, blighted areas, sprawling suburbs, individual commuting to the center, and a tremendous investment in throughways, underpasses, overpasses, cloverleafs, etc.—are beginning to appear in countries that have not yet attained even a decent minimum standard of living. This is another shocking and costly example of the distortion of the pattern of demand.

The developing countries do not question the sacredness of land values as a criterion in allocating resources. Neither do they challenge the right of an individual to go in his car anywhere at any time and to live as far away from his work as he wishes. Rather, they acknowledge the duty to supply him with uncongested vias. The city of Caracas is a replica of a middle-sized American city, with its entire elongated center taken up by throughways and parking lots. In Bogotá it will only be a few years before the small area of level land at 2,600 meters—the Sabana of Bogotá—will be occupied by suburbia. Instead of discouraging this trend, the authorities enforce uniform urban bus fares regardless of distance traveled and encourage both poor and wealthy people to live miles from their work, thus creating obvious problems for the future.

Admittedly, urban concentrations entail heavy expenses for water, light, sewers, telephones, schools, and urban transport, but *up to a certain point,* all of these except transport can be provided more cheaply per capita in cities than in rural districts. Great savings could undoubtedly be realized by careful planning for balanced urban development—planning to avoid gigantism, achieve greater densities with less congestion, and avoid suburban

[27] Compare Carl Shoup et al.: "Expenditure on trunk roads, hotels and the like, probably tend to benefit particularly the richer classes." The Fiscal System of *Venezuela,* The Johns Hopkins Press, Baltimore, 1959, p. 42.

sprawl until at least the bulk of the people enjoy a minimum standard of living. A possible way in which this might be achieved is sketched in Chapter 7.

In this and the preceding chapter frequent references were made to the vicious circle, or the cumulative nature of various forces in developing economies. These interacting and reinforcing phenomena can, of course, act for good or for bad. We do not have the expression "benign circle," but we do say that "Nothing succeeds like success," which presumably implies a benign circle. Needless to say, a most important objective of any national program should be to break vicious circles and to set in motion self-generating or cumulative benign forces. From the point of view of the argument presented in these chapters, any program that plunges the rural dweller deeper into poverty or impedes his ability to move into a more remunerative job contributes to a vicious circle; any action that sets him and his family even on the bottom rungs of the economic, educational, and social ladder is expected to yield ever-increasing returns throughout the years and therefore marks the beginning of a benign circle.

Inadequate Use of Industrial Equipment

Generally in Latin American countries, the work year is short. There are frequent holidays, both patriotic and religious; and if a holiday falls on a Tuesday or a Friday, it is common not to work on the preceding Monday or succeeding Saturday. Consequently, even for the urban fully employed, the work year may not exceed 220 days. With a few exceptions, a single shift is the rule. Thus the bulk of equipment, even where it is fully utilized during working hours, is not in operation more than 20 percent of the year. When we add to this figure the excess capacity resulting from forward planning, mergers, uneven spacing of demand, and the necessity to provide for the peak, it is probable that most equipment is not in use more than 10 to 15 percent of the time; or in other words, an enormous excess capacity exists. This alone makes for a very high—actually unnecessarily high—ratio of capital-equipment import requirements to production.

In addition to the more or less normal concentration of retail sales in the last month of the year, the practice of paying an additional month's salary at that time leads to still greater concentration and so to more uneven use of equipment. Electric utility companies are expected to have sufficient equipment to meet the maximum evening peak in the month of maximum demand.

Other Causes of Low Productivity

One of the costs of chronic inflation without automatic cost-of-living adjustments is the necessity of frequent wage negotiations, with corresponding frequent stoppages of work. Another time-wasting factor is the almost incredible inefficiency with which the routine work of public bodies is carried out. A consequence is that every business or even professional person maintains messengers who spend most of their time in queues. A second small army of necessary but unproductive people are the watchmen that every business, farm, or construction project requires at all times.

Retail selling is another field where the productivity is low, though this is changing. Nevertheless, the excess manpower or disguised unemployment in this field is still very great. Other sources of waste may be found in the faulty maintenance of publicly owned equipment, the overloading of public payrolls, the featherbedding in publicly owned services, faulty planning, and malallocation of funds. While these wastes are common in all countries, they are undoubtedly present to a greater degree in developing countries.

When all these elements contributing to low productivity are added to the fact that there is an army of rural unemployed, the wonder grows not that the countries have a low standard of living but that their standard is as high as it is. Considering the appalling degree of underutilization and waste, it is not surprising that the small technical assistance projects and even loans make little impression.

The economic costs of low educational and health standards are too obvious to need stressing. What is perhaps not so obvious is that, for the working classes, the lack of formal education or skills is not so serious as the lack of proper work habits, the sense of responsibility, and the willingness to accept discipline that are the most valuable by-products of the character formation to which a good early training contributes. It may be noted again that the lowest standards of both health and education are concentrated in rural areas, where they are most difficult to improve.

The Teaching of Economics

I have made much of the existence of economic illiteracy in Latin America, and yet in the countries under discussion there are many thousands of college students concentrating on economics for long four- and five-year terms. How can these apparently contradictory statements be reconciled?

The answer can in large part be found in an excellent study by Howard Ellis, Benjamin Cornejo, and Luis Escobar Cerda.[28] In brief, these writers found that the concentration begins at too early an age; the mortality rate is excessively high; and an attempt is often made to combine economics with business administration. They charge that little active participation by the students is required; weekly hours of lecturing are excessive; and heavy emphasis is placed on mathematics and statistics, so that a certain type of mind is repelled and much of what is taught is irrelevant to actual problems.

[28] *The Teaching of Economics in Latin America,* Pan American Union, Washington, D.C., 1961.

Moreover, they say that graduate students who study abroad frequently receive training which is of little use in their own countries except to teach to others and thus perpetuate another circle which, if not exactly vicious, is not productive.

On the other hand, the subject of economics is relatively new, and in the future the growing number of professional economists may, it is hoped, make a greater impression on the thinking of the governing class in developing countries.

The Efficiency of the Firm versus the Inefficiency of the System

One of the most glaring contrasts, especially in an underdeveloped country, is afforded by the firm where economic motivation has full play, and the economic system, whose calibrations have been distorted in an irrational manner. Let me give one of a thousand possible illustrations.

In a tropical city in Colombia is a relatively small but modern synthetic fiber plant, highly capital-intensive, with air-conditioning, humidifiers, supplementary electric power that switches on in six seconds upon the failure of municipal power, and so on—apparently a very efficient operation. The labor requirements are so small that a taxi suffices to bring and deliver the requisite night shift of women employees.

In the same city, in the main street, twenty-one shoeshine able-bodied men, not boys, were counted in one block.

A well-trained economist would have no difficulty in explaining this contrast in terms of the inequality of incomes and the consequent existence of sufficient demand for man-made fibers, in terms of the capital-employment ratio in that industry as determined by modern techniques, in terms of inadequate saving and capital formation to give better employment with modern technical practices and so on. And yet, rationally considered, the explanation makes little sense.

With a changed calibration of the system or the economic machine—less demand for synthetic fibers, more demand for mass consumer goods, more price flexibility, competition and factor mobility or substitutes to take adequately their place—the same capital (both domestic and imported) could have yielded as high or higher returns and could have been consistent with much greater employment and yielded much greater and widespread well-being. The efficiency of the firm is a splendid thing. But infinitely more important in dealing with the economics of developing countries is the efficiency of the economic system in making the best use of available resources—human, natural, and man-made. The profit motive continues to work to the end that in each plant fewer people can produce more goods. What is not working is the mechanism for picking up the released people (and millions more) and putting them to equally useful, remunerative work.

CHAPTER 5

Various Prescriptions

AS WAS ARGUED in Chapter 2 on objectives, a convenient quantitative way of measuring growth—the increase in the GNP either in absolute terms or in per capita terms—has ended by becoming itself the objective of planning and the criterion by which success is judged. This is a pity, since as I have tried to show, there are other more worthwhile objectives for developing countries. It seems to me that the choice of a plan should depend on the diagnosis of the problem and a sense of values, rather than on the attainment of a compound rate of growth in one of a great number of economic series.

Economic growth, or perhaps a better word would be "advancement," in developed countries in this century and particularly in the past generation has proceeded along various lines: an increase in goods and services per capita, an increase in leisure, and a more equitable sharing of both the goods and the leisure. People are given more protection against the economic hazards of life from the womb to the tomb, health is better, and education is at least continued longer for more young people. In addition, staggering amounts of resources are devoted to military preparedness and space investigation. The diversion of these resources from current consumption and the transfer of other resources to maintain properly an unneeded portion of the farm population are hardly felt. Obviously the objectives have been many. This is perhaps too rosy a picture, but Simon Patten's pain economy is receding farther and farther, and presumably the marginal utility yielded by the steady addition of goods and leisure per capita is steadily diminishing.

It would seem, therefore, that economies attaining this happy state could give some serious study to the large part of the world's population that has as yet shown little ability to resolve its economic problems—where the pain economy still prevails in all its ugliness. While naturally each program has to be adapted to the peculiar conditions of each country, and while specialized knowledge is necessary for this, it will be my contention that the solution to the problem can be found in the evolution of the developed countries themselves—in their mistakes as well as achievements. In other words, we do not have to seek esoteric or original solutions but rather to apply as intelligently as we can the lessons learned in economically advanced countries. Before I enlarge on this point, however, it may be advisable to discuss some of the solutions on approaches that have been and are being offered.

The dominant approach has been the capital formation approach. It singles out two relationships, that between new investment (or saving) and additions to output, and that between the stock of capital and output. The cogent criticisms of various writers have left its primacy undisturbed, probably because the alternatives proposed have been qualitative and have not lent themselves to quantitative treatment. I have, therefore, decided to defer detailed discussion and criticism of the Capital Formation Approach until I have disposed of other approaches and have described the alternative which I believe is desirable. The following brief discussion of the ECLA-Prebisch Approach, which is a simplified variant of the Capital Formation Approach, will be supplemented by an extended discussion in Chapter 9. Discussion of the ECLA Approach is inserted here so that it will not complicate the later discussion of the Capital Formation Approach, which I think is one of the most basic issues raised in this book. I hope that if the reader realizes there is a feasible alternative, he will be more willing to consider criticisms of the dominant approach.

The ECLA-Prebisch Approach

The approach to our problem devised by the United Nations Economic Commission for Latin America under the leadership of Raul Prebisch has had much influence. Its main features are embodied in *An Introduction to the Technique of Programming*, 1955, and they have apparently undergone no significant modifications since they were first set forth in a paper by Prebisch in 1950.[1] The objective is defined quite simply as a rate of growth in the GNP. "The first problem in the technique of elaborating a program consists in determining what are the rates of growth possible for a given economy" (p. 8). Thus solutions to the myriad problems I have touched on in Chapters 3 and 4 are discarded in favor of a rate of growth in the gross product, however distributed, and attained at whatever cost. Rates of growth in education, health, equality, leisure, security, morality—in short, welfare—are of interest only as they aid or hinder one particular rate of growth.

To achieve a rate of growth in gross product, the main reliance is placed on achieving a rate of investment.[2] However, little hope is held out for

[1] *The Economic Development of Latin America and Its Principal Problems,* ECLA, Lake Success, N.Y., 1950.

[2] The general reader may wish to refer to the note on Keynesian terminology at the end of Chap. 1.

increasing investment internally, either through inflation or taxation. Neither is there much hope for an improvement in the terms of trade, since the developed countries are more likely to force a worsening of such terms. Thus we are forced back to foreign borrowing and/or the formation of a defensive trade bloc embracing all Latin American countries. It is not a very inspiring program.

In their elaboration of the Colombian Ten-Year Plan, ECLA technicians were apparently forced or persuaded to include rather large public spending programs in the fields of housing, education, public health, public services, and so on. These, it seems, were expected to increase the GNP because they would be financed in part by foreign loans (increase in investment) and in part by domestic borrowing, which presumably would not act to decrease private investment, since the plan quite frankly stated that internal borrowing would have "possible inflationary consequences."[3] This was the truest forecast in the plan.

Apart from improvement in the balance of payments (the discussion never departs for long from this topic), the Colombian program petered out in a series of measures to encourage expansion of industry, such as tax exemption, the provision of the infrastructure of public services, and campaigns to improve the productivity of agriculture. As in all ECLA programs, the Colombian plan's chief instrument to increase production per capita is increased investment. "If growth depends closely and directly on the quantity of new accumulated capital, since total production is a function of capital, the limiting factors on a high degree of capital formation are also the limiting factors on the rate of growth that can be set" (p. 239). One would naturally expect, therefore, that the Colombian plan would be mostly concerned with ways and means of increasing investment per capita. This is true insofar as foreign borrowing is concerned, but on the much more important domestic front nothing is proposed for increasing saving and hence investment. As the plan states, "This distribution between saving and consumption has strict limits, especially in a democratic society in which one cannot force saving excessively at the cost of satisfying more elemental necessities" (pp. 238, 239). The lack of a design for increasing domestic saving is perhaps the most fatal weakness of the plan, considered strictly within its own conventional limits. To arrive at the goal of a growth of 5.6 percent in the gross product (a goal apparently arbitrarily chosen), a rise in the proportion of gross product (plus imports) saved (and invested) from 15.9 percent in 1959 to 22 percent in 1964 is postulated. This constitutes a rise of 40 percent. (*Net* national saving is projected to rise from 11.1 percent of national income in 1959 to 18.2 percent in 1970—a rise of 64 percent.)

But apart from a postulated rise in gross government investment from

[3] Ten-Year Plan of Colombia, 1961, p. 230.

3.7 percent of gross product in 1959 to 7.2 percent in 1962–1964 (which is in part achieved by foreign borrowing), the rest of the rise in the income saved is merely the result of projections. Of the "planned" rise in government investment, most was supposed to occur by 1961. Similarly, most of the annual foreign borrowing of US$100 million had occurred by 1961. In addition, an increase of 10 percent in the ratio of output to estimated *existing* capital was projected from 1959 to 1962–1964. This is completely unprogrammed—a guess or merely wishful thinking—and expressed in terms of the productivity of the *new* capital, it would appear very high.

The simplicity and complete inadequacy of this type of planning were concealed from the layman by the space devoted to sector projections. The goals and the overall rates of investment postulated were spelled out in a consistent breakdown in all the various fields of economic activity, and a final modification of the goals and investment in the light of the findings of reasonable (or unreasonable) expectations was provided for all the various economic sectors.

For this type of programming, where action is confined to a few public sectors, detailed sector projections are quite useless and are generally out of date before they can be printed. The programming is somewhat similar to that indulged in by the United States, where it generally takes the form of deficit financing of a few billions to absorb a million or so unemployed. To translate these additional billions into spending in all sectors of the economy (including the amount that may possibly be spent on barbed wire) would be considered a terrible waste of time and energy. In poor countries with few trained economists, the waste is indefensible. The puzzling question is why is it done? Does the program appear too thin as it is baldly stated, so that it must be presented in more technical dress to be respectfully accepted by laymen?

The chief weakness of the ECLA-Prebisch Approach in Latin America lies in its failure to grasp the significance or potentialities of the technical revolution in agriculture. Only when we look at this revolution can we understand why half or more of the population is in abject misery, why natural forces cannot bring about mobility and equalization in workers' incomes in time, why increased agricultural productivity, if pushed beyond the growth in demand, can result only in still lower agricultural incomes, and finally why a developing country has within its own grasp the ability to surge ahead—faster with foreign help, but ahead in any case.

This description of the ECLA-Prebisch Approach was based on the *Introduction to the Technique of Programming* and the application of the techniques in the Colombian General or Ten-Year Plan. In 1963 Prebisch restated his position in a long article entitled "Towards a Dynamic of Latin American Development."[4] While the article seems to have been influenced

[4] References are to a reprint put out by the Banco de Comercio Exterior de México.

by earlier criticisms by the present writer, especially in its discussion of agriculture, this is not explicitly stated. In view of ECLA's influence and the fact that it frequently acts as an economic spokesman for Latin America, Dr. Prebisch's views merit careful attention. The article deals with a basic theme and marks some development, or at least change, in his thinking.

As before, the objective is always stated in terms of a rate of growth in the gross product, and this rate of growth is, generally speaking, a function of saving and capital formation. As before, however, little can be done to increase saving. But now the excessive consumption of the rich appears as the villain of the piece. "The upper 5 per cent of the population that consumes 30 per cent spends, per average family, 15 times more than the average family group in the lowest 50 per cent of the population. If this were reduced to 9 times, the rate of growth in per capita income would rise from 1 per cent to 4 per cent" (Prebisch, p. 6). This is at one and the same time a statement of objectives, a diagnosis (inadequate saving), and an implied program (a tax on luxury expenditures?). However, the program remains only an implication. The single specific proposal to increase the percentage of income saved is to expropriate land below its commercial value, with payment deferred and at low interest rates—which in Latin America is expropriation indeed. This procedure, Prebisch's article blandly states, will affect the spending of the expropriated owners but not their incentive to work, and the farmers settled on the expropriated land will have every incentive to work and save, so that the proportion of income saved will rise. Although there is much talk in the article about the necessity of structural changes, this is the only one specifically proposed.

Actually, Prebisch does not seem to place much faith in this program, because he moves quickly back to the double-pronged diagnosis of (1) inadequate internal saving to provide jobs for displaced country people and for the natural increase in the working force, and (2) inability to import sufficient capital goods, an inability which he treats as a fundamental source of disequilibrium regardless, apparently, of the proportion of domestic savings. This is based on a statement that demand for imported capital goods increases faster than the demand for primary products, which are the only products that can be exported. The only way out of the dilemma is the Latin American Free Trade Association, but as the achievement of this is fearfully difficult and time-consuming, we are back to the immediate necessity of foreign aid. "Latin America cannot accelerate its rate of growth without foreign aid" (Prebisch, p. 16).

All this, except land expropriation, is fairly familiar. It is in his attempt to restate agricultural policy that Prebisch introduces some new thoughts. On the one hand, he draws the analogy between rural regions and the primary exporting countries with their unfair and worsening terms of trade, which suggests that there are too many people in agriculture. On the other hand, he insists that agricultural production, which he says has been below consumption for many years, be increased from a rate of physical growth of 3.2 percent to one of 4.2 percent per annum, so that "rapid and massive" Agrarian Reform must be accompanied by technological progress. In some unexplained way, the rate of growth must come from technological improvements which reduce cost *but do not displace manpower.* The choice of technological improvements cannot be left to the individual. All the fruits of the reduction in cost "should" remain with agriculturalists. But again we return to the need to absorb redundant agricultural manpower in the cities. There has to be migration, Prebisch says, but this is a serious and impressive indication of economic and social disequilibrium. If the migrants would only remain in the smaller towns, producing things in a primitive fashion for rural people, disequilibrium would be avoided. A new source of inflation is found in the rural people who are absorbed in urban "services," "where they do not produce an equivalent quantity of goods and services" and so "exert pressure on the goods and services that others produce, thus contributing to the inflationary spiral" (p. 22). In certain cases "restraint" may have to be invoked to prevent rural emigration, "avoiding forms of mechanization that aggravate the problem" (p. 13, footnote).

In short, Dr. Prebisch appears to be rather unclear on the nature of the agrarian problem and has not yet been able to work out a consistent statement, diagnosis, or solution of it. If his view correctly represents that of ECLA, it will be gravely handicapped in its efforts to work out overall plans, since agriculture comprises some 50 percent of the working force in most of the developing countries under discussion.

With no internal plan worthy of the name, ECLA is forced back on foreign aid and the LAFTA. But the Alliance for Progress presupposes that the major effort will be made by the recipient countries themselves. To date it has proved impossible to get LAFTA off the ground since, in the absence of expensive and successful domestic programs, each of the participating countries is desperately anxious to substitute for imports and to protect domestic producers. Underutilized manpower, natural resources, and capital equipment are pervasive phenomena that make the lowering of trade barriers illusory without the certainty of increased sales and guarantees against unemployment and losses.

Insofar as the ECLA-Prebisch diagnosis is based on the alleged difference in the elasticity of demand between primary and industrial goods, it is altogether too simplified. As Raymond Mikesell points out:

> In 1960, the industrial areas of the free world exported primary products totaling $23.2 billion, while the non-industrial areas of the free world exported $25.3 billion in primary products . . . . for a number of relatively high income countries including Denmark, Australia, Ireland and New Zealand, primary products constitute over half of their total exports. On the other hand, in

the case of underdeveloped countries such as India and Israel, primary products constitute less than half of total exports.[5]

Or again:

Between 1959 and 1960 there was an increase in export receipts of primary exporting countries of about $1.6 billion but there occurred a deterioration of the trade balance of these same countries of $1.7 billion. Moreover, sixty out of a total of eighty-seven countries listed as primary exporting countries increased their export proceeds between 1959 and 1960. Out of this group of eighty-seven countries, sixty-five experienced a deterioration of their trade balance and in the vast majority of cases this deterioration was entirely or mainly a result of increased imports.[6]

This is not to deny that the export prospects for certain primary products are unsatisfactory. But before the developing countries or their spokesmen take a position that the world owes them a living, they would do well to analyze the problem more deeply. They would be in a stronger position to ask for help if 60 percent of their working force were not virtually unemployed and their capital equipment were not idle 80 percent of the time, if inequality were not growing, and if national policies were not at least partly responsible for low or declining exports. Similarly, it is not enough to set forth the ideal of a common market to achieve the economies of scale. A careful analysis of the difficulties and obstacles and of alternative approaches is necessary. It is to be feared that such an analysis was not made before this grandiose and highly difficult program was launched.

Despite the manifest confusions and contradictions in the ECLA-Prebisch Approach, it is encouraging to see the new emphasis given to the problems of displaced workers and unremunerative employment, and even to the idea of more intensive use of equipment and the possibility of altering the ratio of product to equipment. Now that these topics are being discussed, it will surely be only a matter of time before a new, consistent, and rational formulation of the problem and its solution is arrived at by ECLA.

The Well-Intentioned Sprinkler Approach

The Alliance for Progress[7] may be characterized in these terms. No one can deny that it is well-intentioned. On the other hand, it is made up of a hodgepodge of objectives, suggestions, sentiments, and prejudices. Large landed estates are bad, except in the United States. Small peasant farms

[5] "International Commodity Stabilization Schemes and the Export Problems of Developing Countries," *American Economic Review*, May, 1963, p. 76.

[6] *Ibid.*, p. 87.

[7] The descriptive phrase "saltcellar approach" is not as apt, because a little salt improves the dish as a whole, but as every farmer knows, a little sprinkle of water does no good.

THE SPRINKLER IN ACTION

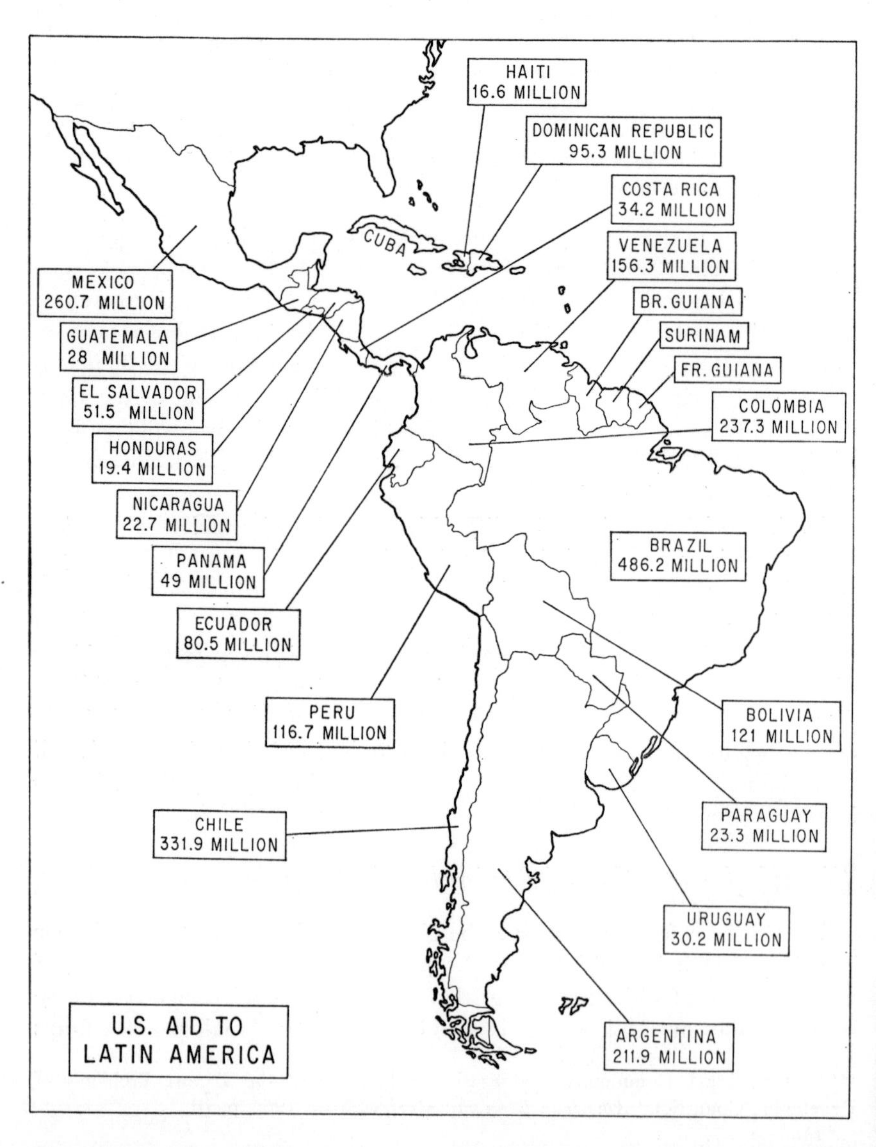

Distribution of aid. The above map, prepared by the United Press, shows the distribution of aid by the United States during three years under the Alliance for Progress, from July, 1961, to January, 1964.

are good, except in the United States. Tax "reform" is good, but almost anything can pass as reform. The difficult and incomprehensible Latins are proud and sensitive, therefore it is better to extend aid in devious ways and avoid any appearance of dictation. Otherwise that dirty phrase Yankee Imperialism may be invoked. Private Enterprise and the Private Sector are good and should be encouraged (particularly with one eye on the United States Congress). On the other hand, the phrase "broad social objectives" has a comfortable sound. Since there is not much money to achieve so many different objectives in nineteen countries, it must be spread thinly. Hence the Sprinkler Approach (in New Deal days a similar theory was called the Trickle-Down Theory).

There is really nothing in all this that an economist would be justified in referring to as either a diagnosis or a program. It is simply an indiscriminate, sentimental, piecemeal approach to a problem that in reality merits the hardest kind of hard thinking on the part of all the partners to the Alliance, which is just what it has not received. For the United States to remove what few strings it has retained would surely not be prudent.

In the case of the Marshall Plan, the situation was quite different. Western European countries had excellent economists, and the problem was more obvious: it was to pay for the necessary imports while the capital structure, both public and private, was being *re*built. In the present case, the economists are missing and the problem is infinitely more complex.[8]

In brief, despite its attractive connotation of irrigation, the Sprinkler Approach as it is being applied could only by a miracle be expected to produce any substantial results. In the end it may even intensify the agrarian problem, which is the gravest problem of all. The United States has economists perfectly competent to diagnose ills and prescribe remedies for individual countries, but they either have not been called in or have given the patients only a cursory glance before returning to their apparently fascinating pastime of writing essays in algebra to each other on the problems of growth and development.

The Individual Project Approach

This is a variant of the Sprinkler Approach, but it is more satisfying to the lender because it permits him to study a project exhaustively and impose conditions on the borrower. Regardless of what may be happening to the country in question, the lender may salve his conscience with the thought that he has spared no effort to ensure that individual projects are "sound." This has been the favorite approach of the International Bank and other lenders.

Despite the fact that on the whole the International Bank has sponsored the best individual projects, mainly in the field of electric power and trans-

[8] The Marshall Plan is discussed further in chap. 7.

port, its policy is open to certain obvious criticisms. For example, it may distort national programming and the determination of priorities, because obtaining the matching funds to assure the foreign load has first priority in framing national budgets. No necessary relation exists between the foreign-exchange requirements of selected individual projects in any given year and the foreign-exchange requirements of a national plan. There is no necessary coordination between the separate loaning activities of different lenders, and there is no relation of the total of all these to the debt-paying capacity of the country. It is as if a number of lenders were loaning to various operating divisions of General Motors. Even though one of the conditions might be that all such loans must be guaranteed by the parent corporation, no loans would be made to General Motors itself to further an overall program.

An increasing awareness that a purely banking approach to the complex problem of development may be inadequate has led the International Bank to set up a more flexible soft-loan subsidiary in the International Finance Corporation, though this subsidiary is still restricted to individual projects. It has also led the bank to try to introduce a policy of country coordination and programming through the device of associating all the lenders. In the case of Colombia, for example, the lenders put up a certain sum to be available for a variety of unspecified projects. This is a distinct advance, but to realize its full potentialities, the device still needs to become an integral part of a soundly conceived and executed national plan.

Agrarian Reform

Although the United States administration was obviously uncertain about a lot of things south of the Rio Grande, it had no doubts about the necessity and efficacy of Agrarian Reform. Were not people hungry? Were they not trying to make a living on rented lands or on tiny holdings? Were not great areas of good land being devoted to extensive cattle raising? Did not the bloody but justifiable Mexican Revolution center on land? What could obviously be more desirable than that the great estates should be broken up and distributed to the poor farmers—legally, or course, and with adequate compensation? Mixed in with the economics was probably the feeling that a sturdy, independent peasant on his own land would be a force for stability and conservatism.

Even in this case, however, and again with the best intentions, the American government misread the problem. While that government was pushing Land Reform for Latin America, its agricultural technicians and scientists were rapidly making peasant farming obsolete. While the drive throughout Western Europe, the United States, and the British Commonwealth was toward consolidation of uneconomic-sized units and the creation of ever larger units, Latin America was to march in the opposite direction. While

5,000- and 10,000-acre farms were becoming common for cotton growing in Texas and California (and one was created with over 86,000 acres), such sized estates were to be subdivided in Latin America. It is to be feared that the Mexican experience was not closely studied—nor, indeed, was any other experience.

In any case, it is not so much the size of the farm that matters as it is the attempt to solve the agrarian problem of too many farmers with too low income by making them all more efficient and productive. One would have thought that at least the American government would have recognized the futility of this, in view of its painful experience in maintaining too many people on the land. In the Latin American country which, for special reasons, launched this program in advance of American urgings—Colombia—there are now doubts that Land Reform by itself can resolve the agrarian problem. There is a widespread feeling, however, that reform can do a useful job in the settling of *some* farmers and in land reclamation. While this may be quite true, there is always a danger that in the zeal of reform, the reformers will divert an excessively large amount of resources to agriculture, thus again intensifying the problem, instead of trying to create other employment for agriculturalists.

Latin American Free Trade Association

LAFTA was another approach launched with great enthusiasm as an answer to the European Economic Community and the restrictive trade practices of developed countries in general. Early hopes have dimmed, and there is a keener perception of the difficulties of developing large-scale trade between a heterogenous lot of noncontiguous countries who all are determined to protect their hard-won gains, whether these are in industry or agriculture. Quantitative restrictions, chronic inflation, and periodic devaluations, all proceeding at different times and rates, make the task doubly difficult and minimize the significance of customs tariff reductions. Venezuela is making vast plans to break into the LAFTA group with heavy metal, aluminum, and chemical products, but it is questionable whether the existing members with their own industries in these fields will take kindly to such imports.

There can be no quarrel with the Association's objective—the creation of a larger market that would permit the economies of scale. But the approach selected has tended to maximize the difficulties. An alternative approach will be suggested later.

An Eclectic Approach

It is possible to envisage a type of program that would include many separate items without giving predominance to any one of them. Such a program would borrow from the experience of developed countries with due regard to the peculiar conditions prevailing in each developing country. For example, it would tackle the problem of the unequal distribution of income not only through the progressive income tax and the inheritance tax, but also through a vigorous program of closing legal and illegal loopholes and doing away with tax exemptions other than personal ones.

An eclectic program could set as its first educational goal a full six-year primary education in cities (to achieve this in rural districts would be extraordinarily difficult for most countries). The health program could be speeded up, along with urban housing. These "social" programs, in conjunction with true tax reform, would bring about some distribution of income and a gain in present and future welfare. Doubtless they could be supplemented by a number of others in transport, agriculture, and public administration, with overall policies in the fiscal, monetary, and exchange fields.

Such a program is reminiscent of the one proposed by the first mission ever organized by the International Bank—that to Colombia[9]—which was followed by many other missions from the Bank and other institutions to other countries. It borrowed heavily, of course, from the many-sided frontal attack then being pursued by developed countries. In following developed countries' practices (at least, the practices of European countries), the eclectic program relies upon (1) the infrastructure being provided mostly by public bodies, (2) small gains in individual productivity in many lines resulting from the pursuit of self-interest, and (3) a wider diffusion of the benefits of such gains through tax and social legislation.

This kind of program lacks symmetry and quantitative precision. Many disparate goals are pursued simultaneously, and at first sight there appears to be no order or scale of priorities. But despite the somewhat messy and disorderly appearance, great gains have actually been made in many countries on many fronts simultaneously. The whole program, if it can be called a program, has yielded truly remarkable results in all the developed countries. Over a generation or so, the governments of these countries have brought about a profound modification in the distribution of income and the pattern of effective demand. For the rest, the program has relied mostly on self-interest and the mobility of labor to achieve the most economic allocation of human and material resources in production (in accordance with the pattern of effective demand, and with the notable exception of agriculture). And the program has generally depended on self-interest to effect a steady increase in individual productivity and decline in the rate of population growth.

Such a program, if pursued over an extended period, would undoubtedly yield benefits in increasing welfare in the developing countries. However,

[9] *The Basis of a Development Program for Colombia,* a report of mission headed by Lauchlin Currie for the International Bank, 1950, Johns Hopkins Press, Baltimore.

the sheer magnitude of the problem, the continuing drag of the population increase, and the lack of economic insight and dedication to the cause of reform, all combine to engender a certain degree of skepticism as to the chances of adoption and successful execution of such a program. At some point the countries which are now developed arrived at the happy stage where the previous vicious circle of poverty—ill health—ignorance—low productivity—poverty was replaced by a cumulative benign circle. It is questionable whether most of the developing countries have arrived at this stage, despite the rise in various economic indexes. This point is of such crucial importance that the next chapter will be devoted to it.

The Wily-Parrot Approach

In his deceptively simply written but actually profound book, *The Backward Society*, Raymond Frost was concerned with societies much poorer than those discussed in this book. The possibility of a Breakthrough or Long Reach Upward (the wily parrot climbing upward, making sure of his new grip before relaxing his old one) is infinitely more difficult for such societies. Frost emphasizes the importance of diversifying and improving the quality of exports (as New Zealand did, for example) and of being prepared to extract the maximum advantage from the periodic export booms when they occur. While this is excellent advice, one wonders whether a country willing and able to accept it would be a backward society.

Conclusion

The discussion in this chapter is an impressionistic rather than an exhaustive country-by-country treatment and pays slight attention to the Capital Formation Approach. It is quite possible that other promising leads might be uncovered in the course of closer analysis. However, since this summary has covered the approaches favored by the main national and international agencies who have assumed responsibility in the field of development, I hope that nothing of great importance has been overlooked.

In brief, the picture is one of floundering and uncertainty. There is a feeling on all sides that the magnitude of the effort since 1949, and particularly since 1961, should have led to greater results and that something must be inadequate in the various approaches, but at this point agreement ceases. It is desperately important that a way out be found before a real crisis develops compounded of (1) increasing manifestations of impatience and resentment which make the functioning of the economic system more difficult (2) the reaching of the safe foreign-debt limit by various countries, and (3) the continued inability to resolve the balance of payments problems in certain countries.

On this point the U.S. Agency for International Development has made some truly alarming studies and projections in its report released April 5,

1965. The following citations are taken from a summary in the *Survey of International Development.*[10]

> The total foreign debt of the less developed countries rose from $10 billion in 1955 to more than $30 billion in 1965, and will reach nearly $90 billion by 1975 at current lending rates . . . in terms of export earnings, repayments will cost the less developed countries 13.6 percent of their foreign exchange income by 1975, compared with 3.7 percent in 1955 and about 10 percent this year.

According to the same survey, Pierre-Paul Schweitzer, Managing Director of the International Monetary Fund, in his report to the UNESCO on March 25, 1965 "stressed that the real need is for both debtor and creditor countries to exercise proper responsibility and restraint to prevent the build-up of excessive indebtedness in the first place."

These calculations and warnings are alarming not in themselves, but in relation to the lack of results. As debt limits are reached by one country after another, and refinancings are resorted to, the program takes on the character of a mass charity operation. That this point may not be far distant is suggested by the rapid growth in debt service. "In 1955, 8 percent of external assistance received was offset by debt service. In 1964 debt service offset 30 percent of external assistance."[12]

Despite the various programs and combinations of programs utilized to date, the rate of population growth in almost all developing countries continues not only alarmingly high but is growing. On the contrary the causal sequences embracing economic, cultural, and political developments appear to be becoming worse. I do not know what further proof is needed of the failure of current efforts to accelerate development. Surely the answer cannot be found in more "soft" loans and in lengthening maturities and reducing loan rates, as suggested in the AID Report, or merely a reduction in the volume of borrowings, as suggested in the IMF Report. Rather a drastic reappraisal of the nature of the problem is indicated before it is too late for such a reappraisal to do any good.

[10] Published by Society for International Development, Washington, D.C., 1965, vol. 2, no. 4, p. 1.

[11] *Ibid.*

[12] *Ibid.*

CHAPTER 6

The Need for a Breakthrough

W. W. ROSTOW HAS made us familiar with the concept of "takeoff," by which he means the attainment of that point or stage from which development becomes self-generating. While it is suggestive, the idea is not satisfying as applied to many developing countries. The difficulty is this: Probably Rostow would say that Colombia, for example, is in the stage of self-generating development. There was a substantial growth in investment and gross national product over the past decade and a much smaller, though fairly persistent, growth in average per capita production and consumption. Urbanization and industrialization, while small in absolute terms, have been taking place rapidly in relative terms. Gross product has grown relative to imports. Mechanization of agriculture has been proceeding rapidly. All these suggest that development has become self-generating.

And yet can one honestly say that the result is satisfying and that a steadily rising standard of living is assured? Here we come to the realm of judgment and forecast where opinions may legitimately differ. There are those who sincerely believe that the cities are already growing too fast—that the provision of public services, education, and housing is lagging and that, if anything, a breathing spell to overcome deficiencies is needed. The objection to this point of view is that it pushes the problem back to a level where the difficulties are multiplied—where remunerative work, public services, decent housing, and education literally cannot be provided, and where the effort to provide them only serves to disperse forces and further diffuse poverty.

To bring about greater equality in incomes and to diffuse the benefits of increasing productivity,[1] the economic machine relies upon the mobility

[1] There appears to be widespread confusion about the relation of productivity to income. As this is not an economics textbook, I will only say dogmatically for the benefit of the general reader that physical productivity per worker has much to do with the *national* real income, has something to do with the difference in *individual* incomes within groups, and is entirely irrelevant in accounting for differences between *groups* or *sectors.* In fact, in the last case, greater productivity in a physical sense may have an inverse relation to income while in the national

of factors, particularly labor. When this mobility is artificially restrained and is insufficient, the inequality, instead of diminishing, may increase. Another element lessening the effectiveness of factor mobility as an automatic regulator is the rapid increase in population. It is this element that accounts for part of our confusion. We all talk about the migration from rural regions to urban, and it is true that there is movement. But—and this is crucial—there may be no *net* migration. Despite mechanization and technification of agriculture, which should "release" people (or make their continual presence and work in the country unnecessary), the rural working force in various countries has continued to grow in absolute terms. This weakens the incentives to mechanize and accentuates a number of the problems mentioned earlier. This lack of sufficient mobility can be a self-generating or self-perpetuating process, but not of development in the sense of permitting a wide diffusion of well-being. For those who distrust verbal formulations, Gustave Ranis and John C. H. Fei demonstrate, in a series of equations of increasing complexity, that under certain conditions inequality between urban and rural income levels may never disappear.[2]

It may be objected that I am confusing the issue by talking in terms of absolute, instead of relative, growth in urban and rural populations. Suppose we start with a population of 16,000,000, evenly divided between town and country. If the percentage of rural workers eventually drops from 50 to 15 percent of the total, one may ask why it matters whether this was achieved by net migration or by a slower rate of growth of the rural poputión. Given a sufficient growth of the urban population, the rural percentage will fall to a point where its income will rise relative to the rise in urban incomes. It may be conceded that although this means a long-drawn-out agony and a needless sacrifice for perhaps generations of the full fruits of agricultural technification, it is, as a matter of arithmetic and simple supply-demand theory, undoubtedly true. The answer must be in political and social terms and from the standpoint of the dynamics of the situation.

In the first place, for the existing 8,000,000 rural and small town population to represent 15 percent of the total would take a growth in the urban population to 53,000,000, which would require many years. Despite the industrial development of Mexico, half the population is still rural, with low incomes and high birthrates. Secondly, we are not dealing only with numbers but with human beings, with emotions. What are they supposed to be doing during this long period of persisting inequality and painfully slow adjustment? Even more to the point, what are their spokesmen supposed to be doing? Surely there would be continuing demands for price supports,

---

scene it has direct relation. Such is the danger in using shopworn and ambiguous words like "productivity" where they are really inapplicable.

[2] *American Economic Review*, September, 1961, p. 533.

government spending in rural areas, and direct intervention of various sorts, all of which would impede the efficient functioning of the economic machine.

Developing countries have no urban policy except that of following in the footsteps of the Americans. They are building slums and creating conditions that will result in horrible losses from traffic congestion or excessive diversion of national savings to urban transport. In a relatively few years, ever-extending suburbs will spread out from all the larger cities. The cities face an indefinite continuance of not quite keeping up with the demand in all public services—of too little, always too late.

It would appear that we dare not wait on natural forces to solve these problems. In Colombia, Dr. Enrique Peñalosa, Chief of the Agrarian Reform Organization, has stated that Agrarian Reform by itself could not resolve the agrarian problem, that it would have to be supplemented by 1,000,000 new jobs outside agriculture (40 percent of the total in agriculture) and 2,000,000 by 1970.[3] Considering the natural increase in the working force, any substantial *net* migration will result only from a deliberate and conscious program.

For these reasons it appears that the concept of takeoff—self-generating development—needs to be supplemented. The various commonly used indexes, mostly reflecting urban progress, may conceal deep-lying and self-perpetuating sore spots in the economy that may effectively prevent it from arriving at the self-generating development stage.

If we could somehow, by a tremendous effort, attain a higher level in a short time, we might break forever the vicious circle of poverty—ignorance—bad health—excessively high birthrate—and so on. We need, in developing countries, something analogous to a breakthrough in the natural sciences. Only in this way can we resolve the paradox concisely stated by Jacob Viner: "It is a paradox of the population problem that on the grounds of historical experience and of theoretical analysis the attainment of high levels of per capita income and of education appear to be almost essential prerequisites of a cure of the problem and that the excessive rate of increase of population is itself the most important barrier to the establishment of these prerequisites."[4]

A dramatic example of the inadequacy of the takeoff analogy can be found in a book by James Street on the tremendous mechanization that has occurred in cotton growing in the United States since 1940.[5] For a

[3] Taken from a speech reported in the press. A similar point was made in the 1963 *Report* of the Agrarian Reform Institute: "The only opportunity that exists for this mass [one million families] to obtain work and sufficient income rests on the ability of the non-agricultural sectors to offer them work in the future," p. 16.

[4] *International Trade and Economic Development,* The Free Press of Glencoe, New York, 1950, p. 149.

[5] James Street, *The New Revolution in the Cotton Economy,* The University of North Carolina Press, Chapel Hill, N.C., 1957.

century and a half, cotton was the principal harvest in the South of the United States. It was a technically backward and depressed industry that depended first on slavery and later on Negro labor which received wages below that of the rest of the country. It did not pay to mechanize. There was a steady movement of labor away from the rural South, but the birthrate was so high that the actual population continued to grow, wages remained below the rest of the country, and education was scanty since the children worked in the cotton fields to supplement the family income. Thus what the author calls the push factor in labor mobility failed to give the desired results.

Then came the Second World War, and the pull factor began. There occurred a tremendous exodus from the rural South to the Armed Forces and the new war industries of the Southern cities. The remaining rural labor force was utilized more intensively and an enormous impetus was given to mechanization. More and more cotton was planted in larger and larger units in the great level stretches of Texas, Arizona, and California. From 1940 to 1950 the rural population in the South declined by 3,600,000, or 22 percent. These totals conceal part of the movement. According to Brown and Ware, "Throughout the old Cotton Belt shifts have been from poorer and hillier areas to leveler, larger and more fertile fields . . . a general shift to the Westward."[6]

And now I come to what is the really exciting part of the story. *The process was irreversible.* Those who left the country remained in the city. Their children remained in school. The birthrate declined. Mechanization continued. Man-hours per bale of cotton declined from 160 to the incredible figure of 10 to 12 in the highly mechanized farms. "The more significant effect of the War, however—the effect likely to have long-term consequences for the process of economic development—is that it brought about full national industrial recovery and an increased level of civilian consumption. Thus it created many opportunities for employment outside of farming while it stimulated the demand for farm goods."[7] In short, the war took the place of a deliberate program of accelerated mobility and job creation. A pattern of one hundred and fifty years was dramatically broken not by natural economic forces but by a crash program. This was truly a breakthrough, and now we can speak with confidence of an assured takeoff. It is not maintained that the Negro "problem" was solved, but that one of the essential links in the chain which blocked the solution was broken.

This concept is not the same as Rosenstein-Rodan's "big push," which stresses the need for initial large investment, particularly in social overhead facilities. Our type of underdeveloped country has long since acquired an infrastructure adequate to support a far higher level of production. What

[6] Harry B. Brown and J. O. Ware, *Cotton,* 3d ed., McGraw-Hill Book Company, 1958, p. 531.

[7] Street, *op. cit.,* p. 177.

we are seeking here might better be called a "breakthrough" that utilizes a strong pull factor in speeding up the mobility of labor so that we may have a better chance of overcoming the drag exerted by too high a rural birthrate, poverty, and ignorance.[8] As Celso Furtado said, commenting on Rosenstein-Rodan's paper, "The main question is not to launch the boat, but to diminish, or avoid widening, the distance that separates it from those that long ago put to sea"[9]—and, it might be added, those that long ago put to sea have lately been acclerating their speed.

Curiously enough, it was a study in 1944 of the status of the Negroes in the United States that led Gunnar Myrdal to formulate his hypothesis or theory of underdevelopment and development whereby the old concept of the vicious circle became a statement that "a social process is cumulative because of circular causation."[10] Myrdal elaborates this thesis with considerable skill and finds in it the explanation for continuing inequalities both within and between countries. He brings out the interrelation of economic and political factors—how, on the one hand, great existing inequality "is inimical to the growth of an effective democracy which would form the power basis for the egalitarian policies" particularly needed, while on the other hand "the more effectively a national state becomes a welfare state—motivated in a way which approaches a more perfect democracy, and having at its disposal national resources big enough to carry out large-scale egalitarian policies with bearable sacrifices on the part of the regions and groups that are relatively better off—the stronger will be both the urge and the capacity to counteract the blind market forces which tend to result in regional inequalities; and this, again, will spur economic development in the country, and so on and so forth, in circular causation."[11]

While Myrdal is unquestionably right in laying emphasis on the importance of the vicious (and benign) circle effect, and while his thesis supports the argument expounded earlier in this chapter about the necessity for a Breakthrough Program, he perhaps overdoes it. In the absence of a means to break into the circular causation, the problem for developing countries is insoluble. Myrdal is forced back to a hope in nationalism, democracy, and education, but the first is obviously a weak reed, and his thesis applies with full strength to the other two factors. Strictly speaking, moreover, his thesis leaves no room for a "creeping progress." It leads him to minimize the importance of disguised unemployment (he mentions it only in passing) and of the lack of mobility of labor. The chief relevance of his work to

[8] See the interesting discussion of this entire concept in *Economic Development for Latin America,* Howard S. Ellis (ed.), St Martin's Press, Inc., New York, 1961, pp. 57–81.

[9] In *ibid.,* p. 73.

[10] *Economic Theory and Underdeveloped Regions,* Methuen & Co., Ltd., London, 1957, p. 50.

[11] *Ibid.,* p. 41.

the argument here is the point that where, in some manner, it is possible to change the causal sequence from a downward to an upward direction, the continuing and augmenting benefits are out of all proportion to the initial costs.

South Italy appears to be another illustration of the failure of the push factor in the face of heavy population increase and of the recent effectiveness of the pull factor. It was not lack of customs protection against the north that kept incomes so low in the south, as Myrdal states, but lack of sufficient movement of labor away from the rural south.

The economic history of Venezuela in the fifties might be cited as a case that casts doubt on the soundness of the breakthrough theory. Thanks to petroleum, the annual rate of growth from 1951 to 1958 in terms of the GNP was at a phenomenally high figure of 8 percent, which one would have thought was sufficiently high to permit a breakthrough to the self-generating stage. Despite this record, however, the rate of growth in the population *increased* to over 3 percent per annum, and in 1959–1962 the growth in the gross product per capita faltered to 0.5 percent.

But on closer examination, the history of Venezuela casts more doubt on the favorable balance of trade approach than on the Breakthrough Theory. The high rate of growth in the gross product was accompanied by great inequality. In 1962 it was estimated that the top 3 percent of the population enjoyed 30 percent of the national income, while the lower 45 percent received only 10 percent. At the same time, health and sanitation programs greatly improved, and the infantile death rate fell to 55 per 1,000 births as against 81 per 1,000 for Latin America as a whole. There was no *net* migration from the countryside, and it is very probable that the continued high rate of population growth is made up of a falling urban birthrate and a falling rural infant mortality rate. The faltering in the rate of growth in the GNP was associated with a decline in the rate of growth of petroleum exports, a decline in the price of petroleum, and a flight of capital.[12] In other words, the 1951–1958 experience could not qualify as a true Breakthrough Program. It is interesting to note that the Venezuelan Plan of the Nation anticipates a fall in the rate of population growth from 3.09 in 1961 to 2.81 in 1975, but the latter is still a very high rate.

Actually, the necessity of a Breakthrough Plan is illustrated by the fact that the rate of population growth rose in Mexico and Venezuela despite the great inflow of dollars and the rapid per capita production growth rates. The counteracting force can be found in the large mass of rural poverty. With a plan designed to abolish this poverty and reduce inequality by a leveling process, the "break-even" point would probably long since have been passed and a declining rate of population increase have been achieved.

[12] This discussion is based on statistics taken from the *Plan de la Nación, 1963–1966*, Caracas, 1962, and the evaluation of the plan by the Committee of Nine, Alliance for Progress, 1963. The inferences are mine.

In the case of Venezuela, however, a Breakthrough Program may require a corresponding program in Colombia because of the ease of passage of migrants over the long, unguarded frontier. Such emigration would not even be a solution for Colombia, as numerous historical examples from high-birthrate countries and regions indicate.

I am indebted to an Indian economist for a quotation from a World Bank mission which he does not identify but which puts the issue so clearly that it deserves to be requoted: "If it was simply a question of trying to achieve the maximum increase in income and output *during the next five years,* a different pattern of investment would be appropriate. But the economy would then be less well prepared for further expansion in subsequent periods."[13] I would amend this to say that a different pattern not only of investment but of demand, production, and resource allocation would be appropriate. If a sustained five-year program would have a real impact on our vicious circles, it would appear that the economy would be better- rather than worse-prepared for further expansion. Without a solution of the rural and population problems, the effect of the continuing heavy investment program is offset by the increase in population and by the growing inequality, and it is difficult to discern any progress toward self-sustaining development.

Lloyd Reynolds has called attention to the paradox offered by Puerto Rico where a highly successful development operation in terms of the growth in per capita income and establishment of new industries resulted in surprisingly little growth in industrial employment and a continued high level of unemployment, despite considerable migration to the United States.[14] Evidence was presented that the steady rise in legal wage minima, industry by industry, may have enhanced the attractiveness of capital-intensive industries and have increased capital investment relative to employment. This was doubtless true, but one is also left with the disquieting query whether in less favorable circumstances a continued adhesion to existing patterns of demand and the adoption of the latest capital-intensive technical processes are compatible with the requisite advance in nonagricultural employment, even if wages are not advanced excessively. In other words, deliberate changes in relationships of the type proposed here may not only be essential to break vicious circles but may also be essential over a longer term to prevent chronic unemployment if (1) demand is centered on products requiring capital-intensive investment, (2) foreign exchange is strictly limited, and (3) the working force is increasing rapidly. In these circumstances even the existence of the classical assumptions of freely moving prices, competition between firms and for jobs, and factor mobility may

[13] H. Venkatasubbiah, *International Development Review,* June, 1964, p. 14.

[14] Lloyd G. Reynolds, "Wages and Employment in a Labor Surplus Economy," *American Economic Review,* March, 1965, pp. 19–39.

not result in sufficiently rapid rises in well-being and nonagricultural employment.

The classical answer would be that sufficiently low wages and competition would in themselves bring about a change in relationships of employment to capital to insure full employment, but under the conditions assumed much of this employment should really be classified as disguised unemployment. In other words, what we are questioning is the efficacy of the classical system that functioned relatively efficiently in what are now developed countries in providing steadily increasing nonagricultural employment, to make sufficient headway against the vicious-circle effect in the developing countries of today. Of course, where the basic classical assumptions do not apply, there is even less possibility that the mere addition to capital formation, supplemented by foreign borrowing, will provide sufficient nonagricultural employment, as the case of Puerto Rico clearly demonstrates. In short, it is possible that continuation of the present indefinite loaning and charity programs cannot provide the breakthrough necessary and can only end in disaster for many countries.

Classical economics gave us not only tools of analysis highly useful and relevant to the problems of development but also some hypotheses bearing on the possible sequence of events that are relevant. The Malthusian hypothesis was one, closely related to the law or principle of diminishing returns. The economies of scale suggested the existence of a different type of sequence—increasing demand, growing market, economies of scale, reduced marginal costs and prices, growing demand. These sequences are directly contrary to each other. Those economists who are inclined to stress the gloomy consequences of the population explosion and the economic vicious-circle effect are the intellectual descendants of Malthus. Those who consciously or unconsciously believe that economic progress is self-generating or self-perpetuating are the lineal descendants of Adam Smith and Alfred Marshall (the advantages of the division of labor as a concept are obviously a forerunner of the economies flowing from large-scale production).

Since most economists are from developed countries, the optimistic view generally prevails. In economic development, the benign circle has many more adherents than the vicious circle.

This sharp division obscures the possibility of a different and more complex sequence in which technical progress, the economies of scale, foreign borrowing, and other expansive factors exist side by side with and outweigh a high rate of population growth, the resort to soils more costly to exploit, and to sharply rising costs of urban public services. In such a sequence rising per capita income may continue *for a time* but vicious-circle effects may eventually outweigh the benign circle effects. For this reason the use of the phrases "take-off" and "self-generating development" may be very misleading. Worse, their use may contribute to a dangerous feeling that current problems will pass and eventual transition to the developed country category is inevitable.

It may be concluded, therefore, that a Breakthrough Program capable of quickly achieving a higher economic and educational level must be one designed to break the interrelated vicious circles of rural poverty and too high rate of population growth. A subtitle to this book might well be "Beating the Numbers Game." The passage of time intensifies rather than ameliorates the problem. A 4 percent rate of product growth may not be twice as good as a 2 percent rate. A rate of growth that permits and indeed encourages a rapid geometrical progression in numbers would be eventually self-defeating.

Growing inequality, cost-push inflation and other obstacles to mobility and industrialization, agricultural technification, preventive medicine, government improvisation of scattered policies, and a worsening relation of population to resources, all tend to create and perpetuate a growing and desperately poor subsistence economy composed of the disguised unemployed. The problem and the effort required to solve it are greater today than they were five or ten years ago and will assuredly be still greater in five or ten more years. The comfortable view that progress is being made, even though slowly, is based on superficial factors and not on a more profound analysis of the working of vicious circles. Even at the risk of being accused of economic terrorism or defeatism, it is of the utmost importance that we challenge the comfortable view, because it is blocking the adoption of anything that could remotely be called a true Breakthrough Program.

Where the combination of factors such as just indicated exists, the need for a breakthrough type of program cannot be determined by reference to any rate of per capita growth in output but by the existence and recognition of factors of an adverse self-perpetuating nature which could, in time, bring per capita growth to an end. This intermediate sequence *could*—I do not say necessarily *does*—even apply to such countries with remarkable growth rates as Mexico and Venezuela, since they have not as yet broken the vicious circle of rural poverty—high birth rate—rural poverty. Until they do, judgment on the permanence of their development sequence must be reserved. For countries not so favored, the prospects, of course, are much worse and a continuance of present-type programs hardly seems the answer. What is needed is a drastic revision in objectives, diagnoses, strategy, and magnitude of effort.

CHAPTER 7

Lessons from Developed Economies

I STATED IN the first chapter that we needed in this field to apply our tools of economic analysis to the problems of developing countries and not try to develop a special economics of development. Although I still believe this to be true, it is also so difficult to escape from old ideas and preconceptions that I find analogies helpful and suggestive. The present chapter, therefore, is devoted to a consideration of certain episodes in the history of developed countries that I believe are relevant and helpful in working out an alternative approach to accelerate development. These are in addition to the examples previously cited of the early Canadian settlers and the wartime changes in the rural South.

I. *The Great Depression*

There is probably not much disagreement among economists today that the fundamental diagnosis of the problem by New Deal economists was correct and that the remedy for the Depression of the 1930s was to put together idle men and idle machines to produce the things the community so desperately needed. Again, in retrospect, the limited measure of success the New Deal achieved in this objective was owing to the small-scale, hesitant, and vacillating policy employed; the failure to slough off shibboleths and misapplied slogans;[1] the mistaken analogies of "pump priming" and "self-generating recovery," adopted with no appreciation of the leakages resulting from wage and price inflation, too rapid an increase in the propensity to save, and so forth. (In recalling these analogies, one is reminded of Joan Robinson's observation, "So economics limps along with one foot in untested hypotheses and the other in untestable slogans.")[2]

[1] One beauty was "You can no more spend yourself rich than drink yourself sober."

[2] *Economic Philosophy,* Aldine Publishing Co., Chicago, 1962, p. 25.

In this pioneer effort, however, much was learned. Professional economists at least took to heart the difference between private and public finance and acquired much more insight into the functioning of the economy. Few succumbed to the lure of subsistence homesteads or cottage industries as generalized solutions. The groundwork was laid in the tax and social legislation for a later profound modification in the patterns of saving and consumption.

Probably the reason why this shattering experience has not been studied more intensively in connection with development problems is that the unemployment in developing countries is in rural regions and remains concealed, and the machines and equipment are idle at night and on holidays instead of during the single shift on ordinary workdays. But these are superficial differences. In essence, the present problem and opportunity are the same as those with which the New Dealers wrestled—namely, the employment of underutilized resources, the creation of effective demand, and the prevention of developments that choke off the growth in effective demand.[3]

II. *Wartime Economics*

It is also curious that so little attention has been paid to the lessons that might be learned from wartime experience, especially in the United States. Given an overriding objective to which everything else is subordinated, the production possibilities are almost unbelievable. The United States, with not much more infrastructure or industrial equipment than in the late thirties, and with 12,000,000 people serving in the Armed Forces instead of being formally listed as unemployed, produced a prodigious amount of goods, not only arming, feeding, and clothing itself but also contributing substantially to the upkeep of its allies.

How was this accomplished? First, not only by rationing consumer goods and discontinuing the production of luxury goods (chiefly motor cars), but also by cutting back all investment that could not be expected to make a marked contribution to the war effort. Unskilled people (especially housewives) were quickly trained for industrial work, and key equipment was utilized on a 24-hour-a-day, 7-day-a-week basis. The same economy that a few years earlier could not provide a decent standard of living for its people now did precisely that and in addition waged a tremendous war on many fronts, building a mighty fleet, air force, army, and merchant marine! In 1942, 1943, and 1944, respectively, 36 percent, 45 percent, and 47 percent of total output in the United States went into the war effort. The GNP, in 1954 prices, rose from $186 billion in 1938 to over $320 billion in 1944. Despite rationing, per capita consumption rose throughout the war. Commenting on this record, Dernburg and McDougall wrote: "The fantastic increase in real output which took place was made possible

[3] For the earlier excessive propensity to save, substitute sellers' inflation.

by the existence of a vast pool of unemployed resources at the start of the war and by the willingness of most Americans to work overtime to make up for the manpower drain to the armed forces."[4]

The same simple principles of setting objectives, establishing priorities, cutting back on nonessentials, and utilizing human and material resources intensively are available to our type of developing economies. What is lacking are the will and the desire to use them and, perhaps, the knowledge. There is also the possibly unacknowledged belief that a great effort is really unnecessary because the Alliance for Progress will turn the trick without pain or strain on the part of the beneficiaries.

Allan G. B. Fisher has discussed the possible lessons of the war period from the point of view of developed economies.[5] He concludes that while the productive performance of wartime suggests great possibilities, it is doubtful whether in peacetime we would or should tolerate such a degree of state interference in the pattern of production-consumption. Therefore, he says, we have little to learn from the war experience.[6] He is doubtless right in terms of protracted programs in developed economies in which little slack exists. But for a breakthrough program, and for underdeveloped countries where the degree of idle men and equipment exceeds that in the United States in 1939, the objection would not hold. For such a program the important consideration is not the interference in the pattern of consumption, but the great net addition to goods of mass consumption that is possible and the necessity of quickly attaining a new and much higher plateau of well-being. Moreover, it is to be hoped that when the breakthrough is achieved, the pattern of consumption can be increasingly modified by the more subtle and indirect methods of taxation and social security. Despite Fisher's skepticism, therefore, I still think that the wartime analogy is relevant and has much to teach us.

III. *The Recovery of Western Europe*

This case was a variation of the war-effort theme. The overriding objective was the rebuilding of the destroyed physical productive capacity as rapidly as possible. Much of this was done with internal resources. While the industrial and agricultural capacities were being built up, however, a large deficit in the balance of payments was unavoidable. The great contribution of the Marshall Plan was in underwriting the overall program by making up the balance of payments deficit for a limited period. A viable

[4] *Macro-Economics,* McGraw-Hill Book Company, 1960, p. 15.

[5] See his *Economic Progress and Social Security,* Macmillan & Co., Ltd., London, 1945, in the Spanish edition. The relevant chapter is "The Lessons of the War."

[6] But it is interesting to note that elsewhere he remarks, "One of the most interesting secondary results of the war experience is the discovery of the possibilities, in many countries, of increasing the production of food while decreasing, at the same time, the number of producers of food." Chapter on blind alleys, sec. d.

program by means of which the varous countries of Western Europe were to become self-supporting at a relatively comfortable level in a relatively short period was worked out by European statesmen and technicians. Partly for economic and humanitarian reasons but mostly for military and political ones, the United States not only accepted the program but made the major part of its contribution as a gift. The whole operation was a brillant success—an experiment in economic and political planning on an intercontinental scale embracing many diverse economies and carried out in a superb manner. Probably Western Europe could have recovered without American aid, but unquestionably the aid enormously accelerated the process.

Surely this episode again has something to teach us of the importance of setting limited, understandable objectives, devising a program designed to attain the objectives, and establishing priorities in making a major effort to attain a plateau from which further recovery can be self-generating and independent of outside help. So far, all these procedures are lacking in the Alliance for Progress approach.

IV. *The Broad Pattern of Economic Growth*

The economic development of what are now the developed countries has its roots well back in the eighteenth century. Probably too much emphasis has been given to inventions and industrial development and not enough to the steady growth in agricultural productivity that not only made the rapid population growth possible but also markedly changed the distribution of the working force. The growth in agricultural output per worker released the manpower needed for the great growth in the production of all the other things, and until recent times, the released manpower could be absorbed.

It is natural to assume that the presently developing countries should duplicate this process, but at a much accelerated rate because of the great advances which have been made in agricultural technique.[7] Indeed, the technical progress in the field has recently been too rapid for comfort. The inability to adjust to this rapidity, the reluctance to rely on the demonstrably inefficient and callous working of the push factor in labor mobility, and the readiness to resort to almost any device to avoid the economic adjustment called for, are creating grave problems for all countries, both developed and developing. There is a great difference, however, in degree. What is a headache for developed countries is building up to a disaster for many underdeveloped ones, who stand in danger of losing markets abroad and

[7] Myrdal, on the other hand, appears to believe that little can be learned from the history of developed countries. "All the underdeveloped countries are now starting out on a line of economic policy which has no close historical precedent in any advanced country." *Economic Theory and Underdeveloped Regions*, Methuen & Co., Ltd., London, 1957, p. 102.

whose rural workers cannot earn a decent living at home. It is a situation reminiscent of a Great Depression, when for a time man lost the ability to resolve the economic problems he had created. The halfhearted solutions attempted by various countries are in marked contrast to the brilliant manner in which the war and immediate postwar problems were resolved.

In any case, the lesson to be drawn from the broad pattern of development in developed countries is the tremendous shift from agricultural occupations accompanied, after the 1870s, by a falling birthrate.

V. *Shifts in the Labor Force*

It is generally not appreciated how much of the growth in the GNP in developing countries (and even in some developed ones) is attributable to the distribution of the annual addition to the working force. This is a variant of the broad pattern of economic growth theme just considered, but is so suggestive that it merits separate treatment. The point depends for its validity on (1) there being a marked difference in income among workers, and (2) the new workers joining the ranks of the higher-paid. It can best be illustrated by a simple example.

Suppose the working force in year 1 is 7,000,000, distributed equally between urban and rural activities. Suppose further that the GNP is 15 billion units, of which the urban half accounts for 10 billion and the rural half 5 billion, or 2.860 units per urban worker and 1.430 per rural worker. Suppose that the increase in the working force in year 2 is 3 percent, or 210,000.

Suppose finally that all this force joins either rural or urban activities and that this decision does not affect the present value of production per worker (a very dubious supposition in the case of rural work). The impact of the GNP would be as follows:

If all rural,	210,000 × 1.430 = 300,000,000 = 2% of 15 million
If all urban,	210,000 × 2.860 = 600,000,000 = 4% " " "

In one case the GNP would increase by 2 percent (or less than the growth in population of 3 percent) because of the new workers. In the other case it would increase by 4 percent or by an average of 1 percent *for all workers, solely for this reason.*

Obviously many possibilities suggest themselves. If the discrepancy is greater than pictured—if the addition to nonagricultural pursuits helps in itself to raise productivity of the other workers in nonagricultural work because of, say, greater economies of scale, and if the addition to agriculture results in a further fall in the average gross product in this field—then the difference that would result from different distributions of new workers would be even more spectacular.

Sheahan's discussion of the importance of the redistribution of the working force in recent French history was mentioned in Chapter 4. It would appear that writers on growth and development have not given sufficient emphasis on the contribution resulting from a better allocation of the working force through mobility of labor and competition.

Conclusion

All these episodes as well as others scattered throughout the text have important things to teach us if we examine them with open minds. The wartime and Marshall Plan illustrations show what can be accomplished by subordinating all policies to the attainment of specific and comprehensible objectives other than a rate of growth in the GNP. The Marshall Plan, in particular, may be contrasted with the sprinkler approach. The long struggle against unemployment initiated in the Great Depression, and culminating recently in the deliberate stimulation of consumer demand through tax reduction and the adoption[8] of incomes policies, has much to teach us once we accept the hypothesis of mass unemployment (in a strict economic sense) in some developing countries. The supreme importance of agricultural technology and the optimum distribution of the labor force is brought out in the other two illustrations concerning the economic growth of developed countries and the distribution of the annual addition to the working force.

Japan is one of the few countries that in this century have safely entered the developed-country category. Analyses of the remarkable Japanese experience indicate that the elements which have to do with self-help, with diverting resources out of agriculture, with forcing overall effective demand while restraining income inflation, and with pushing exports, are all highly relevant. Publications of the Japanese Planning Office show a high degree of economic sophistication. The birthrate is falling. Some of the difficult legacies from the past lie in the tiny size of farms, the widespread practice of part-time farming, and the difficulty of mechanizing such farming—all of which problems Latin American countries might take to heart. When Japanese speak of the agrarian problem, they mean the difficulty of modernization and of making it worthwhile for part-time farmers to retire and sell their properties. And they are concerned with this problem even though the rural population has fallen to 12 percent of the total and the emigration of agricultural workers to other occupations continues.[9]

All these examples and others that could be cited illustrate the thesis of Chapter 1 that our principal task in developing countries is to apply known theory and experience to special cases.

[8] In Great Britain and various European countries.

[9] *Economic Survey of Japan, 1962–63,* Japanese Planning Agency, Tokyo, p. 113.

CHAPTER 8

An Alternative Approach: The Breakthrough Plan

Recapitulation of the Nature of the Problem

It was argued in Chapters 3 and 4 on the diagnosis that a large proportion and, in some of our countries, even a majority of the workers are, economically speaking, virtually unemployed. These are the people engaged in a primitive type of agriculture, as well as the workers in small towns who are dependent on this form of agriculture. To this total may be added many more workers in towns and cities which have no industrial base. Owing to the frequent holidays, the minority who have regular employment probably work no more than some 220 days a year. It is obvious that people out of work, or working little, cannot enjoy a high standard of consumption.

It was also argued that remunerative employment in agriculture could not be created for this labor force—that the future of agriculture, as in developed countries, lies in mechanization and technification, requiring much less land and much fewer people. Further, it was pointed out that the translation of felt demand into effective demand and hence remunerative employment—an effective working out of Say's Law—is prevented by numerous powerful elements which impede mobility of labor, as well as by mistaken government policies.

It was argued that the failure to break the circle engendered by intense and hopeless poverty could bring the whole development process to a stop—that the forces of regression can be as self-generating as constructive forces. Finally, it was implied that the various approaches or programs that have or are currently being tried offer little hope of success, though extended treatment of the Capital Formation Approach was postponed to Chapter 9. Therefore a breakthrough plan is necessary to attain quickly a higher level from which the constructive self-generating forces can gain the ascendancy.

Even if a country has arrived at a point where continuing development appears assured, a policy of acceleration may still be justified to relieve misery and suffering. Thus in the United States a program to abolish the remaining poverty has been adopted. If this is a desirable and humane objective in such a relatively rich country as the United States, there would appear to be hardly a country in the world where an acceleration in the production of goods and services and more equality in consumption are not desirable. Thus the approach suggested here does not depend exclusively on the breakthrough argument.

The nature of the problem suggests the elements of a plan. It is simply to bring together idle men and idle equipment to produce goods and services to satisfy felt needs, to channel resources to this end, and to subordinate other objectives to the early attainment of a decent minimum standard of living for the masses. Stated thus, there can surely be little disagreement. It is in the elaboration of a program to accomplish these objectives that difficulties arise.

Elements of a Plan

The program described here is in essence a very simple one. Instead of trying to secure an increase in productivity of all workers in their present occupations, it proposes that the least productive (the virtually unemployed) be given an opportunity to secure more remunerative work. It suggests that we provide incentives or a pull to overcome the sluggishness in the mobility of labor and that we remove existing deterrents to such mobility. Instead of setting the objective as a certain rate of growth in the GNP, it proposes to tackle directly the problems of wider employment and inequality by setting the objective as the creation of a certain number of new nonagricultural jobs in a given time. It also suggests taking action to ensure that the bulk of these jobs will be in the provision of urban housing, public services, and wage goods, so that the additional people will be in part employed in making additional goods they themselves need. Insofar as the objective is attained, the overpopulation in rural districts is reduced and the effective demand for foodstuffs is increased. The plan proposes that the initial major emphasis be placed on raising the consumption of the poorest sectors of the community rather than on increasing investment. It seeks to achieve a greater measure of equality in consumption by a process of upgrading on the one hand and a better enforcement of progressive individual taxation on the other.

This, then, is the objective based on the diagnosis of widespread underemployment, particularly in rural areas and small towns. In general terms, the objective would be the same for our whole group of developing countries; in specific terms (such as the number of jobs and the length of the work year), it would vary according to the degree of underutilization of existing equipment, the availability of foreign exchange resources, the magnitude of the problem, and the will to do. When the breakthrough plan was first proposed in summary fashion in Colombia in 1961, the public impression, perhaps because of faulty presentation, was that the essential point consisted of the migration of labor to the cities. Actually, of course, the keystone is the provision of new and better-paid jobs. Migration would be a consequence rather than the initiating factor. It is just as important to provide work for the urban unemployed as for the rural.

Presented in this way, the plan appears perhaps deceptively simple. Actually it would require economic programming of a high level of technical competence. Just as its inspiration owes a good deal to wartime experience, so in its mechanics it relies more heavily on direct controls and rationing than most economists in developed countries would probably care to invoke in the absence of war.

For example, to restrain the importation and/or production of luxury goods (expensive homes, cars, and so on) little reliance could be placed initially on the taxing arm. Stopping tax avoidance and closing up loopholes are the fruit of persistent years of effort. A short-term program would depend mainly on the exercise of the authority to grant or withhold building licenses, to control imports, and to ration available exchange.

The exchange licensing authority would be confronted with many applications claiming that they would save $\$x$ exchange in the form of future importations, create x jobs, utilize national raw materials, and so forth. Such applications would have to be subjected to very close study. The following questions should be the main criteria for this type of war in which the enemy is dire poverty: (1) How much use of existing equipment can the applicant show? (2) How much more use of the existing equipment will the new imports permit? (For example, will they enable the applicant to pass from one shift to two?) (3) Will the imports increase the capacity to produce wage goods or goods of mass consumption immediately?

Applications receiving high priority would be spare parts in general; goods that permit passing from one to two or three shifts daily; new cotton textile machinery in cases where operations are already on a three-shift basis; equipment for water, sewer, and electric plants in cities expected to show large population increases; hand tools; equipment for the construction industry; and so on. If capital is scarce, preference should be given to investments yielding immediate returns. When the emphasis in exchange rationing is shifted from more roundabout capital investments to those permitting intensive use of existing capital, the increase in returns can be enormous.

If criteria such as these were adopted, I believe that the ratio of production to the stock of capital could be sharply raised, the productivity of new investment could be greatly increased, and the ratio of employment to capital could be radically altered in a short period.[1] It seems to me that the

[1] Some writers seem to think that the ratio of capital to employment—the amount of capital it takes to create one new job—is fixed and is so high as to make

limitation on production imposed by shortage of foreign exchange suggested by a study of historical relationships would not apply, at least for a time. Exchange licensing, then, would become one of the chief arms of policy.

Another main policy instrument would be housing, a topic which brings us to the actual mechanics of getting the program under way. Although the plan's overall objective is the creation of nonagricultural jobs for agriculturalists (which could well be an objective for developed countries also), we are in a moving situation, with population and the working force increasing at a rapid rate. Thus before we can effect a net shift of population from rural to urban surroundings, we must first provide, say, a yearly 3 percent increase in jobs for the natural increase in the working force. If the gainfully employed are distributed roughly 50-50 between urban and rural activities, and it is desired to reduce the rural force from 50 to 40 percent of the total in three years, there would have to be an increase in urban jobs of around 15 percent of the total working force, or 30 percent of the original urban working force. Though not an impossible goal, this is certainly one requiring a tremendous effort, and an effort which few countries would probably be prepared to embark upon. Yet if the goal is set too low, we may do little more than provide for the natural increase in the working force. An objective that would show great results would be, say, a 4½ percent decrease per annum in rural employment continued for three years—the breakthrough period—and lowered to 3 percent thereafter. Even this program would, under our assumptions above, mean an increase of 31 percent in urban jobs and a decline in the rural population only to a little below 40 percent of the total. In countries with a lower rural excess, the numerical objectives would be reduced.[2]

If this should be chosen as an overall objective, then the immediate aim would be the provision of adequate urban housing for the expected addition. And here we come to a very important difference between the breakthrough program and the New Deal problem of providing employment. In the New Deal's case, the listed unemployed were already in the cities, with housing of a sort. Hence the pump priming had to be sought in public works of various kinds. But in the breakthrough program, housing and public services provide the obvious object of pump priming. This phrase is perhaps not very appropriate, since housing and public services would remain the main items in the investment segment as long as the program continued.

The nature and financing of the housing program will be considered below. Here we shall continue with some of the overall planning problems

---

it impossible to have many new jobs without a tremendous increase in saving and borrowing. They are unconsciously postulating the continuance of present inefficient practices and patterns.

[2] As this study was being completed, references were appearing in the press to the Spanish Plan of Development, designed to reduce the proportion of rural population from 40% to 33% in four years.

involved. If a recent business or employment census is available, and if national accounts have been maintained for some years, the choice of a numerical objective of nonagricultural jobs will enable us to forecast the probable impact on the gross product and on its various parts (except where past relationships are changed because of the imposition of new controls). It will also be possible to predict the distribution of employment by localities and hence the need by years and by city for additional housing and public services.

What cannot be accurately forecast is what rate of increase in aggregate investment will be compatible with the physical ability to produce while avoiding inflation. On the one hand will be the unknown net effect of the addition to the working force, more intensive use of equipment, the nature and extent of the bottlenecks, and the effect of rationing exchange. On the other hand, there will be the multiplier effect of increased investment on aggregate consumer demand, additional saving out of the additional income and the success of an incomes policy. In short, in determining the rate of acceleration, the planners have, as it were, to feel their way, pushing the economic machine as rapidly as they dare, but not to cause such a degree of overheating as to result in a runaway price situation. It is a familiar problem, on a smaller scale, in developed economies, and compromises and mistakes are unavoidable. One can only take comfort from the fact that doing nothing is the greatest mistake of all. Past global and static relationships of investment and gross production are probably not too helpful in a developing situation where marginal increments are more important. Another development that will require careful watching is the elasticity of supply of agricultural production and the relative price incentives that may be necessary to call forth the requisite supplies. In a country whose climate permits two or more harvests a year, the response can be more rapid.

An increase in employment and output may result from an increase from the proportion of income saved and invested, from a decline in the proportion saved but an increase in the absolute amount, or from a constant amount of investment but an increase in consumption. These surprising changes in the relationship of investment to gross output can result from greater efficiency or employment of hitherto unused factors. The relationships are clearly much more complex that generally appreciated and there appears to be no way for forecasting changes in the relationship with any certainty. Since, however, increased employment will necessitate more housing (which is included in investment), public services, and goods in the pipeline of production, it will doubtless result in an increase in the aggregate volume of investment. The issue becomes whether this increase should be completely or partly offset by a forced decline in other investment, or whether the volume of saving will increase to permit a net increase in investment. It appears difficult to determine in advance with any assurance the probable change in the ratio of gross saving to gross product and the absolute amount of additional saving out of additional income resulting from the additional employment. This is not a criticism of the breakthrough approach as it applies with equal force to the capital formation approach.

Even with a reasonably good incomes policy, *some* rise in investment (in money terms) and prices is probably unavoidable to secure the additional employment desired and to provide sufficient incentives to increase agricultural production to meet the additional effective demand. Up to now, recoveries from depressed conditions in developed countries have always been accompanied by some price advances. In the Second World War in Britain and the United States, with rationing and high taxes, the rise in prices was restricted to 50 percent despite the tremendous withdrawal of manpower from production and the almost intolerable pressure to produce.

Various possible ways of tackling this problem suggest themselves. One is to avoid the sudden imposition of a large housing–public services program on top of existing programs in these fields and, through the control of licensing, to proceed for a time with the substitution of middle-class and upper-working-class housing for luxury housing and other types of construction. In this way the total of construction may be increased more slowly, allowing time for assessment of its impact on wage goods and service industries. However, since the volume of savings (and probably the ratio of savings to the increase in income) will tend to expand almost immediately, it is to be expected that the total volume of investment will also increase.

The second approach would be to enlist the cooperation of industrialists and trade-union leaders in those segments of industry that have in the past been most prompt to take advantage of any growth in monetary demand. Thus the overall instruments of control for the large sectors of the economy where competition is still dominant (agriculture, services, construction, parts of transport, and commerce) could be supplemented by direct appeals in the monopoly sectors. Such appeals are generally not very effective, but they sometimes work for a time and in particular circumstances.

The greatest threat to the proposed program is indoubtedly inflation of incomes and prices—an inflation initiated not so much by excessive monetary expansion as by price and wage markups. Later monetary restriction is a clumsy and unsatisfactory way of dealing with this type of inflation, because once it has been permitted to occur, forcing prices and wage rates down is virtually impossible except by creating heavy unemployment. Therefore, much emphasis is placed here on educational propaganda and appeals and on restraining the increase in the total volume of new investment. Since the industrialized and unionized sectors are generally quite small in our group of developing countries, it might be possible to back up the moral suasion approach by a positive incomes policy wherein the government would participate in wage negotiations and would try to limit advances so that they did no more than compensate for rises in the cost of living and give workers a modest share in the increase in productivity. The unions would probably not be prepared to accept these terms unless they applied also to profits and dividends.

Alvin Hansen's ingenious suggestion of prohibiting a price advance for six months after a wage advance[3] would be somewhat drastic for Latin American countries, which are not yet even conscious of the problem. At least allowance would have to be made for the chronic rise in the cost of living resulting from monetary (demand-pull) inflation.

There is some feeling that the workers in an industry are entitled to wage advances corresponding to the increase in productivity in that industry, regardless of its origin. Even if this did not cause the prices of the products of that industry to rise, the owners would expect a share of the benefits, inequality among workers would grow, and prices would have to rise where gains in productivity were below the average (as in services). The final result would be a steady advance in the price index, which would again require monetary or fiscal expansion to arrest the growth in the unemployed or maintain the rate of growth in employment. A better policy would appear to be the one on which President Johnson's guidelines for wage negotiations are based. This policy is to focus on strategic industries where imperfect competition prevails and to try and limit their wage advances to the national average gain in productivity. In individual cases where productivity gains are above the average, this should mean lower prices.

It may be noted that such a policy would be inconsistent with that of profit sharing, which is sometimes advocated in Latin American countries. Not only would profit sharing absorb all the gains from growing productivity, but if it led to profits falling relative to the general return on capital, forces would be set in motion to redress these relative falls. In other words, prices would rise also on this score.

Up to now, government intervention has generally favored wage increases far in excess of the goals mentioned above. The development of a rational incomes policy would, therefore, be a task of considerable difficulty. However, concerning the application of price controls in France in the remarkable upsurge of the 1950s, Sheahan says, "It is standard practice, emphasized repeatedly to unions and to firms, to refuse authority to pass on [to the consumer] wage increases in the individual industry going significantly beyond those in manufacturing generally."[4] To this policy Sheahan attributes the ability of the French economy to operate from 1953 to 1957 at a level of 98 percent employment without a significant rise in overall prices.

[3] *Economic Issues of the 1960s,* Harvard University Press, Cambridge, Mass., 1960, pp. 37–38.

[4] John Sheahan, *Promotion and Control of Industry in Post War France,* Harvard University Press, Cambridge, Mass., 1963, p. 36.

A third line of approach to the problem of price advances would be to institute studies in each industry with the objectives of anticipating investment requirements and of determining at which points in the growth in physical demand bottlenecks might be expected to emerge. Of course, action would be taken well in advance to avoid stoppages from these sources.

Still another avenue, again suggested by wartime experience, is the exploration of alternative means of meeting demand. An example might be the substitution of long-distance railroad hauls for truck hauls, or the substitution of artisan-made furniture for factory-made. Economizing in the demand for electric energy during peak hours would be another form of rationing. Cutting back on public investment that might be expected to make a small or a negative contribution to the overall program would be another means of permitting an expansion in the program.

Regarding the analogy of a wartime economy and the possible consequences of a similar large increase in demand, the conceivable desirability of generalized price controls naturally suggests itself. For all practical purposes, this means freezing rather than controlling prices. While it appears unjust, unnecessary, and dangerous that bottlenecks should touch off rapid price rises which might become generalized, the danger of not providing adequate stimuli for the production of important items must also be kept in mind. Perhaps a working solution would be to (1) remove all controls where there is abundant competition, as in foodstuffs, bricks, and transport, and (2) impose temporary controls until bottlenecks are broken in industries where little competition exists, or where a rapid increase in production is considered unessential and/or too costly in foreign-exchange requirements.

The objective of the breakthrough program is threefold. It is concerned not so much to achieve an increase in the GNP as to secure the maximum increase possible in a short time in housing, urban public services, and goods and services of mass consumption. It aims to resolve the agrarian problem by decreasing competition in agriculture, especially between colonial-type farmers and commercial farmers, and by increasing effective demand. Finally, it hopes by a great effort to pass the point of no return: i.e., that point where enough of the people are being educated, are enjoying better health, and are coming to have good housing, remunerative jobs, viable farms, and so on, that the forces of development are truly self-generating and the birthrate may be expected to decline.

In other words, to convert this program into a rate of percentage growth in the GNP is to miss the main point. More important than achieving a certain rate of per capita growth in income is achieving a much greater equality in per capita consumption, especially when this can be done without calling for a redistribution of income—a leveling up rather than a leveling down. It is more necessary to overcome the drag of the population increase by a sudden and dramatic rise in well-being of the most depressed half of the population, which has hardly yet been touched by the industrial and scientific revolutions except as its resentment and bitterness have been aroused.

The incentive which the breakthrough program relies upon for industrialization comes, as in wartime, from the side of demand rather than from tax exemptions, which generally appear *after* profits are made, as a bonus. The one exemption would be a depreciation schedule graduated according to intensity of use of equipment.

Another way of characterizing this approach is to say that it offers a means of permitting Say's Law—i.e., that the product of one man's work is the demand for the product of another man's work—to operate effectively by enabling men to produce something which other people want rather than, as now, something which they do not want. Sidney Dell puts it succinctly: "An underdeveloped country's first concern is to find useful employment for those of its citizens who at the present time are adding little or nothing to the national real output and income."[5] Still another characterization would be to say that the program suggests a way of correcting the faulty functioning of natural economic forces by substituting the pull for the push element in the mobility of labor and by overcoming the resistance to that mobility offered by the growth of monopoly elements in industry and labor. It provides the appropriate economic response to agricultural technification and paves the way for further and accelerated technification.

This last point brings us to the question of what happens after the breakthrough. Given the correctness of the diagnosis, probably most economists would concede the theoretical validity of the short-term program and would not be concerned over the maintenance of demand and employment after the initial housing program came to an end. Backlogs would have been built up in luxury housing and office and commercial buildings, and the demand for wage goods would continue if investment was sustained. What would cause them real concern, to repeat, would be the source of new capital and intermediate goods once the existing equipment was being utilized intensively. One cannot pass from a third to a fourth shift![6] So although it is clear that much more can be done with actual resources, we cannot escape indefinitely from the problem of the balance of payments. For the continuance of the program, even on a reduced scale, we are forced back to the necessity of increasing exports of goods or services, substituting for imports by domestic growth or manufacture, borrowing, attracting foreign investment, or qualifying for grants.

Balance of Payments Policy

If, as is here argued, developing countries suffer from unemployment, it becomes economically justifiable to take actions that could be criticized

[5] Sidney Dell, *Trade Blocs and Common Markets,* Constable & Co., Ltd., London, 1963, p. 163.

[6] But the continuance of three shifts means that every additional unit of equipment imported is equivalent to three units on the previous single-shift basis.

if labor were well distributed and truly gainfully occupied. So far as it goes, this is an argument for import substitution. One difficulty is that industrial protection frequently requires expensive capital imports, gives little employment, and increases local costs of production. It may make more sense to push exports of primary products, though of course more resistance will be encountered. If the country is a small producer, it may develop exports without making enough of a nuisance of itself to arouse the developed countries to impose quantitative restrictions or take other restrictive measures. If it is a larger country and can hope to develop an internal market big enough to permit obtaining the economies of scale, protection may be a better device.

The ways and means of increasing exports must generally be treated on a product-by-product and country-by-country basis. It may be noted, however, that by incurring wage inflation which has brought wage costs in certain fields far above the national average, some developing countries have sacrificed whatever advantage in exporting they have derived from lower wage costs.

If a country is blessed or cursed with monoexportation, a strong case can be made for at least two rates of exchange applicable to different exports and imports. If the country suffers from great inequality of income and disturbed political conditions, it may be justified in taking measures to make the export of capital difficult and costly. There is no single or "correct" foreign-exchange policy applicable to all countries in all stages of development.

Some doubts were expressed earlier over the LAFTA approach because of the technical and political difficulties involved. There is, however, a variant of this approach that might help some countries to achieve the desired larger market and foreign exchange. This would be a common market between two contiguous countries whose economies are in part complementary. It is believed that such a market may be possible for two countries when it is not for, say, twenty because a *sine qua non* is assurance that the existing demand in each country will continue, at least for a time, to be met by local industry and agriculture, insofar as they are now meeting it. In other words, the common market arrangements would apply to future *increases* in demand. This should not be beyond the wit of technicians to work out in terms of varying exchange rates, exchange licensing policies, and tariffs between the two countries, with constant adjustments for differing courses of the two domestic price and cost levels. If the market were extended to many, however, the arrangements would become impossibly complicated. It will be noted that this policy could be combined well with the breakthrough approach, which implies a considerable increase in overall demand in a relatively short time.

A final topic under this general heading is the policy indicated in relation to borrowing abroad. A curious attitude prevails that any borrowing for any purpose on almost any terms is justifiable. This statement may be a little extreme, but not much so.[7] The attitude has its origins in several characteristics of our type of developing country: in the fact that the internal rate of interest has never completely reflected the fall in the value of money, so that internal borrowing has normally proved profitable; in the rapid turnover of cabinet ministers and managers of public enterprises, which gives rise to the desire to show immediate results without concern over future repayment; and in the lack of cultural patterns which encourage a feeling of responsibility for the nation in general, particularly for the nation's future.

It is difficult to compare returns in pesos (which may be greatly influenced by, say, tariff decisions in the case of transport and public service companies) with interest payable in dollars. There are in reality two sets of considerations to bear in mind: one is the internal economic justification of an investment, regardless of who finances it, and the other is the country's capacity to repay.

It is not necessary that net foreign borrowing be linked directly to increased exports or import substitution, but it is desirable that the two developments take place at the same time. A grave weakness of the Ten-Year Plan of Colombia is that it called for an increase in net borrowing which had no relation to any specific program of increasing exports.

In the absence of national plans worthy of the name, it was probably a good thing that the main single lender, the International Bank, confined itself for so many years to lending for transport and electric power generation, and that it spent a long time studying each application and setting conditions to be met. But now, with a number of additional sources of loans, and the International Bank disposed to increase its operations, the absence of a carefully worked out plan may be very dangerous for the future of borrowing countries. For example, housing loans of which not a dollar goes into housing but, say, into financing foreign travel or capital remittances in the free market, mean that the country is incurring a debt with little or no offsetting benefit. In addition to the lack of planning connected with loans from these official sources, there is little ability or inclination to control private short-term borrowing.

The following discussion of the desirability of a foreign single underwriting of a portion of the foreign-exchange requirements—a variation of the Marshall Plan—is taken almost verbatim from an article I wrote in 1961.[8] While it referred specifically to Colombia, I believe it is applicable to various other countries.

> It should prove feasible to work out a fairly dependable relation between the expansion of gross product and increased capital and raw material require-

[7] Even Venezuela, the greatest exporter of petroleum in the world, borrows from abroad.

[8] *Operación Colombia, Bogotá,* pp. 29–30. (Edition of the Colombian Chamber of Construction.)

ments, even though past relationships may have to be modified by the peculiar nature of the Operation. It must be kept in mind that a large growth in industrialization after the initial stage is an integral part of the Operation, as well as a stepping up of the process of mechanization of agriculture. It is for this reason that so much emphasis has been placed on steps to expand exports.

In the initial phases, however, foreign financial assistance is absolutely indispensable for various reasons. In the first place, it is necessary to bridge the gap before increased exports can be obtained. Secondly, as will be explained later, it is a highly desirable means of effecting a relatively painless transfer of internal resources to the purposes of the Operation. Thirdly, it offers a means whereby international lending agencies may participate in overall national programming. Fourthly, it offers a means whereby continuity in the prosecution of the program may be assured.

Not only is such assistance desirable and indeed necessary, but in order to accomplish the above purposes it is also essential that it take the form of underwriting the additional exchange requirements of the Operation *as a whole,* rather than of individual projects, as in the past.

Individual project foreign-exchange financing is open to various objections. It is a time-consuming process and during the past ten years [i.e., up to 1960] new loans have barely kept pace with repayment. It is generally restricted to public projects, and it has proved difficult to finance the foreign-exchange requirements of hundreds of smaller private projects that may be better prepared. It is difficult to coordinate such financing with overall national programming, as it is only an accident if the exchange requirements of a project bear any relation to the exchange requirements of the nation. Since there is always a bias in favor of borrowing, even if it is only for 10–20% of the total cost of a project, the bias is introduced in national programming in granting priority for the remaining peso financing.

The difficulty in matching foreign loans has given rise to requests for peso financing. But this does not make much economic sense, as it merely means lending foreign currency and selling such currency for pesos. The dollars finance the importation of other goods that may or may not be essential and, in any case, are not related to an overall program.

Since the Government underwrites such loans there would appear to be no sound reason why the loans should not be made directly to the Government to help in the financing of an approved overall program. The present practice would be analogous to a bank loaning to specific entities of a large corporation for specific purposes under specific conditions, but not to the corporation itself regardless of how good its credit may be and what its general program may be.

Finally, individual project financing is difficult to combine with participation in overall national planning. The separation of loaning from technical assistance has proved unfortunate for both programs.

Recently, the creation of new loaning agencies that have sought to combine their operations with technical assistance, and the stepup in the technical assistance programs, have led to a somewhat chaotic situation where missions have been falling over each other, duplicating work and issuing contradictory recommendations. Viewed from the perspective of an underdeveloped country, it has become rather an unedifying spectacle and one is discouraged by the apparent absence of any Grand Design in this uncoordinated activity.

It is most heartening that the American Administration has shown awareness of this lack of coordination, of the previous absence of emphasis on overall programming, and the paucity of results achieved to date. It is believed, therefore, that the present program may be welcomed, as it seeks to correct these shortcomings.*

To do this, however, it is absolutely indispensable that the loaning agencies form a consortium and undertake to finance the foreign exchange requirements of the overall program, provided, of course, they feel that it is a sound national program.

This might be done in the following manner:

1. The Colombian Government would set up an agency—called for convenience here the Operation Colombia Fund—to receive and administer the loans, a portion of which would be supplied by, say, the World Bank, the Export-Import Bank, the Interamerican Bank, and the United States Government.

2. The Fund would be established as a semi-independent agency on the model of the Banco de la República [the Central Bank] with local representatives of the foreign loaning agencies a minority on the Board.

3. The Consortium would presumably form its own Review Committee to follow closely the development of the Operation on the basis of reports from its representatives on the Fund.

4. The Consortium would agree to loan dollars up to a certain figure to cover the actual and near term future exchange requirements resulting from the Operation.

5. The Fund would sell these dollars to the Banco de la República as needed for pesos (these pesos, in actuality, would come from private and public importers and would, in part, represent a transfer of buying power from the private sector of the economy to the Fund).

6. The Fund, in turn, would loan these pesos to individuals and entities whose activities are vital to the Operation—to municipalities and public service companies, to the mortgage bank, to regional authorities, and even to private individuals and companies the extension of whose activities is essential to the success of the Operation, and who could not finance expansion in other ways.

It is apparent that this system would have many advantages over the project financing system. It ensures coordination at the level of national programming. It provides a smooth, almost automatic manner of providing exactly the amount of foreign exchange *nationally* required for thousands of individual items. And it resolves the problem of internal peso financing.

If we assume that the Operation necessitates additional dollar requirements of US$100,000,000 a year, this would also provide a peso fund for the peso financing of a variety of activities related to the Operation through an

* This was much too optimistic a statement.

agency somewhat divorced from excessive political influences, and yet with the Government retaining the decisive voice.

It may be objected that certain lending agencies have either committed project loans or are in an advanced state of negotiation, which it would be inconvenient to cancel. These loans might be continued. However, since the drawing upon of these loans in the form of imports would give rise to no peso receipts for the Fondo, it would be preferable if the Fondo assumed the obligation and the Consortium increased its loan to the Fondo as the goods were imported.

As mentioned earlier, the above suggestion owes some of its inspiration to the Marshall Plan. It was adopted in part by the World Bank, which headed a group of lenders for Colombia; but the limited funds made available for unspecified projects were turned over to a Colombian entity for administration without any foreign representation or any relation to an overall plan. Consequently, whatever benefits may have resulted were lost in the general picture.

Little has been said in this study of the role of foreign investment. I must confess to a degree of uncertainty that makes generalization difficult. Clearly, such great and risky investments as oil exploration need foreign investment. But in others, such as luxury-goods manufacturing where there is a high measure of protection, the exported returns may be disproportionate to the national benefits.

There have been cases in Colombia where the initial foreign investment was comparatively small and thereafter growth was financed through depreciation reserves or by borrowing from Colombian banks. In certain cases it is possible to borrow funds arising from the sale of American Government surplus foods and to remit the resulting profits. This comes dangerously close to bypassing the original intent of Public Law 480 which provided that the receiving country need pay only in pesos if it elected this course. (Of course, paying diplomatic and other expenses with the pesos resulting from sales of surplus agricultural products, which otherwise would require the import of dollars, is actually another form of repaying in dollars.)

After pursuing a free policy in the matter of foreign investment for years with apparent benefits, Canada is moving to reduce the high percentage of foreign control of its industry. In the early stages of the type of program proposed here, where the emphasis is on housing, public services, and mass consumption goods, there would appear to be little need for private foreign investment. In later stages, where the manufacture of more capital, intermediate, and semiluxury goods may become desirable, and where a strong national entrepreneurial class exists, every effort should be directed to securing the maximum of foreign technical know-how with a minimum of foreign investment. However, much would depend on the individual case, the current balance of payments, especially exports, and the availability of fixed interest loans.

A National Urban Policy

A national urban and housing policy that I favor as being appropriate for a developing country and consistent with the breakthrough plan differs radically from the course (one cannot call it a program) pursued in the United States. There, the wealth, the abundance of land, and the earlier laissez-faire attitude combined to produce the all too familiar features of American urban life. In the United States it is probably too late to change those features significantly. One of the few advantages of being a developing country, however, is that there is no need to repeat other countries' mistakes. Perhaps a better way of putting it is that one can plan urban development in the light of many countries' experience.

The objective of the breakthrough plan is to provide the bulk of the people with a decent minimum standard of living before making more luxuries available for the few. Individual motor car transport for the urban worker and separate transport for his family are definitely in the luxury category. When all the public and social costs are included, this is probably the most costly single item of expenditure in an American family's standard of living (in such a context "the family breadbasket" has a quaint, archaic sound). When people lack a balanced diet, decent housing and clothing, and primary and secondary education, and when they must get to and from work in inhumanly crowded conditions, it appears indefensible to allow the American pattern of individual motor transport to develop, with all that this implies in terms of road expenditures, expensive public services, blight, congestion, and waste.

The following model urban plan is therefore suggested for developing countries.

1. Physical and population limits should be placed on cities, the limits being set at those points where the per capita costs of transport and public services begin to rise sharply.
2. The agricultural and rural character of the land close to cities should be strictly preserved.
3. The ownership and use of the private car should be made very expensive.
4. A conscious effort, involving subsidies if necessary, should be made to provide housing for people within walking distance of their work, whether it be in the center of the cities or around factories.
5. During working hours the center or core itself should be banned to cars other than taxis.
6. Fast, comfortable public transport should be provided from existing suburban districts to a ring around the core, with the fares steeply graded according to distance from the core.

7. Blighted areas near the centers should be redeveloped in large units as permanent residential areas, freed from the tyranny of the grid system of streets.

8. The new housing should be planned for middle-class and upper-working-class people instead of for the very poorest groups and the recent arrivals, as it is now. Otherwise we will be committed either to build slums to be replaced in a few years or to give impossibly high subsidies. The new arrivals could be aided in finding housing in the units being vacated by people passing to the new high-rise apartments or to single-family dwellings near the core or the factories.

9. Large cities should be surrounded, where feasible, by a circumferential highway to reduce traffic within cities. Wholesale markets and meat processing plants could be located on such highways.

10. We should decide now that cities are permanent, not a passing fad, and that more and more of us will spend our lives in them. They should therefore be built for beauty and permanence, not to be replaced every thirty years. They should have adequate systems of parks, playfields, stadia, and so forth.[9] Urban dwellers in developing countries will not be able to live in rural surroundings and work in urban (and this is becoming daily less possible for Americans). Accordingly, cities should be planned to serve as homes.

11. There should be a system of incentives and penalties to encourage balanced urban development and avoid gigantism. The consequences of the absence of such a policy can be seen in Tokyo, Mexico City, and Buenos Aires, as well as in the belated and futile efforts of London to limit its growth.

It is hoped that this program will not be dismissed as utopian or unrealistic. There is not an item in it which has not a precedent or is not under serious discussion in some existing city.

Paris, content for many years with the beautiful and harmonious center which it had preserved, suddenly came to and realized that it had lost control of the suburbs. It is now making strenuous efforts to limit further growth. The Dutch, probably because of the limited land, appreciated more quickly than other people the consequences of *laissez faire* in urban development. They took action in time to limit suburban sprawl and preserve the rural character of most of the Netherlands. In rebuilding Rotterdam they increased densities while minimizing congestion, and they preserved a large shopping area for pedestrians. The British, with 50 million people

[9] Compare Hansen: "We have no tradition of city planning, no deep sense of aesthetic values, of spaciously laid-out squares with fountains, landscaping, flowers, shrubs or trees, no pride in architecturally satisfying public building." *Economic Issues of the 1960's*, p. 183.

in a small area, have just now grasped the full implications of the unchecked use of the automobile and in the Buchanan Report of 1963 have set forth the alternatives in uncompromising terms.

The 1970 Plan for Forth Worth includes a central area reserved for pedestrians. Most of the American literature on urban planning, however, seems helpless before the fact and concentrates on palliatives—slum clearance, renovation of blighted areas, and more and better roads. Possibly only the United States could afford the colossal price involved and could permit half of its most fertile class 1 land to be devoted to suburbs.[10] It is said that two-thirds of the center of Los Angeles is now devoted to streets and parking space.[11] Possibly they are waiting to see what happens when 100 percent of the space is so devoted.

In Caracas, the relative prosperity is shown in widespread car ownership. It is curious that although there are a great number of high-rise apartments and few of what Americans would call sprawling suburbs, a good part of the center of the valley in which the city is located is devoted to throughways and cloverleafs. Even so, the congestion is striking. Apparently the private car is used for short hauls, and it is still not possible for most people to live within walking distance of their work.

The suggestion on the type of housing to be undertaken (see no. 8 in the list above) will probably shock many urban planning professionals, who have taken it for granted that new housing must be provided for the poorest classes even if this means building slums far out in the suburbs where land is cheaper. Here, however, is a case where sound planning and common sense join hands. Let us reduce the enormous bill (in perpetuity) for urban transport by spending more now to locate the potential car owners near their work. It makes no more sense to try to build new houses for the very poor, when there are used houses that can be made available, than to try to make new cars for this same class when there are used cars available.

Building houses for the poorest or most recently arrived people, if it is to involve no subsidy, means building slums, with the hope that eventually they will be improved. Moreover, it entails seeking cheap land, extending the area of the city, and creating more transport problems. Building better houses for these people closer to the center may involve a substantial subsidy, and the justice of this may very well be questioned.

The compromise suggested[12] is to build for the classes that can afford

[10] William White, *The Exploding Metropolis,* Doubleday & Company, Inc., Garden City, N. Y., 1958, p. 122.

[11] Lewis Mumford, *The City in History,* Harcourt, Brace & World, Inc., New York, 1961, p. 510.

[12] Lauchlin Currie et al., *Una Política Urbana para los Países en Desarrollo* (An Urban Policy for Developing Countries), Ediciónes Tercer Mundo, Bogotá, 1965, p. 188.

decent housing and to make their vacated homes available for the less well-off, and theirs, in turn, for the poorest. In this process of upgrading, everybody get something better than he had before, so that the benefits of the housing program are widely diffused. At the same time, no more slums are built and the city and nation save greatly by placing more and more workers within walking distance of their jobs, in permanent homes that add distinction to the city. This appears to be the appropriate solution of the problem in qualitative terms.

However, combining this type of housing program with the overall economic program does mean that a larger proportion of resources must be devoted immediately to the housing program. This in turn means cutting back more sharply on other types of construction or taking measures to increase saving and so reduce the multiplier. It also means that more temporary dormitories may have to be built because of the time lag between increased employment and additional permanent housing. While these measures make the program to provide additional jobs more difficult, I believe that the permanent gains in welfare more than offset the added expense and difficulty. Even if single men have to be housed for the time being in barracks (as in wartime), their work will be of more lasting benefit when they are building a properly planned city than when they are erecting slums that have a high social cost and will shortly need to be torn down.

Another reason for combining the objectives of creating new jobs and initiating a new urban housing policy is that both programs need the cooperation of existing urban employees. It is unrealistic to expect these workers to abstain from wage demands that will cause price rises and to ask them to undergo the inconveniences of overcrowding and overloaded public services just for the sake of providing new jobs for new arrivals. They must be shown that they can expect some rise in income resulting from increased productivity, promotions in passing to a second or third shift, work on the Double-Pay Days that replace former holidays, and the opportunity to acquire better housing on attractive terms. All these are solid inducements to gain cooperation and acceptance for the new incomes policy so badly needed to facilitate industrialization.

To economize foreign exchange and time, it is essential that the breakthrough program raise the ratio of employment to capital goods, which means utilizing existing equipment more intensively in night and holiday work. Since the existing equipment will be found mostly in a few large cities, initially the breakthrough will further unbalance urban development. This will bring the day closer when the population and area limits (see no. 1 in the list above) will apply to the largest cities. Thus a program that provides incentives for the growth of a number of smaller cities is imperative. With the possible exception of Mexico City and Buenos Aires, the larger cities in most of the developing countries have probably not yet reached their optimum size, so that some further immediate growth would not be undesirable. In any case, there does not appear to be any other course open if more intensive use of existing equipment is desired.

A continuance of accelerated growth would facilitate later balanced urban development. The more rapid the growth in demand, the more economic it becomes to think in terms of additional factories rather than additional machines or small extensions to existing factories. The state can offer incentives to locate new factories in smaller centers and can discourage their location in the cities approaching their optimum size.[13]

Agricultural Policy

While the goal in agriculture should be a complete conversion to commercial-type farming, with all the instruments of the state utilized to further this objective, the magnitude of the task and the numbers of people involved in some countries suggest that we must expect the continuance of colonial-type farming for a considerable time to come. The stimuli necessary to meet rapidly increasing urban requirements may even make conditions more tolerable for the small farmer and lessen the incentive for him to try to engage in different activities. In any case, the bulk of the middle-aged rural population cannot be expected to move.

In the reorientation of policy, more emphasis would be placed on aiding commercial-type farming. Technical assistance programs have tended to concentrate too much on generalists and extension workers and not enough on scientific aid. For example, it would be valuable to have some of the world's leading agricultural scientists, in both the economic and the more technical fields, come to developing countries for terms of work. When successful, this type of aid has the advantage for capital-scarce countries of increasing yields and improving quality without necessitating great capital investments. A successful silage operation may obviate the need for irrigation in well-defined dry seasons, and so on.

The aim should be, as always, to attempt to secure the maximum result with the minimum effort. Great Britain, with one of the most efficient agricultures in the world, meets the bulk of its foods requirement with an annual investment amounting to 3.5 percent of the total investment.[14] Great land reclamation projects may be economically justifiable, but a country which has sufficiently good soils, land, and climates to make them unnecessary is to that extent better off than one which must resort to them. Insofar as the state can guide the expansion of production in the more accessible

[13] An excellent illustration is given by Tinbergen in his *Design for Development* of how the Netherlands government influenced the location of an industry to take advantage of existing facilities. Johns Hopkins Press, Baltimore, 1958, p. 62.

[14] Edith H. Whethem, *The Economic Background to Agricultural Policy,* Cambridge University Press, London, 1960, pp. 97–98.

areas along established lines of communication, total costs can be held down. In most of the type of countries under discussion, marketing and distribution can be greatly improved.

A difficult point arises in connection with especially depressed areas. No general rules apply, but in many cases it would appear more economic to bring people to jobs than try to create jobs in unfavorable and costly circumstances.

Throughout the world, technology is daily enlarging the optimum size of farming units, and in certain European countries the state has intervened to further this process.[15] An English agricultural economist remarks that "the appropriate policy for a Government aiming at economic efficiency is to encourage the outflow from farming and the amalgamation of farms by all methods short of creating an intolerable political uproar."[16] It is to be hoped that in our group of developing countries contrary policies will not be advocated and carried out.

Few of our countries are conservation-conscious. Poverty in the countryside is too prevalent and dire; people cannot be prevented from burning and destroying the natural resources and exposing the topsoil to erosion by improper practices. Not much headway can be made to conserve the forests, fisheries, and topsoil until the agrarian problem itself is resolved, along with the interrelated population problem.

Prices and Cost-of-Living Adjustments

It is surprising that in the course of time more departures from organizational forms and procedures appropriate to economies with relative stability of prices have not occurred in economies characterized by chronic inflation. People in the latter countries are exhorted to save at low fixed interest rates when obviously this makes no sense whatever. Bonds can be sold only with lottery and tax-exemption features. No mechanism has been worked out for a smooth adjustment of the external to the internal value of the money; this takes place through a series of nerve-shattering jolts (devaluations) that bring much injustice and economic maladjustment in their train. The real value of public investment is constantly being eroded, as is the real value of all mortgages. There is enormous pressure to borrow from banks (and for them, in turn, to borrow from the central banks), because

[15] "In Sweden, since the second world war, the State has scheduled certain holdings as uneconomic so that, when they fall vacant, they cannot be transferred or sold in the open market, but have to be combined with others in the vicinity." *Ibid.*, p. 113, quoting F. Meissner, "Agrarian Reform in Sweden," *Journal of Agricultural Economics*, vol. XI, no. 4, 1956, pp. 444–456.

[16] Whethem, *op. cit.*, p. 113.

generally bank rates, though nominally high, still do not reflect the earnings resulting to capital from a constant rise in prices.

Securing a mortgage at a fixed interest rate is like securing a winning lottery ticket. Consequently, the only funds available for home building are (1) one's own capital, (2) a small amount of institutional lending at fixed rates, (3) government funds, and (4) AID funds. The last alternative is particularly questionable, when not linked to a Marshall Plan type of operation, because under AID neither dollars nor goods for housing enter the country or are necessary. The dollars are disposed of in the exchange market by local authorities for local currency, and the buyer may very possibly invest these dollars in foreign stocks. In no type of transaction does the "money veil" so completely hide the real nature of the economic transaction. The borrower benefits by receiving his house in the course of a few years as a virtual gift (because of the steady rise in prices and incomes); the local public authority is aided in transferring some local currency resources from some other use to low-cost housing; American authorities feel, quite mistakenly, that American dollars have been used to "build" low-cost housing, and they wonder why greater results do not flow from annual appropriations for the Alliance for Progress.

Possibly, the reason why procedures have not been worked out for a situation of chronic but varying inflation is that underdeveloped country authorities are always embarking on programs of austerity to stabilize prices. Obviously such a happy result would be eminently desirable, but in the meantime it would appear that no harm and much good would result from the adoption of a system of cost-of-living adjustments to (*a*) the principal and interest of fixed-interest-bearing loans, (*b*) wages and salaries, and (*c*) exchange rates. Applying this procedure to institutional loans (loans by banks and insurance companies) would raise difficulties, since their liabilities (other than capital) are also fixed. They might be omitted at the start, provided the central bank rate was raised to more realistic figures to discourage the well-nigh irresistible pressure to borrow.

If a really substantial amount of money is to be attracted to financing of housing, private lenders must be given assurance that their principal will be protected in terms of purchasing power and that the interest received will be well in excess of the decline in purchasing power. Under these conditions home financing would become advantageous, because the present refuges for capital (stocks, land, office and apartment building, and dollars) all have certain drawbacks. Stocks may not go up; land may be expropriated; rents may be frozen; land and buildings lack liquidity; dollars earn little.

From the point of view of the borrower, it is believed that smallness of down payment and length of term are more important considerations than fixity of payments. If government and institutional funds were combined with private money in one large mortgage pool, they could be used to provide longer terms than private lenders would offer and to lessen the amount of the cost-of-living adjustment to the borrower.[17]

It may be objected that a generalized cost-of-living adjustment will result in a cost-price spiral which will intensify rather than ameliorate the problem of stability. This is highly questionable. For one thing, the absence of the adjustment has not prevented the spiral effect. For another, the certain knowledge of the adjustment that will follow a rise in prices may strengthen the hands of those who favor a more conservative course in monetary and fiscal policy. Finally, it is to be expected that wages and salaries in general will rise more than the cost of living if there is any increase in productivity per capita. In this circumstance, a rise confined to the rise in the cost of living would be deflationary in the sense of effective demand falling short of productive capacity. One aspect that would have to be investigated carefully is the effect of the adjustment in relation to the numerous fringe benefits given workers. Most of these benefits are expressed as percentages of the wage. In some benefits, however, the last rise is retroactive, so that total remuneration might rise more than the cost of living from this factor.

Education and Health

There should be little need to stress the supreme importance of adequate education from both an economic and a social point of view. The problems of illiteracy and non-school attendance are both concentrated in the rural part of areas.

More economically advanced countries have come to place first emphasis on prolonged, universal, and obligatory training of their youth. A highly educated people is not only a desirable end product of a high standard of living, but also a cause. Its importance in the latter connection was dramatically shown by the reemergence of West Germany from the economic ruin and social chaos of the end of the war.

In primary schools, at least, character formation is probably even more important than formal knowledge. To learn good working habits, punctuality, regularity, and acceptance of discipline is to acquire qualities that make for social stability and for successful industrialization and mechanization. Widespread deficiency in these qualities takes its daily toll in lowered productivity in the developing countries.

It would seem clear that a society made up of a relatively small class of well-educated, well-to-do people on the one hand, and an overwhelming

[17] For a more detailed treatment, see Chap. 14. The applicability of the suggestion to individual countries would call for detailed study. J. G. Gurley and E. S. Shaw, in a path-breaking article, point out how lack of appropriate financial instruments and institutions may inhibit growth. "Financial Aspects of Economic Development," *American Economic Review*, 1955, pp. 515–538.

preponderance of illiterate and poverty-stricken people on the other, is highly unstable, and indeed cannot last. Unless the directing class can close this great gulf, as it has in various Northern countries, it will be obliterated by revolution, as it has been in much of the rest of the world. From the viewpoint of the preservation of free democratic institutions, this is undoubtedly the key problem. Those who benefit from and strongly believe in democracy and private enterprise will not be able to breathe freely until it is solved.

In the rural areas where the problem is concentrated, eradicating intestinal parasites, providing schools, and securing competent teachers are costly and difficult. The parents' extreme poverty and lack of ambition must also be contended with. One or at most two years of school, with an incompetent, dispirited teacher, and with the children suffering from parasites, amoebas, and malnutrition, will not yield worthwhile results.

The solution proposed here is twofold: (1) bring a much larger proportion of the children to the cities, where it is physically and administratively feasible to provide better health care and better education, and (2) elevate the standard of living of the families remaining in rural areas, so that it will become feasible to think in terms of better education and better personal hygiene.

This program is believed to be within the capacity of the type of country under discussion. Just as a thoughtful father, after providing for food, clothing, and shelter, will place the health and education of his children next in importance in the family budget, so the country could do likewise. The father has no doubt that he is making an investment that will pay off in the earning capacity and happiness of his children. So, likewise, the country need have no doubt. The intermediate group of countries have now advanced to a point where the margin above the primary necessaries of food, clothing, and shelter is more than sufficient to permit the requisite investment in the health and education of the next generation—or they could advance to this point if they put their idle resources to work. Health and education costs should not be regarded as expenditure comparable to armaments to ward off communism, but as a truly economically productive investment that will yield large returns in increased productivity and welfare.

The Labor and Social Security Laws

These laws are compounded of modern phraseology and ancient concepts. The elaborate procedures, which must be scrupulously followed, and the placing of various burdens on the employers such as payments for death, accidents, and occupational disease, reflect cultural attitudes and the absence of contributory workmen's compensation systems. Many of the fringe benefits are in reality delayed wages (bonuses, severance pay, vacation compensation). Then there may be family allowances and payroll deductions for apprentice training. Doubtless most employers are able to pass these various wages and benefits along to the ultimate consumer as uniform percentages of the basic wage.

In the case of the surcharge for night work, not all employers may be able to pass it along as it applies to only a few, and it must be listed as an important deterrent to intensive utilization of equipment. Where an activity is participated in by both employers and the self-employed, the labor laws penalize the employers, who are generally doing a more technically advanced operation. Possibly the worst effect of the multitude of benefits provided by law and subject to frequent change is that the worker looks to the government for more benefits regardless of whether they are earned. Hence raising wages by decree is common. On the one hand, this situation favors the competitive position of the artisan and colonial-type farmer at the expense of the more technified operations. On the other hand, it penalizes the self-employed worker insofar as he is a consumer of industrial products.

The Labor Code is generally politically sacrosant. Probably all the changes that can be hoped for are a reduction in the surcharge for night work, the conversion of a number of holidays into Double-Pay Days, and where the union requests it, the suspension of the code in a completely unionized activity. Many union officials feel that the existence of the code weakens their bargaining power. Instead of the few workers with strong unions being provided with further programs for retirement at an early age, and other benefits, the self-employed should be given additional security in the case of sickness and accidents and additional help for their dependents and survivors. This would substitute the reality for the shadow of social security and lead to large gains in welfare.

Tax Policy

Although the breakthrough plan proposes to accomplish a better distribution of consumption by direct means, this does not lessen the desirability of securing a more equitable distribution of available income after taxes. The situation varies from country to country, but generally the most urgent need is to end tax exemptions and tax evasion. There is no point, and indeed much harm, in raising the progressive income tax schedules when few taxpayers actually pay such rates.

The tax program will not be improved until the nature and motivation of economic activity are better understood, because there is now widespread conviction that tax exemption is an effective instrument to induce industrial or agricultural expansion, regardless of the state of demand. Similarly, resolving the problem of tax evasion requires a great improvement in public administration, as well, of course, as a determination to enforce the tax laws. Merely to call for tax reform, and be put off with assurances, is much too easy a way out.

Although Alvin Hansen stated the issue with his usual succinctness in the following quotation, he unfortunately and doubtless inadvertently omitted the word "effective" before the words "income tax": "Without an income tax, the distribution of income would rapidly become oppressively concentrated. An income tax is essential for the preservation of a democratic society."[18]

Financing

As in wartime, the real limitations on a breakthrough program are physical rather than financial. The additional investment and the additional production of consumer goods result in part from increased productivity and in larger part from the employment of hitherto idle men and equipment. Sidney Dell puts it very well when he writes, "The problem [in an underdeveloped country] is then no longer one of allocating fixed resources to the most economic uses—as in a fully employed economy; rather it is one of finding productive employment for resources not otherwise used."[19] The function of financing, therefore, is to bring about this additional employment as smoothly as possible.

It will be recalled that in order to prevent the increase in housing expenditures (and the subsequent increase in the demand for wage goods) from outrunning the physical capacity to produce, it would be prudent to *shift* resources from other types of construction. The smoothest way of accomplishing this would be to shift the corresponding financial resources. Such a shift would be one of the purposes of the new mortgage institution prepared to make the requisite cost-of-living adjustments on money invested in its notes and bonds.

A second source of financing would be from the budgets of public entities, particularly their funds formerly destined for long-range reclamation projects, rural roads, and municipal services in small towns. Projects that take three or four years before any returns may be expected could be the first candidates for delay. Insofar as good land is available near existing means of transport, its development should be given preference in any rational system of land use.

In countries with highly progressive individual income taxes, collected at the source, a rapid growth in incomes would be immediately reflected in an even more rapid growth in tax receipts. In our group of developing countries, the tax receipts are more likely to grow at the same rate as the growth in production. This could be another source of financing.

Financing could also be provided by foreign aid. By pooling such aid

[18] *Economic Issues of the 1960s,* p. 110.

[19] Dell, *Trade Blocs and Common Markets,* p. 162.

in underwriting a breakthrough program, foreign lenders would be assured that they would receive the maximum return on their loans, that the government would assume the exchange risk, that the disadvantages of uncoordinated specific project financing could be avoided, and that the country in question would be aided not only in covering the foreign-exchange portion of its program's requirements but also in corralling the requirements in local currency (as in the case where dollars are sold to a local power company for local currency).

Another source of financing could be the considerable monetary expansion that would become permissible with the sizable expansion in gross product resulting from the additional employment. If through the temporary device of the 100 percent reserve system (the requirement of 100 percent reserve on deposits above a certain figure) secondary expansion were avoided, the program-financing agency would be enabled to borrow all the newly created deposits. Strictly speaking, the commercial banks would in this case be entitled to compensation, since their expenses would be increased relative to their earning assets.

Still another way to finance industrial expansion, and one which would have other desirable consequences, would be to permit depreciation allowances in certain industries to rise up to a certain limit with a rise in the volume of production relative to fixed capital. This would be another inducement to move to second and third shifts as well as a longer work year. The yield of corporation taxes would for a time be lower, but not lower than they would have been if the companies had stayed on a single-shift basis. The longer-term yield would be much higher. In this manner the necessary increase in saving and investment in the industrial sector could be secured. The accelerated allowance could be combined with an incomes-price policy to secure the maximum degree of employment per unit of existing and new capital investment.

A variant of this proposal is in effect in France, where depreciation allowances are varied proportionally to production.[20] According to Sheahan, "Usinor [one of the largest steel firms] did report a loss in 1957, but its depreciation charges fully covered a record high level of investment expenditure, as they did for the whole six-year period from 1953 to 1958."[21]

This is a form of forced investment, secured partly at the expense of government revenue and partly at the expense of consumers. However, where this policy is combined with an incomes policy and an appropriate monetary policy, prices need be no higher than they were. The increased "saving" would arise from the increased volume of sales. With more well-paying jobs and more production of consumer goods, the end result would

[20] Sheahan, *Promotion and Control of Industry in Post War France,* p. 74. The various upper limits are expressed as percentages of sales.

[21] *Ibid.,* p. 84.

be the attainment of a greater measure of equality by a process of upgrading.

The magnitude and proportions of the different forms of financing resorted to would, of course, vary from country to country. We are here concerned only with the several possibilities in qualitative terms. In regard to the analogy of war, it must be admitted that most countries' wartime financing record left much to be desired. In almost all cases, they should have had more recourse to diversion and rationing and less to monetary expansion. In the case of the developing countries, the need for extreme haste is not so urgent, and it is not proposed to impose great additional demands on a fully employed economy, but rather to take up existing slack. Therefore, at least in theory, it should be easier to avoid monetary inflation than it proved to be in wartime.

Conclusion

The fact that a large pool of underutilized labor constitutes an opportunity as well as a problem has been put very well by Richard Fry:

> All the previous "miracles" started with a large reserve of labour which was absorbed as the pace of economic growth quickened. West Germany began, after the currency reform of 1948, with more than five million unemployed and until 1960 received a constant inflow of refugees from the east; in addition she made use of a large army of foreign workers which at times reached a million. France had similar numbers of foreign labour, first Italians and Spaniards, then Algerians and, more lately, repatriated French people from North Africa. Both Germany and France had (and still have) a backward, overmanned agriculture which was able to release people for urban occupations at a great rate. In Japan, too, rural overcrowding provided an almost unlimited supply of labour for expanding industries and services. In Italy, ten years ago, unemployment was heavy even in the developed industrial North, while the problem of finding work for the millions of poverty-stricken people of the South had baffled Italians for generations. In each of these countries exceptionally rapid economic growth was sustained for a number of years by the absorption of these manpower reserves.
>
> Britain has no such reserve to draw on. The additional work involved in raising national output would have to come from increasing output per worker, which involves intensive investment in labour-saving plant and equipment as well as accelerated transfer from low-output to high productivity industries.[22]

Obviously the developing countries with which we are concerned have the requisite reserve of labor which, if employed, could bring about the type of economic miracle Fry is referring to. It is not even necessary that

[22] "The Next Economic Miracle," *Midland Bank Review,* London, November, 1963, pp. 4–5.

this labor be very efficiently used, but only that it be more efficiently used than at present. As Sidney Dell says:

> Insofar as the output of industrial products can be increased by an underdeveloped country without reducing the output of agriculture, this represents a net gain of real income to the economy. And this is true *no matter how inefficient the industrial production* may be . . . inefficient production is better than no production at all.[23]

The preceding chapter gave some arithmetical illustrations of the importance of the allocation of the annual new addition to the work force in raising or lowering per capita output. Returning to these illustrations, we may now add to the new workers an additional modest shift of subsistence farmers to urban jobs. Under the previous assumptions, the average per capita production increased by 1% (or the GNP increased by 600 million, or 4%) solely because all the net addition to the labor force went into the higher-paid urban occupations. Now assume that there is an additional net shift of workers of 3% per annum from the lowest-paid rural to the average-paid urban sectors. Assume that the subsistence farmers are credited with a former 500 units of income per year. The 105,000 former rural workers will earn 2,860 units per worker, or 300,300,000 additional units, which represents a net increase of approximately 250,000,000 additional units and an increase in the gross production of 1.7%. Assume further that the remaining agriculturalists (3,395,000) produce an additional 3%, at no advance in prices, to meet an additional 3% increase in urban demand. Production per agriculturalist will rise to

$$\frac{5{,}000{,}000{,}000 + (3\% \text{ of } 5{,}000{,}000{,}000)}{3{,}395{,}000}$$

—or to 1,520 units from a previous 1,430, a rise of 6.3%, which in turn means an additional 1% per capita for all workers. Thus we have the effect on the GNP of

1. The new labor force	4.0%
2. The shift from subsistence farming	1.7%
3. Greater production per agriculturalist	1.0%
	6.7%

—plus a "normal" growth of, say, 1.5% in the productivity of the formerly employed resulting from new and improved capital formation, better organization of work, and so on, for a grand total increase of 8.2%, or 5.2% per capita. More significant than this overall figure is the fact that the

[23] *Op. cit.*, p. 162.

former and actual agriculturalists, whose average income before was only half that of nonagricultural workers, would experience a rise of 250,000,000 + 150,000,000 or 400,000,000—that is, 114.30 per capita or 8%, plus whatever rise might occur because of "normal" growth. Even this is a global figure, and the rise would be even greater for the poorest segment of the agricultural population. Continued for only three years, this trend would represent a significant structural change in the distribution and incomes of the working force and would permit an enormous increase in well-being, or decrease in ill-being. Other aspects of this suggested approach will be considered in Chapter 14, where it is specifically applied to Colombia.

One of the great and cumulative benefits resulting from the success of the breakthrough plan would be the increased opportunity it allows for specialization and for the fuller utilization of human potentialities. One actual example is that of an illiterate rural worker in Colombia who became the administrator of a mechanized dairy farm which had the highest average production per cow in Colombia. If the opportunity had not been offered, he would probably still be a day laborer. In general, the larger the market, the greater the opportunity to specialize and to utilize human potentialities.

When there are great areas of unemployed or underutilized labor combined with rich and underemployed resources, the continuance of intense poverty is both unnecessary and indefensible. A program which aims to raise everyone's productivity, the course most economists prescribe for developing areas now, would be applicable only in conditions of full employment in the true economic sense of the term, and, as Fry says, is the most difficult course.

Some writers have found the effective brake on development to lie in the inability to import enough capital goods, which is owing in turn to the sluggish demand for the primary products that most developing countries have to export. A recent ECLA publication, which was discussed in Chapter 5, makes much of this point, and it is also emphasized by Sidney Dell in his stimulating and provocative *Trade Blocs and Common Markets.* Dell believes that the problem justifies whatever protection may be necessary so long as there are underutilized factors of production. ECLA, on the other hand, on the whole disapproves of protection, thinks that the possibilities of import substitution are strictly limited, and looks for the answer to borrowings and LAFTA.

Their fears cannot be lightly dismissed in view of recent world trade trends. The type of breakthrough program proposed here suggests escapes from the import limitation by a variety of measures: more intensive use of existing capital resource, modifications imposed on the pattern of consumption and investment, strict rationing of exchange, continued import substitution, stimuli to exports, borrowing, foreign investment, and, where feasible, the formation of a common market with a neighboring country.

The use of some of these measures is limited—as, for example, in the case of continued borrowing without increasing exports. Also, the increase in the total of all exports from developing countries is of course dependent upon the willingness of the rest of the world to accept more exports from them. But it is obvious that a variety of possible measures exists. Imports can continue to be rationed and used with the maximum intensity; the pattern of consumption is subject to further modification until a relatively high standard of living in terms of essentials is attained by most; if necessary, imports can continue to form a smaller and smaller percentage of the national product; and there are always possibilities of pushing exports, or of making more capital goods at home when the market justifies it. Initial successes make further successes easier.

There are, in short, many things that can be done by one or two countries acting alone or in concert before the two limitations emphasized by ECLA—inadequate saving to create sufficient jobs and inadequate exports to secure the necessary volume of imports—take effect. To ignore the possibilities and stress the rigidity of the limitations is to play into the hands of the ever-present forces of inertia and to encourage the defeatists who maintain that nothing can be done through a country's own efforts, that it is the victim of uncontrollable outside forces.

The temptation is natural to make the picture as black as possible in order to secure foreign loans and to enhance the chances that the measures necessary to make LAFTA a success may be accepted. However, the welfare of too many people is at stake to gamble on one or two relatively painless solutions. The greatest service an economist can provide is to show a country that to a very large degree its destiny lies in its own hands, that it can mold its environment if it cares to. What is unforgivable is for developed countries and international agencies to encourage attitudes and pursue policies that can only perpetuate poverty and misery for a large segment of the world's population—that make conditions sufficiently tolerable to excuse the political leaders of developing countries from the necessity to seek basic solutions, and that foster the idea that developing countries can do nothing to help themselves.

Is accelerating development by means of breakthrough or crash program worth the effort? The answer depends on one's values and the apparent urgency of a program or the consequences of a lack of one. The technical difficulty is not, in the writer's view, the main objection. The real drawbacks are rather to be found in the unavoidable stresses and strains of accelerating development—in the overcrowding of cities, the deficiency of public services, the temporary bad living conditons for many, and the restraints on individual freedom of action. For urban people who are now living comfortably, and who are not impressed by statistics, the idea of better-paying jobs for people they do not know, and the prospect of improving conditions out in the countryside, will not appear to compensate for the inconveniences they will have to undergo. Paradoxically, the more successful the program, the greater will be the strains and inconveniences.

As in wartime, the enemy—poverty, suffering, ignorance, lawlessness, high birthrates—must be dramatized and made the object of hate and even fear. The consequences, even for the children of the well-to-do, of progressive and unrestrained increases in population, destruction of natural resources, and policies of drift, all would have to be stressed to win support. Unless the program can be vivified and dry statistics made to live, the strains and stresses may appear to many people to be indications of failure and to prove that conditions are actually worse than before. If such beliefs are allowed to multiply, the program will sooner or later, and probably sooner, be stopped. For this reason an active educational campaign, both in advance of the breakthrough program and concurrently with it, appears indispensable. Urban people must be warned what to expect, what statistics are to be criteria of success, and what the consequences of failure are for them and their children. Undeniably, a program which forces the excess rural population into subsistence farming while providing a few model rural settlements for a tiny minority has greater appeal in the short term than a crash program.

The danger of overdoing the breakthrough appears remote because of the built-in adjustment mechanism. A continued rise in relative agricultural prices, or a relative rise in agricultural incomes to a point that discourages further movement of workers out of agriculture, would be a warning signal for slowing the movement because of the overheating of the motor. While this possibility must be kept in mind, it appears that the real danger would lie in another type of overheating—that arising from sellers' inflation, which would pinch off the movement before a decisive breakthrough had occurred.

The acceleration of labor mobility has played an important role in most economic upsurges, but it has not generally been appreciated and has been regarded as a consequence rather than a prime moving factor. What is needed is a single successful acceleration of natural forces, during which the tendencies to growing inequality and imperfect competition are kept in check. Theorizing can never carry the conviction that would follow a successful demonstration.

My knowledge of conditions and possibilities in southeast Asia is so limited that I hesitate to say whether the approach outlined in this chapter is in any way applicable there. It is possible that population is already pressing too hard on resources and that the magnitude of the breakthrough effort required is too great. This, of course, is saying that the problem is insoluble, i.e., that the vicious circles cannot be broken and that there is no alternative to vast agricultural slums. An Indian writer implies this by greatly minimizing, in my view, the magnitude of disguised rural unemployment, by accepting a highly inefficient man-acre ratio as consistent with rural "full" employment, and by rejecting the concept of the total labor surplus which could be withdrawn from the agricultural sector without a decline in its output.[24]

The difference between Mathur's attitude and mine, since I regard disguised unemployment as both the problem and an opportunity, is strikingly brought out by his statement:

> In the context of economic development policies, the main objective of measuring disguised unemployment is to ascertain the concealed labor potential which could be mobilized during the process of development *when the need arose*. However, in the immediate future the pool of open unemployment itself is likely to be more than *sufficient* to provide the manpower *requirements*—the Indian Five Year Plans have not been able to provide jobs as yet even to all those belonging to this category. (p. 188; italics added)

It is to be hoped that this negative attitude toward what I believed to be the real problem of development—breaking the vicious circles of rural poverty and high birthrates—is not shared by all Indian economists. Apparently, the successive Five-Year Plans have had little to do with the continuing problem.

In this continent, Raymond Vernon, in his profound and disturbing treatment of Mexico,[25] considers very briefly a type of approach analogous to that proposed here. More than most economists, he is concerned with political roadblocks, and principally on these grounds he appears to accord such an approach little chance of acceptance.

> It is theoretically conceivable, of course, that vigorous government action aimed at altering the distribution of income could regenerate the expectation of rapid growth in the minds of businessmen. Such measures, however, would have to take a form which businessmen would ordinarily regard as hostile and antibusiness in character, such as increases in minimum wages, increases in taxation aimed at reducing sumptuous living or idle hoards, and increases in subsidies on mass-consumed commodities and services. One is then led to ask whether the Mexican government can be expected to take vigorous measures which might be construed as being blatantly antibusiness.

Thus measures which he thought would "ordinarily" be regarded by businessmen as "hostile" become, in the next sentence, "blatantly antibusiness." This, of course, is a matter of judgment, of specific measures, and of presentation. The tax reduction in the United States to stimulate aggregate demand and employment could not be called "antibusiness" or regarded as such in any way. Neither, it seems to me, would the term neces-

[24] Ashok Mathur, *The Anatomy of Disguised Unemployment,* Oxford Economic Papers, Clarendon Press, Oxford, 1964, pp. 161–193. See also comments below, p. 166.

[25] *The Dilemma of Mexico's Development,* Harvard University Press, Cambridge, Mass., 1963, p. 184.

sarily be applied to a carefully worked out program to stimulate demand for mass goods, to restrain sellers' inflation, and to encourage mobility out of the ranks of the poverty-striken country people. If the objectives of the plan are well understood, even an increase in the income tax, or better, a whittling down of exemptions and evasions, may not encounter too much resistance. It may very well be that the Mexican government will prefer to try to penetrate the Latin American market instead of cultivating the enormous potential market that lies within its own borders. But the latter possibility need not be antibusiness. Surely the infinitely more difficult task would be to persuade that government to see its agrarian problem as it appears to a fresh observer free from the symbolism of the Revolution.

It is ironic that the further consequences of the great land grab in Mexico in the latter half of the nineteenth century should now, because of the nature of the subsequent reform, condemn millions of country people to a subsistence type of life. Yet that reform became the source of the intertwined vicious circles of rural poverty and excessively high birthrates that up to now Mexico does not appear to have been able to break despite a long-continued and high growth in per capita production.

It has been suggested that a crash program is both unnecessary and undesirable in developing countries and that individual elements of the breakthrough plan here proposed could be gradually incorporated in existing programs. But without a radical change in objectives, priorities, and emphasis, the adoption of individual elements would have little effect. For example, many years ago the Colombian cotton textile industry made the transfer from a single- to a three-shift basis. This move has saved the country hundreds of millions in exchange and has altered the ratio of employment to investment. In the absence of other necessary policies, however, it did not have sufficient impact *by itself* to place development on a safely self-generating basis. By now we cannot utilize this particular piece of ammunition for the breakthrough effort.

Similarly, the World Bank adopted the earlier suggestion of forming a group of lenders to make loans available to Colombia for unspecified projects. But instead of using this device to underwrite the balance of payments deficit resulting from the adoption of a carefully worked out national program (as in the case of the Marshall Plan), the amount so loaned was limited to the arbitrary figure of $40 million annually and was not linked to any recognizable plan. Its effect, therefore, was lost in the general picture. The same would probably happen with a stepped-up program of urban housing or public services, or even with a gradual change to a three-shift basis in industry.

One of the most difficult and most important aspects of the problem of accelerating development lies in the necessity of concentration of effort. A characteristic of an underdeveloped country is the superabundance of urgent problems all calling for attention. All have their advocates who naturally feel that reforms and increased resources should be devoted to the particular problem in which they are concerned, whether it be roads, public services, or administration, primary or university education, agriculture, and so on. In a paper I read[26] before the Third Congress of Colombian Economists in 1963, I listed eighteen such urgent problems confronting Colombia, and the list could easily have been extended. Foreign agencies and technicians quickly get enmeshed in particular problems or fields and take part in the frantic struggle for attention and funds.

Such a diffusion of effort is natural and actually not harmful in a developed economy where the self-perpetuating growth forces are strong. In our group of countries, however, who have not safely made the transition to the developed category and where resources are scanty, such diffusion can only lead to most disappointing results. Concentration of efforts is indispensable. One must seek out the most important problems in the diagnoses and decide what are primary and must be cured and what are secondary or derivative and can be expected to be improved with a solution of the primary problems.

Of the many adverse and self-perpetuating causal sequences that can be encountered in developing countries, I have given primary emphasis to that of rural poverty—high birthrates—rural poverty. Many of the other problems or sequences can be traced to this one, or are more easily subject to solution if this is solved. Its solution does not guarantee that the country in question will thereby automatically gain control of its environment. Failure to resolve it, however, certainly obviates any possibility of gaining such control. None of the proposed solutions to the problem of development suggested or tried has provided for a requisite concentration of effort on breaking this primary vicious circle. For this reason, I have called the solution offered here the breakthrough program. For this reason, again, I believe we need a fundamental reappraisal of the primary objectives of development, the diagnosis of the problem, and the strategy indicated to attain the objectives.

To wage a war gradually and absentmindedly on many fronts is to court defeat. Similarly, to do just enough to reduce mortality rates and to keep excess numbers on the land is also to risk eventual defeat. To replace vicious by benign circles quickly requires the combination of all elements in a massive program pursued with single-mindedness to achieve specific goals. To omit one element, say an adequate incomes policy, would ruin the whole program. On the other hand, perhaps the only way to secure such an incomes policy is to convince companies and unions that what they are being asked to accept is part of an overall comprehensible plan to save their economies and to benefit all. To use up all the available ammunition in a piece-

[26] Reprinted in Lauchlin Currie, *Ensayos sobre Planeción* (Essays on Planning), 2d ed., Ediciónes Tercer Mundo, Bogotá, 1965.

meal fashion without having broken the vicious circles would be a very dangerous strategy.

Not only does the war analogy apply to the productive effort involved, but elements of military strategy itself are relevant. Thus committing one's reserves and equipment bit by bit on many fronts is generally condemned. The custom of making up a national budget with "something for everybody" offends against sound strategy, which calls for the establishment of strict priorities and for concentration of effort. The priorities in turn depend on the definition of objectives. There is room for variation in tactics. However, for quick success in abolishing poverty and gaining meaningful control over the environment, it is doubtful whether there is much room for wide variations in the choice of objectives and strategy. Administrative arrangements are of such crucial importance that they will be taken up in Chapter 10, the final chapter of Part One.

CHAPTER 9

The Capital Formation Approach

CHAPTER 5 TOUCHED ON the capital formation approach, but since it is the dominant approach, more detailed consideration of it was postponed until after the discussion of a possible alternative. The argument of this chapter is that the development of the Keynesian concepts and terminology and the development of statistical data to fit certain growth models have led to the identification of planning with programming in a narrow sense. This in turn has fostered excessive emphasis on the capital formation approach to development problems.[1]

Keynes was obviously concerned with the problem of unemployment in developed countries. The application of his framework of analysis to the developing countries was made possible, in the theoretical field, by the pioneer work of Harrod in 1939 and Domar in 1946. These writers took into account the effect of an increasing stock of capital on income. In the applied field Government accounts were reclassified into "investment" and "consumption" expenditures.

One of the first and clearest applications of the capital formation explanation of growth in developing countries, and one that had much influence, was made by Ragnar Nurske in lectures delivered in 1950 and published in 1953.[2] It was a great pity that Nurske initially focused his attention on capital formation rather than on the broader subject of development or poverty, since this led to excessive preoccupation with saving as the means of development. For example, on the vicious circle of poverty, he says, "There is the small capacity to save, resulting from the low level of real income. The low real income is a reflection of low productivity, which in

[1] See note on terminology at the end of Chap. 1.

[2] *Problems of Capital Formation in Underdeveloped Countries,* Oxford University Press, Fair Lawn, N.J., 1953.

its turn is due largely to the lack of capital. The lack of capital is a result of the small capacity to save"; or again, "The low level of productivity . . . is the result of the small amount of capital used in production" (Nurske, p. 5).

This preoccupation led Nurske to miss the full significance of rural underemployment, which he recognized from the works of Rosenstein-Rodan, Mandelbaum, Warriner, Cleland, and Issawi as existing throughout southeastern Europe, Egypt, and southeastern Asia but which, curiously enough, he thought was not characteristic of Latin America. He was most insistent that the displaced agricultural labor should be used in primitive capital formation (mostly public works) and fed from the surplus agricultural product. "There is hardly any need to stress the obvious point that it is not enough to get labor released from agriculture, that is, 'saved.' The labor must at once be employed for productive capital formation, that is, 'invested.' Otherwise the manpower released will be wasted and the advantages derived from the increase in productivity lost" (p. 53). He did not consider its possible use in producing other consumer goods. This is an extreme example of the tyranny of words, in which "investment" is good and "consumption" is bad.

Once Nurske has stated baldly that "the country's incremental saving ratio . . . is the crucial determinant of growth" (p. 142), it follows logically that all policies and actions must be judged by this criterion. "The general problem is to maximize the marginal saving ratio, i.e., the proportion of any increment in income that is saved. This is perhaps a perfectionist view; some immediate relief of the crushing weight of poverty is probably unavoidable and may even be desirable for the sake of development itself" (p. 142).

Thus he was led to overlook the possibilities for increasing the output of consumer goods by utilizing underemployed labor and capital resources, and he ignored almost completely the distortion in the patterns of investment and consumption that could result from gross inequality in income. He refers to the theory of using taxation to mitigate the inequalities of wealth as being "rather old fashioned now and in any case beside the point . . . not a change in the inter-personal income distribution but an increase in the proportion of national income devoted to capital formation is the primary aim of public finance in the context of economic development" (p. 147).

Nurske quotes Prebisch's 1950 paper with approval, but whereas the latter felt that little could be done to increase capital formation internally and that main reliance must be placed on foreign loans and investment, Nurske was skeptical of this recourse unless it was implemented by measures to increase internal saving. He frequently cited the example of Japan with approval in this respect. In that country, early capital formation was entirely national, was based largely on the land tax, and was accompanied by little inflation.

This preoccupation with internal saving and capital formation also led Nurske to overlook the possibilities in a transfer from unproductive to productive occupations. Such a transfer, he says, "begs the question of capital formation . . . which must be solved first" (p. 51). Here he seems to accept the position that there is a rigid relation between capital and employment, which, of course, is not true. Moreover, he overlooked the possibility that labor may be "unproductive" not because of lack of capital but because of lack of effective demand in relation to supply. A girl's labor may be worth almost nothing in agriculture but be quite remunerative as urban domestic labor, while utilizing no more "capital." What has apparently happened here is that the Keynesian identification of saving and investment by definition, which was a useful and intellectually satisfying tool of analysis, acquired a mystique of its own and resulted in a neglect of factors bearing on development which cannot be handled satisfactorily in the saving-investment and subsequent growth formulas.

Nurske concedes that improved terms of trade will increase incomes and consumption but questions whether there exists any automatic mechanism that will ensure an increase in capital goods imports. For this, deliberate action through taxation to increase saving is necessary. This may be true by his assumption of an agricultural economy with supply conditions generally inelastic in the short run. But in the type of economy with which we are concerned in this study, an initial increase in consumption of agricultural or nonagricultural goods may be expected to generate saving (concealed in the price of consumer goods) and the demand for capital goods, part of which will be drawn from abroad. On the other hand, it may be conceded that in the absence of deliberate policy, part of the increase in exchange resources resulting from improved terms of trade will be used on consumer goods imports. What happens, however, if imports of such goods are restricted?

Nurske raises doubts about the efficiency of exchange rationing as a means of increasing capital formation, on the grounds that capital formation must be matched by saving and that it is at least questionable whether restricting the import of, say, luxury goods actually increases internal saving. "So long as there is no increase in saving, there can be no increase in total net capital formation. An increase in saving can come about in the present case only in the form of forced saving resulting from inflation" (p. 113).

Perhaps he was led to this position by his initial assumption of "a position of equilibrium in which imports are equal to exports and national income is at a level corresponding to full employment without inflation" (p. 111). Suppose, however, that there is (1) great inequality of incomes, (2) a strictly limited supply of exchange, and (3) slack in the system. In these circumstances the *rate* of exchange at which a "natural" equilibrium takes place may be very high. At a much lower rate made possible by rationing, the demand for capital goods in terms of foreign currency may be much higher, though not so much higher in terms of local currency. In this case little, if any, increase in local saving purchases a larger *volume* of capital goods. The formula may show little change, but capital formation in real terms may be increased.

Actually, saving in terms of local currency is probably increased. If one cannot, for example, secure a secondhand car except at a very high price, a well-to-do person may be influenced not to employ more servants but rather to "buy" an apartment nearer the center. In this case, however, the additional saving is matched by additional internal investment.

To meet Nurske's objection, one would have to think of cases where the restriction of imports of luxury goods leads to increases in saving. This would be the case where the inability to buy a car does not lead to alternative consumption but to saving, which is certainly conceivable. Or we can depart from the unrealistic assumption of full employment. If, as here maintained, there is a large pool of underemployed human resources, increased local expenditures and an increased volume of imported capital goods can lead to more remunerative employment *and* more production, with an increase in domestic saving. We do not have to invoke inflation.

Nurske tended to think of saving as being mostly by individuals—the 25 percent or less of the well-to-do. While this is undoubtedly an important source, most of the saving is probably an immediate by-product of business operations. In a study of a group of cotton textile companies in Colombia from December 31, 1956, to December 31, 1962, it was found that expenditures on plant and equipment amounted to 191 million pesos. In the same period depreciation and other reserves increased by 253 million pesos. The shareholders paid in an additional 38 million pesos in capital but took out 317 million pesos in dividends, of which a substantial part doubtless was "saved."[3] One can speak of this as savings by a few shareholders. From another point of view the savings were made possible by the many consumers who were not consciously saving at all. In this six-year period, sales of these companies to their agents and distributors and to processors amounted to nearly 3½ billion pesos. (What the final consumer paid was considerably more.) Out of this sum, as we have seen, the companies retained 250 million pesos and the stockholders over 300 million pesos. In addition, growers of cotton received over 1 billion pesos, out of which they financed machinery purchases and improvements. The relatively highly paid textile workers received over 700 million pesos, part of which was certainly saved, if only in acquiring homes. Part of the remaining 1 billion pesos

[3] Lauchlin Currie, *El Algodón en Colombia,* Foundation for the Progress of Colombia, Bogotá, 1963.

paid out in other purchases, taxes, and other expenditures was doubtless "saved." So the process of consumption of textiles in itself provided a large pool of saving.[4]

Another work that has had great influence in this field is the *Design of Development* by Jan Tinbergen,[5] elaborated from a series of lectures given at the International Development Institute. This is an excellent and stimulating little book, full of profound and daring observations. The author shows appreciation of the importance of rural underemployment. He is also aware that the market or going rate of wages may be above the rate compatible with full employment, that the interest rate may be below an equilibrium rate,[6] and that distortions may thus be introduced. "We have to accept, therefore, in a number of underdeveloped countries that the market price structure is not the correct guide for taking decisions" (Tinbergen, p. 40).[7] Although I arrived at the same conclusion independently, I am happy to acknowledge that Tinbergen applied the concept of wage or cost-push inflation to developing countries several years before I did. He even mentioned the possibility of altering the capital-employment ratio by working more shifts, but in my opinion he minimized the significance of this because it could be done only once (p. 76). Thus he overlooked the breakthrough effect and the fact that the great increase in productivity, if continued in the future, would be equivalent to a great and continuing increase in exports.

Unfortunately, Tinbergen identified well-being with national income, both present and future, though he envisaged "possible corrections for its distribution over social groups or regions" (p. 36). Instead of developing this modification, he, like Nurske, was led off at this point to the importance of investment as the determinant of income. "The desperate situation of large parts of the population may be said to be due to lack of capital" (p. 49). Or again, "The quantity of product obtained is practically proportional to the quantity of capital . . . [and] the ratio between capital and product seems not to depend on the degree of development of a country" (p. 75). To increase the national income per capita in a country with a population increase of 3 percent would require a rate of saving of over 20 percent; 12 percent is necessary merely to maintain income per capita in such cases (p. 14). He says, "Part of the population cannot be

[4] See also the example of the French steel industry cited by John Sheahan, *Promotion and Control of Industry in Post War France,* Harvard University Press, Cambridge, Mass., 1963, p. 13.

[5] Johns Hopkins Press, 1958.

[6] His use of the phrase "accounting rate" to indicate the economic or equilibrium rate would not, however, appear to be a happy choice.

[7] See also Myrdal: "The price system does not give rational criteria for economic planning," *Economic Theory and Underdeveloped Regions,* Methuen & Co., Ltd., London, 1957, p. 89.

gainfully occupied for lack of complementary means of production, land and capital," (p. 76)—forgetting, for the moment, his point on the influence of too high wages.

So, despite a number of excellent suggestions, the final impression Tinbergen leaves is profoundly discouraging, since the volume of saving necessary to raise the standard of living of a rapidly growing population is so large. It is a pity that Tinbergen did not develop more fully the implications of his criticisms of the role of market prices in allocating resources. This could have led to more fruitful results than the emphasis on capital formation.

Few economists have insisted more than Gunnar Myrdal on the need for new approaches and on the irrationality or irrelevance of much of current economic theory to the problems of underdevelopment. His provocative *Economic Theory and Underdeveloped Regions* is mostly concerned with the causes and implications of growing inequality, but in the few pages devoted to planning he is surprisingly conventional. For example, "There is no other road to economic development than a compulsory rise in the share of the national income which is withheld from consumption and devoted to investment. This implies a policy of the utmost austerity. . . . This frugality, which must be applied to the level of living of the masses of the people for the simple reason that they are the many, becomes a much more difficult policy in the under-developed countries to-day than it ever was in the now highly developed ones in their early stages of economic development. This is so both because of their much greater poverty and also because of the new ideology—which had no real counterpart in the earlier history of the developed countries but has now been spread with their generous support—that the purpose of economic development is to raise levels of living for the masses of the people . . . undoubtedly democracy . . . makes it more difficult for governments to hold down the level of consumption *in the degree necessary for rapid development*" pp. 82–83; italics added). Or again, "This approach, if effectively carried out, will in the practical sphere dictate reasons for an economic policy of suppressing the temptations to raise levels of living rapidly" (p. 91). Here he is implicitly adopting the assumptions of a fully employed, well-distributed, and more or less equally paid working force—all assumptions which he had explicitly rejected as being uncharacteristic of developing regions.

In this manner he illustrates dramatically his own warning against carrying around implicit assumptions as part of our mental luggage. Once we change the assumptions above to those of a labor force largely idle and badly distributed, with great inequality in earnings, and once we assume the existence of heavy consumption expenditures by the very rich, then to talk of increasing saving and holding back a rise in consumption of the masses makes no sense.

With this background I shall now attempt to show how planning is becoming identified with a special kind of programming which, in turn, is more and more identified with the saving–capital formation approach. It is always possible to cite exceptions, but we are concerned here with what receives the emphasis.

Reference was made in Chapter 1 to the report *Programming Techniques for Economic Development* by a distinguished group of experts for the United Nations.[8] It is an extraordinarily interesting work, because it illustrates very well the difficulty of combining a strategy of development with quantitative programming. Needless to say, they must be combined if we are to make progress, but it is my belief that in some way programming must be rescued from an excessive preoccupation with the saving–investment–income, capital-output ratios approach and that planning must be given the dominant and initial role.

The actual danger may be brought out by a number of quotations from this important report. At the beginning it remarks that the fact that the technique of programming is concerned with quantitative estimation "does not mean that the use of the more qualitative kind of analysis in the work of planning is denied or overlooked . . . . it is useful for planners to formulate, at an early stage, what may be called the broad strategy of development" (United Nations, p. 3). As might be expected from the choice of words ("denied," "useful"), the qualitative treatment that follows is cursory. It then passes on to the choice of objectives or targets and lists seven possibilities. Immediately, however, it moves back to a single objective: "The objective of a rapid rise in per capita income should always be given high priority for the simple reason that the source of all material well-being is the availability of goods" (p. 6). Could "the simple reason" be that this objective lends itself to the capital-output approach?

After these perfunctory remarks, the report goes on to what really interests the authors. The section "Planning the General Rate of Development" comes out flatly with the statement, "The final goal of development programming is . . . to design the most efficient and optimum rate of capital accumulation" (p. 8). A momentary doubt entered here: "It would be an over-simplification, of course, to regard economic development as a matter of capital accumulation alone" (p. 8). But this doubt was resolved by the bland statement that other things, such as entrepreneurship and worker training, are "seldom possible without some increase in the stock of capital. Therefore capital accumulation may very well be regarded as the core process by which all other aspects of growth are made possible" (p. 8). The choice of the words "may very well be regarded" and "core process" is curious. In any case, in one short paragraph, planning and programming became synonymous with a restricted and particular kind of programming.

[8] E/C.N., 11/535, 1960.

The rest of the discussion follows in large part the now familiar pattern that has almost become identified with the word "programming."

There are, however, some interesting departures, perhaps because the group of authors were supposed to be particularly concerned with Asia and the Far East. Thus the report shows an unusual awareness of "overcrowding" and low productivity in rural areas and the possible necessity of finding alternative employment for some of the people now engaged in peasant agriculture. However, this problem is cited merely as a justification for a "model" consisting of Farm versus Industrial Sectors. On the problem itself, the report is basically pessimistic: "If land is very scarce and non-agricultural employment increases by less than the growth in the labor force, non-agriculture may grow relative to agriculture as a whole, and yet the shift from 'farming' to 'industrial agriculture' may not take place" (p. 29). This development may, in turn, check industrial development because of inadequate agricultural production. The report has recourse at this point to increased investment in both sectors and to a possible reduction in consumption (p. 31). Elsewhere, in a short chapter on manpower and education, it is remarked that a shift from lower-paying to higher-paying occupations improves the position of those who shift and those who remain and that "it may well be a wise policy to pursue greater income equality as an end in itself, within certain limits, in order to arrive at healthier social conditions" (p. 74).

There are also passing references to the possible desirability of rationing consumer goods (p. 67), to the desirability of seeking new techniques which require less capital to produce the same amount of output (p. 14), and to the possibility that "in some countries, the problem of unemployment may be so serious that targets must be set primarily in terms of employment creation" (p. 13). But no one of these and other promising leads manages to get itself incorporated in the programming technique, which is overwhelmingly based on the capital-output growth model.

The conclusion I derive from a consideration of the work of the "programmers" appears, at least to me, to be of basic importance. It is that planning must be restored to its preeminent place and that programming must assume its proper role of furnishing the statistical tools and other techniques of implementing a plan.

It appears that the opposite has happened, that planning which does not lend itself to being fitted into the "Fundamental Equation of Economic Growth" (p. 82) is relegated to perfunctory comments. In effect, the programmers would have us subscribe to a standard highly simplified plan, that of securing "growth" by increasing saving and capital formation. Actually, a plan, with its objectives deliberately chosen and its strategy based on a fully considered diagnosis, should determine the nature of the program and the necessary techniques; not vice versa. The fact that welfare eludes precise measurement is no justification for discarding the concept. Poverty, pain, inequality, and ignorance *do* exist, and at least for the developing countries of the world, the economists are under some obligation to propose the most feasible plans to lessen their pervasiveness, even if such plans entail very difficult problems of implementation.

For developing countries, it appears that too much emphasis has been placed on increasing the percentage of income saved. From a dynamic point of view the provision of more remunerative work, whether in investment or consumption, leads to an increase in the value of production, in income, in consumption, in saving, and in investment. From the cotton textile example cited above it can be seen how an increase in consumption permits an immediate increase in saving, which in turn finances more investment. On the other hand, an increased investment in housing leads immediately to an increase in saving.

What started out in the hands of Keynes as a useful set of definitions and concepts to explain inflation, or the persistence of unemployment, or the emergence of a brake on a recovery movement, is in danger of becoming a mental straitjacket on our thinking about development problems.[9] A more fruitful starting point would appear to be the creation of more remunerative jobs and the adoption of an incomes policy to prevent the increase in demand from petering out in higher individual incomes and prices. If we are successful in this, the incentive to invest and the offsetting saving follow as derivative rather than initiating factors. Keynes' analysis is still useful in indicating that the major expansion in new jobs and additional production in developing areas must be in consumer goods and that, given an adequate incomes policy, the initiation of new investment may have to be restrained so that the combined investment and consumption will not outrun the physical capacity to produce. The saving–capital formation analysis can then be put in its proper, and always useful, place and the way opened for a more dynamic and many-sided attack on development problems. Such a reorientation would have the incidental benefit of enabling us to evaluate governmental programs without having to contrast public "investment" with public "'operating" expenditures, and without having to speak of government "consumption" to cover all expenditures other than "investment."

It is perfectly conceivable that the proportion of income saved and invested may be too high if great inequality prevails and the pattern of demand is distorted from production of mass consumer goods to the production of luxury articles for the few. Greater equality may lead to a decline in the proportion saved and yet, if there is slack in the system, may be compatible with an increase in demand, production, investment, and saving

[9] See J. G. Gurley and E. S. Shaw: "The complexities of a growth model that incorporates the financial as well as the real conditions of growth appear, for the present at least, to defy simple or even systematic conditions of growth." "Financial Aspects of Economic Development," *American Economic Review*, 1955, p. 531.

in absolute terms and with a great gain in welfare. Six percent of one hundred is equal to twelve percent of fifty. Moreover, the composition of investment is important. Equal investment in facilities to produce goods like cotton textiles or goods like automobiles can yield widely different results in terms of welfare in developing countries.[10]

In short, the identity of saving and investment by definition is a useful concept but is by no means a theory of employment or a theory of development. There would appear to be no particular merit in treating all development problems in terms of capital formation, capital stock, consumption, and production, and much can be argued against it. There are obvious advantages in being able to deal directly with welfare, disguised unemployment, income inequality, imperfect competition, factor mobility, population, financial phenomena, incomes policy, and direct controls, without trying to squeeze all these topics into the saving-investment formula. The failure of Nurske, Prebisch, Myrdal, and many others to grasp the full significance of rural underemployment, income inequality, and inadequate labor mobility may very well have been a result of their preoccupation with the Keynesian terminology.

Even the outstanding text by Samuelson, which has had such a tremendous influence, makes the determination of national income a function of capital formation. "Economists are agreed that the important factor in causing income and employment to fluctuate is investment."[11] Although the text makes clear that the discussion is concerned with the *monetary* relation of investment to income, the student can be forgiven for exaggerating the role of investment and forgetting or minimizing the host of other factors that affect or determine the standard of living or *real* income of a people.

In view of the general concurrence of leading economists that the key to development lies in increasing the proportion of income saved—i.e., in increasing investment—and to a lesser extent, in making that investment more "productive," it is with considerable diffidence that I suggest a some-

[10] Viner had the perspicacity to note that according to available data, the propensity to save in poorer countries was higher than in richer. "If capital formation is seriously inadequate in the poorer countries, therefore, it must ordinarily be because average incomes are low rather than because the propensity to save in relation to per capita income is exceptionally low." In the same paper he had the insight (and courage) to question the desirability or necessity of great inequality in developing countries and to ask whether programs of economic development might not aim first at raising the income levels of the poor masses. "Stability and Progress in the World Economy." *Proceedings of First Congress of the International Economic Association* in 1956, edited by Douglas Hague and published in 1958, pp. 49–50.

[11] Note that he says *the,* not an, important factor. Paul A. Samuelson, *Economics,* 6th ed., McGraw-Hill Book Company, New York, 1964, p. 221, in a chapter entitled "The Theory of Income Determination."

what different approach. (However, it is encouraging to note that Domar, one of those whose work led to the endless proliferation of growth models, remarked, "Surely no one imagines that capital formation, even broadly defined, can be the sole explanation and cause of growth."[12]) In my approach, based upon the existing widespread underutilization and malallocation of resources, emphasis is placed directly on satisfying the demand for consumer goods and services by the lower-income portion of the population (assuming housing to be a durable consumer good). To the extent to which success is achieved and effective demand for consumer goods is met, saving and investment will increase (1) to permit three-shift operations for a longer work year and (2) to add to productive capacity in public services, consumer goods industries, and some intermediate and capital goods industries. (This will be even more true if housing is included in investment.) But the increase of saving and investment will be a consequence of the success of the program rather than a cause or an objective in itself. More intensive utilization of existing or new capital will greatly raise its productivity—again, a consequence of quickly meeting existing needs for consumer goods and services of the poorer part of the population.

Since the capital-production approach is so firmly entrenched, it may be worthwhile to point out that my alternative approach *can* be expressed in its terms. More intensive utilization of existing and new equipment in a transition to two- and three-shift operation, and more remunerative and intensive employment of existing labor, can together be expressed as a rise in the productivity of the existing stock of capital and in the new addition. This rise should also have the effect of increasing the annual addition to the stock and may even increase the percentage of income saved.[13] The advantage to be derived from treating my approach in terms of the capital formation approach or in terms of a growth model appears questionable, however. It would seem that there are certain advantages which flow from the proposed shift in objectives and emphasis from the side of supply to that of demand and from investment to consumption. That this is important is shown by the fact that instead of preaching the necessity of austerity, as Myrdal does, I start with the objective of greater consumption per capita, made possible by (1) putting underutilized manpower and capital to

[12] *Capital Formation and Economic Growth: A Conference,* Princeton University Press, Princeton, N.J., 1953, p. 107. Curiously enough, in the same year he wrote, "In underdeveloped countries it is clearly capital rather than labor that is the factor limiting growth." *Quarterly Journal of Economics,* 1953, p. 559. Compare R. S. Eckhaus: "This suggests an observation which is, by now, almost trite: reduction of underemployment in overpopulated areas requires the addition of scarce factors." *American Economic Review,* 1955, p. 547.

[13] These various possibilities could be studied in the light of the provocative ten hypotheses on capital formation set forth by Moses Abramovitz, *Capital Formation and Economic Growth: A Conference,* Princeton University Press, Princeton, N.J., 1953, pp. 658–667.

work, and (2) more equitable distribution of consumer demand and production.

For some peculiar reason, the capital formation approach appears to lead to a more static treatment by placing emphasis on the necessity of initially increasing saving and investment, with consumption being a derivative consequence. Many years ago I remarked that "it is a peculiarity of Keynes' work that he appears always to think of an increase in income as being generated by an increase in investment and never by an increase in consumption."[14] I went on to cite the possibility of reversing the sequence through an expansion of installment credit to buy cars or an increase in public relief expenditures. In my testimony before the Temporary National Economic Committee in 1939,[15] I presented the results of several years' investigation of the distinction between exogenous types of spending and derivative or endogenous types. In the former category were what I then called the net government contribution, housing, and installment selling; in the latter were the great bulk of business and public utility investment. The possibilities of this approach for forecasting (and intervention) were later skillfully explored by V. Lewis Bassie.[16] The implications of the approach for development problems are obvious.

In the present approach we start with the necessity of increasing consumption—i.e., demand—and saving and investment follow almost as a matter of course—i.e., are induced. It is a dynamic approach recently adopted by the United States in its deliberate tax reduction and apparently practiced for a number of years in Japan, where it was particularly effective in drawing down the originally enormous pool of rural labor. It is interesting that Viner, who Myrdal criticized as having a static approach, escaped the trap of static formulations by placing emphasis on the abolition of dire poverty, whereas Myrdal, while stressing the need for a dynamic approach, ended by arguing for a further reduction in the standard of living! Economics is indeed a difficult field.

Another shift in emphasis is my insistence that saving and investment are not good in themselves. They represent costs and sacrifices that should be kept as low as possible consistent with the achievement of our basic objective of increasing the well-being of the many. Placing emphasis on "heavy" industries, petrochemical industries, and "new" industries, regardless of the product or cost, may have made sense in the case of Soviet Russia, or may be desirable if this is the only way of utilizing idle factors. But, as we have seen, it is not the only way. It can make more sense to utilize idle factors in producing what most people want (e.g., cotton textiles

[14] *Some Theoretical and Practical Implications of J. M. Keynes' General Theory*, National Industrial Conference Board, New York, 1938, p. 18.

[15] *Hearings pursuant to Public Resolution 113*, vol. 9, *Savings and Investment*, pp. 3520–3538.

[16] *Economic Forecasting*, McGraw-Hill Book Company, New York, 1958.

rather than dacron) and pushing exports (or subsidizing them, if necessary) to earn foreign exchange to increase the productive capacity of industries catering to mass demand. Even exporting is not good in itself and represents a cost. Its main justification can be found in what is done with the proceeds. Clearly, emphasis and subjective values are of tremendous importance in determining the nature of the program selected.

It will be recalled that the saving-investment formulation is only a tool of analysis. Keynes himself utilized this tool to insist that savings might have been too high in the conditions of his day to be consistent with full employment. There is perhaps no doctrine that has been more ridiculed than that of the "mature economy." The term was unfortunate, it is true. But the basic idea of a long-term possibility of an excessive propensity to save was valid. It was a dilemma of the New Deal that saving tended to increase more rapidly than the demand for capital goods to permit full employment. The dilemma was resolved by the war, and it did not reappear in the postwar period because of the tremendous continuing volume of government expenditures and transfer expenditures, which held the volume of saving at full employment levels under what it otherwise would have been.

This bit of history illustrates another analogy. Just as the proper objective in 1933–1939 was the stimulation of effective demand to meet the need for consumer goods and services, so this should be our objective, modified only to take account of the much greater inequality, in a certain group of developing countries today. To call for diminished consumption was not a rational policy in 1933–1939 in the United States or Europe, nor is it a rational policy new for many developing countries. This affords another illustration that our problem can be resolved by the appropriate application of general economic theory and does not require a special theory of development or growth. Making the appropriate application is sufficiently difficult without having to devise new theories. It appears that the plan proposed by President Johnson to abolish poverty in the United States does not rely on the capital formation approach.

Joan Robinson came very close to the argument set forth here: "The problem can be stated in a straight-forward manner in terms of the need to provide for an increase in necessary consumption while restraining unnecessary consumption. The overall saving ratio . . . distracts attention from the distribution of income between individual families." Or again "The advantage of the handicrafts lies in being capital-saving, not in being labor-using."[17] Unfortunately she did not pursue these leads and reverted to the necessity of increasing saving and capital.

It will probably be objected that experience has demonstrated the existence of a definite relation between gross investment and gross income

[17] *Economic Philosophy,* Aldine Publishing Co., Chicago, 1962, pp. 118 and 122.

and that by abandoning the capital formation approach we abandon our main programming tool for achieving a "given" increase in production. "Even though there are variations, [this approach] is perhaps one of the most useful parameters with a fair degree of stability,"[18] the United Nations experts say. However, the few examples they give show a variation in the capital coefficient from 2.3 for India to 4.7 for Japan, which fails to establish a case for much stability in the relationship.

In their recent evaluations of national plans prepared by technicians who shared this view of programming, missions of the World Bank and the Committee of Nine, which also shared the same view, confined themselves largely to revising the proposed investment upward or downward in various sectors to achieve the same goals. The usefulness of this procedure is doubtful. B. R. Williams[19] compared gross investment as a percentage of GNP with annual percentage growth in the GNP for nine countries for the period 1950–1957 and found absolutely no correlation. Australia spent nearly 30 percent of its GNP in investment and achieved a growth rate of 2½ percent; at the other extreme Greece spent 16 percent and achieved a growth rate of nearly 8 percent. The relation in seven other countries showed no consistent pattern. The returns from investment appear to vary widely.

Similarly T. P. Hill, in a study of the relation between the growth of investment and the GNP for seventeen countries, found variations ranging from the case of Greece, with a rate of growth of 7 percent and investment of 17 percent, to that of Norway, with 3.5 percent and 29 percent, respectively.[20] It is interesting that he found absolutely no relation between the amount spent on construction and the growth of the GNP on the one hand, and a low rate of return on services on the other. But he points out that in the richest country of the world, 60 percent of the product originates in services, and two-thirds of gross investment in recent years has consisted of construction![21]

These findings are in contradiction to the widely held belief in the consistency of the relation between investment and income, a belief dating from the earlier quantitative work of Colin Clark and Simon Kuznets. As summarized by W. Arthur Lewis, "On the average an investment of £1,000 is associated with an increase in national income by between £25 and £33 per year; or . . . raising national income by 3 percent per annum cumulatively is associated with an annual net investment of between 9 percent and 12 percent of national income."[22] It is a pity that this does not appear

[18] United Nations, *Programming Techniques,* E/C.N., 11/535, 1960, p. 11.

[19] Of the Manchester School of Economic and Social Studies. Quoted from *The Times* (London), Feb. 7, 1964, p. 20.

[20] *Economic Journal,* June, 1964, p. 295.

[21] *Ibid.,* p. 304.

[22] *The Theory of Economic Growth,* George Allen & Unwin, Ltd., London, 1955, p. 201.

to apply to all economies at all times with differing compositions of investment, since in that case growth, if not economic well-being, would be simply a matter of arithmetic.

The new evidence of the absence of any consistent relation between gross investment and gross production is extraordinarily interesting to me because I believe that I was perhaps the first to attempt to use Keynes' concepts quantitatively (apart from Keynes himself) on the basis of Kuznets' data.[23] For the period 1919–1934 in the United States, I found that "on five occasions [years] net investment and income moved in opposite directions; on two other occasions the increase in income was less than the increase in investment. Similar computations based upon two or three year aggregates show but little greater consistency. From 1923 to 1929 the national income increased by nearly $14 billion, yet the absolute propensity to consume increased. In other words, national income increased throughout this period with virtually no increase in the yearly figures in net investment."[24]

The widespread belief that there is a stable relation between incremental investment and production tends to lead to reduced emphasis on the quality of investment, particularly in the public sector, and to a highly unreal treatment of public programs. Roads going from nowhere to nowhere obviously should not be accorded the same real production-generating quality as textile machinery to be used on a three-shift basis. The criterion for judging a public education program should clearly not be that afforded by the investment-production approach. In fact, it may be questioned whether the extension of these concepts to the public sector has not done more harm than good. As pointed out earlier, the enormous expenditure by the United States on weapons (including warships, rockets, missiles and military installations) are all included by Kuznets in "investment," with the implied effect on real per capita income. Possibly some such classification is necessary in order to give quantitative meaning to growth equations, but at least we should be aware of the disadvantages and dangers involved. It may be a case where what should be our servants are becoming our masters.

One of the major differences between a highly developed and a developing economy lies in the character of investment. In the former, the sheer volume of investment prevents mistakes and individual undertakings from having undue influence on the grand totals. In an economy at an early stage of development, very large individual government undertakings may dominate the picture and result in wide variations in the capital coefficient. In Colombia two relatively large investments, the Atlantic Railroad and a steel plant, took years to get into operation and to arrive at a stage where they were earning. The investment under way in the Orinoco region

[23] *Some Theoretical and Practical Implications of J. M. Keynes' General Theory,* National Industrial Conference Board, New York, 1938.

[24] *Ibid.,* pp. 21–22. Also *Hearings,* "a more or less stable volume of capital expenditures supported a rising national income" from 1923 to 1928 (p. 3537).

of Venezuela is a tremendous one relative to current national investment. To rely on past capital-output ratios, or worse, to assume, as most plans do, a rapid *rise* in the ratio, appears to be very hazardous.

One grave weakness of the global capital formation approach lies in the fact that for the most part, the area of positive action is restricted to public investment financed in various ways. The connecting links to the much larger totals of private investment and gross product are weak and the results are extremely hypothetical.

Various authors can be cited on the danger of exaggerating the role of capital formation in the growth process. After examining several attempts to separate the respective effects of technical progress and the growth of capital, Everett Hagen[25] wrote that he preferred the technique employed by Robert M. Solow.[26] Solow estimated that of the increase in output per man-hour in the United States from 1904 to 1949, not more than 13 percent was due to increase in capital, while 87 to 90 percent was due to other changes. If this finding can be sustained, it is one of tremendous importance and should effectively dethrone King Capital. As Hagen remarks, "indeed, if creativity ceased, and capital formation in the United States were limited to producing additional machinery and equipment embodying methods already known, it is a reasonable guess that increase in output per man-hour and the accompanying steady rise in our level of living would probably decline almost to zero within two decades."[27]

Solow in turn cites Salomon Fabricant, who estimated that over the period 1871–1951, about 90 percent of the increase in output per capita was attributable to technological progress.[28] Finally, J. K. Galbraith, though he does not give the source, refers to calculations made under the auspices of the National Bureau of Economic Research for the period 1944–1953, according to which "the net output of the American economy increased by an average of 3.5 percent a year. Less than half of this (1.7 percent) is explained by increases in the supply of capital *and labor*."[29] On the basis of this finding, Galbraith concludes: "We now get the larger part of our industrial growth not from more capital investment but from improvements in men and improvements brought about by highly improved men."[30]

Gottfried Haberler, after referring to the outpouring of models, stated, "There can hardly be doubt any more that so far the results have been

[25] Everett Hagen, *On the Theory of Social Change,* Dorsey Press, Homewood, Illinois, 1962, p. 49.

[26] *Review of Economics and Statistics,* August, 1957, pp. 312–320.

[27] *Op. cit.,* p. 50.

[28] *Economic Progress and Economic Change,* 34th Annual Report of the National Bureau of Economic Research, New York, 1954, p. 317.

[29] Italics added. *The Liberal Hour,* Houghton Mifflin Company, Boston, 1960, pp. 35–36.

[30] *Ibid.,* p. 36.

most disappointing. The multiplicity of more or less inconsistent models, many of them based on broadly plausible assumptions, and if of the econometric type, fitting the data from which they were derived fairly well—but none of them standing up to the test of extrapolation beyond the period from which the data were taken—is a spectacle that is not calculated to inspire confidence."[31]

To this goodly company of skeptics may be added Kindleberger, who, after analyzing various serious conceptual difficulties in the use of the capital-product ratios and the erratic statistical results obtained, concluded that the relation "in its present rudimentary stage is hardly a planning device."[32] He considered that the relative stability in the relation *over long periods* was probably the result of the law of large numbers in which opposing movements cancel out.[33] However, for most planning purposes in developing areas, we have to deal with small numbers and short periods.

Hirschman is still another skeptic. "A model based on the propensity to save and the capital-output ratio is bound to be far less useful in underdeveloped than in advanced countries. Its predictive and operational value is low."[34] Finally, in the words of Henry J. Bruton, "It must, therefore, be emphasized that the growth process must be viewed in a larger context than simply the arithmetic of capital-output ratios, savings-income ratios, and population growth rates."[35] He concludes his excellent review of the literature on growth by declaring, "A strong argument can be made that the problem of underdevelopment will not be solved until economics has achieved a more compatible marriage than now prevails with other social sciences"[36]—heretical words indeed.

It is, again, significant that nobody would dream of advocating the capital formation approach to wage a war, where the productive efforts required dwarf normal peacetime goals. It may be objected that the analogy does not apply, since the economic essence of waging war is a sacrifice of future production for present, while what is needed in development is the assurance of larger future production, which only more roundabout production can provide. But is this certain? What is most urgently needed to break the vicious circle is an *immediate and substantial* rise in the level of consumption of the poorest people. This cannot be accomplished by decreasing con-

[31] *Stability and Progress in the World Economy,* The Macmillan Company, New York, 1958, p. 161.

[32] Charles Kindleberger, *Economic Development,* McGraw-Hill Book Company, New York, 1958, p. 47.

[33] *Ibid.,* p. 46.

[34] *The Strategy of Economic Development,* Yale University Press, New Haven, Conn., 1958, p. 32.

[35] "Contemporary Theorizing on Economic Growth," in Bert Hoselitz et al. (eds.), *Theories of Economic Growth,* The Free Press of Glencoe, New York, 1960, p. 267.

[36] *Ibid.,* p. 242.

sumption now for the benefit of more roundabout methods of production, but by putting idle resources to work immediately and by immediately securing a much better distribution of disposable income and consumption. So the analogy to war does appear to apply.

The discussion in this chapter points to the conclusion that criticism of the capital formation approach is not enough. It will continue to be used as long as quantitative alternatives are not available. What is urgently needed is the development of new programming techniques directed toward the attainment of new national goals. For developing countries, techniques based on the capital formation-output approach to attain per capita output goals have proved ineffective and indeed dangerous. Is it asking too much that other techniques to attain other goals be at least given a trial?

Some of the elements in such techniques are indicated in Chapter 19. From the point of view of statisticians who like to make projections on the basis of past relationships, the necessities for identifying sectors that will require capital and exchange resources quicker than others, for modifying the pattern of past demand and resource allocation, and for attempting to assess quantitatively the effect of such structural changes over the near term, are admittedly defects.

Again, we can have recourse to a wartime type of programming.[37] There appears to be no good reason why quantitative techniques in this field should serve only one goal. The farreaching quantitative implications of the utilization of hitherto underutilized resources in the creation of *x* number of new jobs a year in nonagricultural occupations certainly should offer an inviting challenge to the quantitative programmers. Indeed, considering the sorry record of the capital formation approach, it is very likely that more precise results can be obtained by starting with the goal of a better allocation and utilization of factors. What must be insisted upon, however, is that the purpose of such programming is not to arrive at a certain figure of average per capita output but to attain quickly a plateau of well-being for the masses from which self-generating advancement in the widest sense is assured.

Both qualitative planning and quantitative programming are necessary, but the latter need not be restricted to the capital formation approach, and certainly the former should not be.

The issue of this chapter is well pointed up by Stonier and Hague, who justify a new edition of their excellent and widely used textbook by remarking that a body of doctrine is emerging on the theory of economic growth and that they have done their best "To summarize that part of growth theory on which there is now agreement."[38] Turning to the accepted

[37] An example is given by Kindleberger of the use of input-output tables to estimate all factor requirements to produce 10,000 airplanes. *Op. cit.*, p. 143.

[38] Alfred W. Stonier and Douglas C. Hague, *Textbook of Economic Theory*, 3d ed., Longmans, Green & Co., Ltd., London, 1963, preface.

doctrine we first find, as was to be expected, the exaltation of the rôle of capital and the fundamental growth equation, with a number of somewhat incautious statements on the necessity of an increase in capital as a condition of growth.

The authors then take up technical progress and surprisingly remark that "technical progress therefore turns out to be even more essential to economic growth then is capital accumulation" (p. 534), and that productivity could rise without any change in the stock of capital assets (p. 538). The final blow, however, is the statement that technical progress makes it impossible to measure changes in capital and that "Some economists, particularly Mrs. Robinson, go so far as to hold that it is not really possible to talk of 'quantities' of capital at all: capital cannot be measured" (p. 543). In the face of the formidable lack of agreement on accepted growth theory the authors rather lamely conclude, doubtless to the confusion of thousands of students, that while we must not forget this difficulty (inability to measure capital), "It has clearly not prevented us learning a great deal from these simple models of economic growth" (p. 543).

It appears that they are like the fallacy of composition—no validity but we can learn something from it. Finally they assert that "A decision to spend money on education . . . is an investment decision in just the same way as is an entrepreneur's decision to build or buy a new machine" (p. 553). Should we then include all or part of education expenditures in investment?

Exactly where then are we left with our theory of growth? To me it appears that growth or development cannot be divorced from welfare or "illfare," with all the complexity and even messiness that those terms evoke. To identify welfare, particularly in underdeveloped countries, with a rate of growth in the summation of the gross or net value of product, without an adjustment for distribution (and how would one adjust?) seems to be an unforgivable simplification. Even if we commit the unforgivable, and then acknowledge that "progress," with all it implies, is more important to this concept of growth than capital accumulation, what becomes of our growth theory? That "growth" arises from "progress"? A perspicacious student might be forgiven the question: After twenty years of labor, is that all the mountains have brought forth?

If, as Joan Robinson remarked, the corpus of science at any moment consists of the theories that have not been disproved, it appears that Stonier and Hague may have been a little premature in including the capital output approach in the corpus of our science, or, to follow Mrs. Robinson, in our branch of ethics. Clearly, it is possible to apply the basic concepts of economics to the problems of growth or development; what is not so certain is whether there is such a thing as *growth or development economics.*

CHAPTER 10

Prerequisites

As STATED EARLIER, the truly difficult problem in accelerating development is not technical, difficult as that is, but rather the lack of will and knowledge. Few, if any, governments in developing countries would have the faith, courage, and ability to adopt and execute a sophisticated program such as the one set forth here, with its apparent paradoxes and the necessity of avoiding income and price inflation at crucial points. Some of these paradoxes can be briefly listed.

To resolve the agrarian problem, we must industrialize and divert expenditures to the cities.

To create new jobs, we must restrain wage (and dividend) advances relative to prices.

To encourage industrialization, we must start with housing and urban public services.

To create more jobs, we must work more, not less.

The objective is to spend less, not more, in agriculture and to engage fewer people on less land.

To make additional housing available for the very poor, we should build for the middle class and upper working class.

To prevent the harmful effects of inflation, we should provide for periodic cost-of-living adjustments instead of attempting to freeze prices, wages, interest payments, and exchange rates.

We should give priority to consumer goods (including housing) rather than to heavy and capital goods industries; and so on.

This by no means exhausts the list, but it serves to make the point. It would be unrealistic to expect the adoption and execution of such a program without powerful assurance, guidance, and pressure from outside. It would be even more unrealistic to expect the adoption of such a program in the face of opposition from foreign lenders. We are not dealing here with a relatively straightforward problem of rebuilding and reequipment, as in Europe after the war, but with a terribly complex problem in a difficult cultural milieu complicated by a population explosion. If, instead of being under outside pressure to adopt unpopular and little-understood programs, governments find that they can get all the financial assistance they can reasonably expect by merely going through a few motions of planning and reform, they will naturally do so.

The entities that must first understand the problem and be convinced of the nature of the solution are not, therefore, the governments or political parties of developing countries but rather the international agencies—and indeed, the governments of developed countries who ultimately influence the international agencies. Only if they provide leadership can the developing countries be expected to make the requisite effort. Otherwise it seems evident that we will continue with the sprinkler approach, supplemented by ineffectual changes in land tenure and halfhearted tariff negotiations. When debt-paying capacity becomes overstrained, presumably refinancing will be resorted to and the process will continue.

If the international and foreign national agencies should arrive at the diagnosis of the problem set forth here, the next task will be to influence the development and execution of an appropriate program as unobtrusively and yet as effectively as possible. Preferably this would be carried out first in a single country where the chances of success appeared favorable.[1]

One possible device would be for the underdeveloped country to set up a development fund as the main administrative device though which money for the program would be channeled, and for the consortium or consulting group of lenders to accept minority representation in the fund upon invitation. In that way they and their technical assistants could exert a continuing influence on the program. Actually, foreign agencies (the Monetary Fund and the International Bank) do this in a sporadic and *ad hoc* fashion today. All I am suggesting is that this guidance be systematized and related to a definite countrywide program of which coordinated foreign assistance would be an integral part.

Doubtless it will be objected that the cry of imperialism or excessive paternalism would be raised. It is, however, difficult to accuse an international agency of imperialism. No country has to accept the agency's advice—and aid—and no country has the divine right to insist on being given aid which the lender is convinced is doing it no particular good. Some developing countries have come dangerously close to blackmail or to arriving at a state of mind in which they convince themselves that the world owes

[1] Although our treatments differ significantly, Hirschman and I appear to be close on this most fundamental of diagnoses: "If backwardness is due to insufficient number and speed of development decisions and to inadequate performance of developmental tasks, then the fundamental problem of development consists in generating and energizing human action in a certain direction." Albert Hirschman, *The Strategy of Economic Development,* Yale University Press, New Haven, Conn., 1958, p. 25. The difficulty lies in securing agreement on the direction.

them a living. This is nonsense. Lender agencies and nations do not have to surrender their right to lay down certain conditions for loans. The real danger is that they themselves do not know what conditions will do the borrower the most good. Since in this case they might do more harm than good, the suggestion about the development fund is made with a good deal of hesitation. Perhaps a safeguard against the danger of bad advice would be to set up a trial in one or more countries that were prepared to be test cases of different approaches.

A further advantage of the fund device is that it removes the execution of the program one step from the ministries, where the level of public administration is generally low, and protects the program from excessive sectional pressures to which the ministers are presumably more susceptible than the technically oriented board of the fund. The fund would be a small policy-formulating group which conducted studies to furnish a basis for allotting funds and foreign exchange to break bottlenecks and to secure the maximum use of equipment in the creation of new jobs. Regular reports would be desirable to the country's president, to his planning organization, and to the consortium of foreign lenders. This suggests the early need for developing current statistical series on urban employment, production and/or sales, housing, exports, imports, etc. Such data would also be necessary to maintain public interest and support.

Obviously, the feasibility of having such a joint operation varies from country to country. There are some that would accept no conditions and others that would welcome working with international agencies. What would be most desirable would be a successful pilot operation.

It will be noted that under the country's president, the main reliance for the administration of the program is placed on the development fund and the central mortgage institution. In carrying out a national urban policy, a ministry of urban affairs, such as President Kennedy once proposed for the United States, might be desirable. Other fields where coordination with the work of ministries would be desirable would undoubtedly come to light.

Interesting precedents for the administrative device suggested above can be found in episodes that occurred in Colombia some years ago. Upon the publication of the first International Bank mission report, I returned to Colombia and organized a nonpartisan group of distinguished persons (appointed by the President) to review the report. I headed the technical staff, the foreign members of which were supplied by the bank. It was, in short, a sort of royal commission, instigated and supported by the bank. All are agreed that it was a great success, kept the report from gathering dust on the shelves, and led to implementation of many of its recommendations. The original idea was that upon the completion of the commission's report, the bank and the government would decide which parts they could respectively support and finance, achieving in this way a joint program that would include health, housing, and education, as well as electric power and transportation. Unfortunately, at the last moment the bank decided that such a course would take it too far from the individual project approach and a grand opportunity was lost, even though much was done in electric power and transport.

The other episode followed a study of the state of Atlantico in Colombia.[2] It was also directed by me, for the new Colombia Advisory Central Planning Office. State economic studies rarely result in concrete achievements, and in the course of this one, I had to deal with three successive governors and eight successive mayors of the state's largest city in the course of a year. Since the prospects of implementation appeared unusually hopeless, I conceived the idea of incorporating the proposed program of works into a contract between a subsidiary of the central bank (Banco de la Republica) and the Barranquilla Waterworks Company, a public entity. This contract provided that the governor should appoint a distinguished watchdog committee with a full-time secretary to make monthly reports to the central bank on the implementation of the plan. This so impressed the rapid succession of governors and mayors that about 90 percent of the program was faithfully carried out.

The willingness of man to suffer needlessly is a subject of constant wonder. It is possible that we could drag along for an incredibly long time with the rich getting richer, with most of the poor staying the same, with army and police appropriations growing annually larger, and with the ratio between resources and population steadily diminishing. In this way, if we relied on "natural forces" and the push factor in mobility, the process of adjustment and response to agricultural technification could be stretched out over one or several generations. It is not a pretty prospect, but it is possible. The pity is that too often aid has been sold as a means to stave off revolution and its success has been judged in this way. Perhaps it is utopian to ask the international agencies and governments of developed countries to adopt other criteria. If so, the only hope of breaking through the vicious circle that poverty engenders lies in the developing countries themselves, possibly in the rise of new opposition parties in search of a program that is not merely demagogic, pronationalistic, and anti-Yankee. This, however, will take time and unnecessary suffering, and the outcome is by no means sure. In any case, it is difficult for a country to adopt a program that either does not have the approval of international lending entities or is actively opposed by them.

In this crucial matter of activating an effective program quickly, I must take sharp issue with Myrdal, who looks to the young economists of develop-

[2] States in most Latin American countries are variously called *departamentos* or *estados*. I shall refer to them as states.

ing countries to form their own programs and advises them to pay little attention to the economic theory being taught in developed countries. This, I believe, is dangerous advice.[3] The problem we are wrestling with is one of the most difficult in the world—far more difficult than problems in the natural sciences. For the truth of this statement we need only to contrast the progress in the two fields and to look at the inability of the leading economists to agree on goals, diagnoses, or programs. Economists in developing countries generally have little prestige, they have almost no incentive to do scientific investigation, and they have great difficulty in reaching a scientific audience. It is to be hoped that in time this situation will change. In the meantime, however, developing countries desperately need better help from the world's ablest economists (even if the countries do not always realize it). This help can be forthcoming only if the economists themselves can make significant advances on basic themes and can work out and apply at least one successful pilot operation. In the latter task, support from international lending agencies would be invaluable for securing a country's active cooperation in speed of programming and persistence in execution.

Another paradox to add to the list given earlier is that the countries which most need national economic planning are the least competent to plan, while the most competent have the least need. The tendency is for the level of public administration in a developing country to decline instead of improve. Raymond Frost's illuminating explanation for this is that the government assumes more and more detailed tasks of a kind that would better be left to the forces of the marketplace. The less efficiently the economy functions, the more the bureaucracy undertakes to remedy its malfunctioning, and the less efficiently both it and the economy function.[4] Viner has noted that "each new set of direct controls in a particular sector of the economy tends to make necessary the establishment of supporting or protective direct controls in the neighboring sectors if the first set of controls is not to be evaded or to have intolerable economic repercussions."[5] He also points out that central planning has frequently been associated with inflation.

Clearly, the tremendous difficulty of the task, particularly in a mixed economy, should not be minimized. And yet there does not appear to be any feasible alternative to planning. With conditions as they are in the developing countries, *laissez faire* clearly cannot be relied upon to break the numerous vicious circles. All we can do is seek to make the planning as

[3] It is particularly bad advice for Myrdal to offer, because it would lead to a lack of appreciation of his own contributions, particularly in his discussion of growing inequality, and his stimulating book *Beyond the Welfare State,* Yale University Press, New Haven, Conn., 1960.

[4] Raymond Frost, *The Backward Society, op. cit.,* pp. 65–86.

[5] *International Trade and Economic Development,* The Free Press of Glencoe, New York, 1950, p. 98.

soundly based as possible, simplify the administrative machinery, and utilize the possible incentives and deterrents to the fullest extent rather than resort to direct controls that require individual and detailed intervention by the state. Actually, few new or additional controls are proposed in the breakthrough plan. For the most part, what appear to be necessary are changes in the criteria on which existing controls are based—exchange control, building licensing, foreign lending, home financing, labor laws, urban planning, taxation and tax enforcement, and the national budget. The only completely new elements (i.e., new for developing countries) are a soundly based incomes policy, which is a necessary complement to a new-jobs program, and an accelerated depreciation policy. In large part, the changes proposed are in objectives and emphasis. It is not believed, therefore, that Viner's strictures on central planning apply more to the proposed program than to existing programs, and it is hoped they are less applicable. In any case, it was Viner himself who wrote, "If a relative shift in demand makes employment in agriculture less productive than other employment, resources should be guided out of agriculture to these superior uses."[6]

The need to accelerate development is urgent. The means of doing it are at hand in many countries. The activation, however, probably requires inspired leadership, mostly intellectual but partly financial, by the developed countries and the international agencies.

The Alliance for Progress does not appear to be the most appropriate vehicle for the kind of highly technical and tough-minded programming proposed here. Rather it should probably grow out of the experience of associations of lenders, first in one and then in another country, until an assured means of quickly raising the standard of living of the most depressed class is worked out.

This general treatment can be concluded with a warning from Viner: "Given, however, the utmost help from these external factors which there is any reasonable ground to expect, the problem will not even begin to have a practicable solution unless the under-developed countries dedicate their own resources, human, physical, and financial, to a sound, large-scale, and persistent attack on the basic internal causes of mass poverty."[7] These wise words were written in 1950. They are even more relevant today. The proper use of foreign aid and foreign lending, therefore, is not to add to the total of capital formation in developing countries—they can rarely be large enough or sufficiently long continued to have more than a temporary effect—but rather to induce and reinforce national programs appropriate to achieve the breakthrough effect.[8]

[6] *Ibid.*, p. 146.

[7] *Ibid.*, p. 150.

[8] It was estimated that net foreign borrowing of US$120 million a year in Colombia's 1962–1966 plan would equal only 10% of the gross investment. Vernon points out that relatively large borrowing may amount to no more than a percentage

A deliberate country by country program to concentrate efforts and resources to achieve breakthroughs and place country after country safely in the category of the self-generating development or "benign circle" ranks would not only be infinitely more effective than the existing program but would also, in the long run, cost much less.

Another Way to Help

Throughout Part One I have argued that, with the exception of the vicious and the benign circles, the problems of the developed and developing countries differ more in degree than in kind. I have also suggested that "aid," unless linked to a comprehensible plan like the Marshall Plan, may do more harm than good. I may conclude this part, therefore, by pointing out that the type of accelerated development planning proposed here is also applicable to developed countries, and if adopted by them, would in turn be of tremendous help to developing countries.

It has been instructive to watch the jerky and scattered attempts by the developed countries to speed up growth in recent years, as well as the resulting alarming extension of international restrictions on trade and finance—a process aptly called stop-and-go. It would seem that what is urgently needed is a new type of concerted and coordinated expansion program, worked out jointly by the leading developed countries, that would be based on (1) simultaneous expansion in effective demand, (2) similar incomes policies, and (3) a calculated increase in imports from developing countries. This would supplement the approach of the GATT (General Agreement on Trade and Tariffs) round of tariff reductions and replace the approach of the international trade conventions with their accompanying generally useless exhortations and recriminations. If Western Europe, the British Commonwealth, the United States, and Japan were assured that internal expansionist programs could be safely undertaken without a weakening of their international competitive position because of simultaneous expansion programs by their traditional competitors, and if they knew that similar incomes policies would prevent a worldwide rise in prices, they would not need to fear a rise in imports from the developing countries. Such a rise would be immediately translated into a rise in exports to these countries.

In other words, the degree of economic sophistication in developed countries would appear to have reached a point where it is surely feasible to think in terms of *concerted* expansion programs instead of shifting competitive positions, stop-and-go, independent emergency measures to improve individual balances of payments, and so on. In the absence of concerted expansion programs, no generalized tariff reductions, removal of quantitative

---

point or two in the proportion of Mexico's gross national product devoted to capital formation. *Op. cit.*, p. 186.

restrictions, or reduction of subsidized farming and dumping would appear to have much chance of success. In other words, part of the solution for developing countries lies in the readiness of developed countries to take concerted action to accelerate their own development.

The first step might be an exploratory meeting of economists of EEC, EFTA, the British Commonwealth, Japan, and the United States to consider technical papers on the general theme, "What common policies could be taken to permit the adoption of internal expansion measures without the hitherto accompanying worsening of external competitive positions?" While it is not difficult to envisage the adoption of simultaneous internal expansionist policies by this group of countries, there would still remain the possibility of a weakening of individual countries' trading or financial positions arising not from differing cost trends but from other sources.[9] New techniques may have to be devised to permit continued internal expansion in such cases. Even if they took the form of a slackening in the rate of expansion, this would be preferable to the present tendency to resort to restrictive practices.

In short, it appears that the developed countries are approaching agreement that the key to internal progress and stability lies in a combined policy of increasing effective demand and avoiding cost-push inflation, a policy which has a certain resemblance to the policy suggested here for developing countries. The next step would logically be the removal or mitigation of the deterrent of worsening external competitive positions by the adoption of concerted expansionist programs. This step would also facilitate the policy recommended for developing countries. Such a fresh approach would seem infinitely preferable to the contrary trends toward autarky which are inadequately offset by loans and gifts and which result in the world as a whole operating far below capacity. The phrase "reduction of barriers" misplaces the emphasis. First should come concerted and planned expansion of demand, *followed* by reduction of barriers.

It undoubtedly sounds presumptuous for a writer from a small, unimportant country to proffer advice to the advanced countries. Yet from this particular vantage point, the advanced countries are not behaving in as advanced a fashion as they might and the advice is not disinterested. In the general unedifying scramble for the exits, it is the underdeveloped countries that stand in most danger of being trod upon. The United States is

[9] Contrary to the general impression, this appears to have been the case with Great Britain in 1964. The rise in consumption (2.7%) was modest, and the rise in exports at 4% was satisfactory, following a 4.3% rise in 1963. What brought on the crisis was the sharp rise in imports (14%) followed by the flight of capital. The bulk of the increase in imports appears to have gone into stocks or "capital formation." It is not believed, therefore, that this case vitiates in any way the need for the working out of common expansion policies among developed countries. What was discouraging was the insistence by international lenders on the adoption of measures to curtail aggregate demand in Great Britain.

the worst large offender in subsidizing, dumping, and restricting, and in forcing its economic machine to hobble along far below its productive capacity. On the other hand, in the accumulation of their enormous gold holdings, France and Western Germany have created disequilibriums and tensions that have in turn adversely affected the developing countries. The worldwide movement to increase exports, reduce imports, and reduce foreign lending on the part of the developed nations, originating in the American gold loss and the run on sterling, could be watched only with deep apprehension by the undeveloped portions of the world.

PART TWO

Application of Breakthrough Plan to Colombia

CHAPTER 11

Introduction

I HAVE CHOSEN to use Colombia to illustrate the breakthrough plan not after an exhaustive examination of a number of countries, but simply because I happened to be most familiar with Colombian problems. I believe that the choice is an apt one, however. Colombia was the first country studied by a foreign mission of an international agency. The report of the mission, based on a piecemeal sector approach, was a model for countless other missions and studies. Enough time has elapsed to show the inadequacy of this type of approach, despite its relative success in a few sectors.

Colombia was also a testing ground for the ECLA "programming" approach.[1] It required much less time to show the inadequacy, and indeed disastrous results, of this procedure. For two years, however, the Alliance for Progress thought it had found its model in Colombia, particularly since the country had also passed farreaching agrarian reform legislation. Colombia was also chosen by the International Bank for Reconstruction and Development as the test case in Latin America for an attempt at coordinated lending through a consulting group of lenders.

Thus it may be seen that the country already has a relatively long history, and not too happy a one, as a testing ground. In Chapter 12 the situation will be presented in some detail. Here I shall briefly outline the main factors that appear to make Colombia an admirable place to attempt a breakthrough.

It is a country of some 17,000,000 people, divided roughly half and half between urban and rural dwellers. However, "urban" includes a number of small towns. Some 20 percent of the population lives in the four largest cities. The largest, Bogotá, is thought to have some 1.7 million people. The agricultural sections are characterized by a few mechanized farms, with productivity approaching or excelling the average of farms in developed countries, and the overwhelming bulk of farms still practicing a colonial type of farming on very small holdings. The most important crop and export

[1] *The Economic Development of Colombia,* E/C.N. 12/365 Rev. 1, 1956, *The Ten-Year Plan of Development,* Bogotá, 1961.

is coffee, a hand culture in a medium climate where there is almost no level land. The great bulk of the cleared land is in pasture, natural and improved, and devoted to a primitive, backward form of cattle raising.

On the nonagricultural side, the country has a small but generally efficient industry, mostly in consumer goods and building supplies and materials. The petroleum industry is also extensive enough to fill all domestic requirements and make some exports. Equally important, Colombia has an excellent entrepreneurial class, quick to take advantage of profit possibilities.

The remarks in Part One about the prevalence of inequality, poor public administration, lack of economic insight, and lack of a sense of patriotism or dedication, all apply to Colombia. Violence has been rife, and one-quarter of the national budget has on occasion been spent on the army and police. Deep poverty, poor health, almost complete lack of education, and lack of respect for the law characterize most of the rural regions and exist, though in less degree, in the cities. The country is being deforested and heavily eroded. The rate of population increase is estimated at 3 percent, which if continued, would result in a population of 75 million in another fifty years.

Exchange is derived mainly from coffee and borrowings. There is one rate at which coffee is exported, another at which exchange is licensed to import "essential" imports, and a third "free" rate (actually pegged through 1963 and most of 1964) for minor exports, tourism, remittances, etc. In 1965, flight of capital caused this rate to soar. Legitimate trade with neighboring Venezuela is virtually nil.

The economic vicious circle is obviously at work and includes an interaction of adverse economic developments with cultural and political developments. The country is most certainly not exercising a conscious and beneficent control of its economic, social, or even political environment.

Obviously the country presents a challenge, with its rich natural resources and the coexistence of an efficient industry and agriculture with artisan shops and colonial-type subsistence farming. Colombia has been a favorite of international lending agencies and the object of numerous studies. Withal, it has a low rate of growth and probably growing inequality. A solution of its problem would, it is believed, provide the solution of the problem of many countries where these conditions exist in different degrees.

CHAPTER 12

Diagnosis of the Problem

THE DIAGNOSIS PRESENTED here does not rely for its relevance on being up to date or complete. For one thing it is difficult to keep pace with all phases of the cumulative deterioration since 1961. It should be regarded rather as a case study included for the purpose of illustrating the arguments of Part One. Even here, the treatment of the all-important cultural framework is implicit rather than explicit. The basic explanation in these terms of why a country does not gain purposeful control of its environment must be the subject of another book drawing on the contributions of historians, sociologists, psychologists, psychiatrists, and others as well as economists. The treatment here is selective and refers roughly to conditions in the early sixties. The actual adoption by any country of the breakthrough approach would, of course, have to be preceded by a careful appraisal or reappraisal of the diagnosis in qualitative and currently quantitative terms. While it will become evident, I hope, that the argument is based not only on theory but on observation, at this stage the important thing is theory.

It would appear a simple task to diagnose the economic sickness of Colombia, but actually it is most difficult. The many and various diagnoses, most of them implicit, remind one of nothing so much as the famous descriptions of an elephant by a group of blind men. All are agreed that the per capita standard of living in Colombia is low and is rising too slowly. After that, however, the explanations offered include overall low productivity; unfavorable terms of trade; faulty monetary, tax, exchange, or fiscal policies; and so forth. Generalized low productivity is hardly a diagnosis, and the other explanations, while doubtless affecting the *rate* of growth, can hardly account for the low level.

The diagnosis offered here resulted from an attempt to identify and localize the areas of low productivity and to analyze in more detail the nature of productivity. It is generally known and agreed that the standard of living is lowest in rural regions and that the population of the larger cities is growing relative to that of small towns and rural areas, though this was widely attributed for some years, in part at least, to a flight from violence in rural areas.

What is not generally appreciated is the impact of the technical revolution in agriculture and transport, both of which began around 1950. A contract from the Banco Cafetero to study the coffee industry in the framework of Colombian agriculture in general permitted, for the first time, an analysis of the causes of low incomes in agriculture. Section A below is derived from the general agricultural part of that study.[1]

I. *Localization and Causes of Low Productivity*

A. In Agriculture

Up until relatively recently people generally thought that agricultural production was "too low" and that, possibly for this reason, it was possible and desirable to settle hundreds of thousands of additional workers on the land. A colonization program to settle 50,000 families in five large projects was approved by an American mission as late as 1960. While this particular plan was dropped, many people still feel that agricultural production and employment could be considerably expanded. The projects of the agrarian reform make no distinction between improving the conditions of individual farmers and extending farming in general.

The first part of this section on agriculture is analytical and general in nature; the second part, quantitative and statistical.

Characteristics of Colombian agriculture. There can surely be no agriculture in the world about which it is so difficult to generalize as that of Colombia. Actually, because of wide differences in climate, terrain, soils, and rainfall, and because it is in a process of violent transition. Colombian agriculture is a mosaic made up of bits and pieces of almost every type of agriculture in the world. Products range from coconuts and mangoes to potatoes, barley, and apples; methods of production range from the highly mechanized and technical to the most primitive imaginable; land tenancy includes every form—renting, sharecropping, informal occupation, and ownership ranging from tiny to enormous holdings. When it is considered that the accuracy of statistics also varies, the difficulty of exact description becomes apparent.

An agriculture in transition. For many hundreds of years the pattern of land use, products, and types of farming varied little, the main variation being the increase in *minifundia* (small holdings) as the demographic pres-

[1] *La Industria Cafetera en la Agricultura Colombiana,* (The Coffee Industry in Colombian Agriculture), Bogotá, 1962. A study directed by Lauchlin Currie for the Foundation for the Progress of Colombia and published by the Coffee Bank.

sure increased. The first major technical changes came about in the first quarter of this century in cane sugar growing in the Valle del Cauca and banana farming in the state of Magdalena. However, even these technical advances originated and still exist side by side with large extensions of completely unmechanized plantings of *plátanos*[2] and of cane sugar for panela.[3]

In the 1950s there were two developments which had a terrific impact on Colombia and whose consequences have not yet been fully grasped. One was the coming of the technical revolution in additional branches of agriculture; the other was the construction of a network of highways and, more recently, the termination of the Atlantic Railroad, developments which one might characterize without exaggeration as constituting a technical revolution. These two factors are reshaping Colombian agriculture, and indeed the country.

Within a relatively short period of ten years, the cultivation of one product after another shifted off the hills to the flatlands, not only in the older areas of the Sabana (plains) de Bogotá, Tolima, and the Valle del Cauca, but also in newer areas near Montería, Villavicencio, Codazzi, and the Middle Magdalena. Thus we are witnessing the rapid breakup of a pattern of land use that lasted for centuries and the emergence of a new mechanized type of agriculture.

As remarked earlier, the full impact of the revolutions in technology and transport has not yet been felt, even though they made it possible to feed and clothe 3,000,000 more urban consumers in the decade of the fifties, to substitute for varous imports, and to begin certain new exports, all with no advance in prices relative to those of nonagricultural goods. In addition to technical advances in sugar and banana farming, mechanization is taking place in virtually all other crops with the exception of coffee and yuca.[4] Cotton, rice, wheat, and barley, as well as improved pastures, are well along. The mechanization of such basic crops as potatoes and corn is under way, as it is also for such traditional hand crops as vegetables and tobacco. There appears to be no technical reason why yuca, *plátano,* and other crops cannot be mechanized. It is now simply a question of economics—which brings us to the next topic.

Competition between commercial and colonial farming. A fierce struggle of which city people are hardly conscious is taking place between the old agriculture and the new. The astonishing thing is that the government itself and various spokesmen for agriculture have seemed unaware of this struggle, aggravating it in every way possible and doing little or nothing for the victims or losers. It must be said that, on the whole, the various measures

[2] A type of banana for cooking.
[3] A coarse brown sugar in blocks.
[4] A starchy tuber.

of the government in improving seeds and varieties, improving transport, and making exchange and loans available for machinery, have favored commercial farming. Even help for the small farmer, to be effective, must take a form that at least looks toward converting him into a commercial farmer. The major effort of the agrarian reform lies in the drainage or irrigation of great tracts of land, which should have the effect in general of increasing production, provided the new holdings are not too small for efficient operation.

In the meantime the competition continues and is bad for both types of farming. The desperate efforts of the colonial farmer to produce tend to hold down prices and delay advances in technology and improvements in quality, which are often expensive. In turn, the relative high productivity of the machine, and the use of better techniques in commercial farming lower the return the colonial-type farmer can gain and make it even less practical for him to do all the costly things that would increase his productivity. The threat of expropriation in agrarian reform initially spurred the large holder to compete without regard to returns; later, the threat was affirmed to discourage costly improvements.

Competition, of course, is basic to a free enterprise system and is one of the means relied upon to spur the individual to improve his productivity and reduce his costs. However, in other forms of economic activity, the state has long since acquiesced in measures to mitigate the harsher consequences of competition. Thus most industries compete in advertising, service, credit terms, quality, etc., but not in price. Trade unions prevent competition among their members in wages, hours, and so forth. Various organized professions have forbidden certain types of competition among their members. Banks and insurance companies have limited the areas of competition. Even the Colombian Economic Association has protested against competition from foreign economists! In short, although the economic system relies on competition for its efficient functioning, nobody likes it, and all who can, seek to escape from it or to limit its range and effectiveness.

All, that is, except the farmers and certain other unorganized groups. The farmers are expected to compete in price in products that by and large face an inelastic demand, i.e., a demand that does not increase much with a fall in price. The government forces competition in a way it would never dream of doing in industry—although it does not so characterize its activities of forcing land into cultivation by threatening expropriation, by parceling farms, by reclaiming land, by extending credit to farmers, by building penetration roads, and so on. These activities are described by the more attractive phrases of "increasing production" or "productivity," and the farmers themselves are so bemused by what is happening that they usually approve such procedures. It is true that some attempt is made to place a floor under the price of some products, but this had most success when done privately, by the beer companies for barley.

One consequence of unrestrained competition in agriculture, although hardly a desirable one, is the resort to a self-subsistence type of farming, i.e., the farmer grows things not for the market but for his own consumption and picks up a little cash income to buy the things he cannot produce through odd jobs, selling "improvements" (which usually means destroying natural resources), stealing, and so on. It has been said that it is easy to live in Colombia, but difficult to live well.

It is difficult to estimate the size of the subsistence economy (and the term itself is not precise). In traveling through the country and flying over it, one is impressed by the number of little clearings and shacks far removed from any road or market and by the army of squatters restlessly moving over the more recently opened parts of the country. This is a Colombia practically outside the money economy, and yet it is an integral part of Colombian agriculture.

Apparently some people are hopeful that the hundreds of thousands of subsistence farmers can be rehabilitated and reincorporated into a settled type of farming for a commercial market. But the number of people involved; the amount of land, capital, and technical assistance necessary; and the increase in production that would occur if the effort were successful, give one pause. To mitigate the consequences of competition, it hardly makes sense to increase competition.

Despite the rapid extension of technology, a common complaint is that it does not pay to utilize much capital when wages are so low. Actually, from a national economic point of view, there is a fallacy underlying this observation. If there were much greater mobility of labor and hence less difference between urban and rural wages and incomes, so that rural employers would have to pay higher wages, it would suddenly become economic to use more machines. From this illustration, it can be seen that the more the incomes of the colonial-type farmers are depressed, the more the advance of the commercial type of agriculture is impeded.

Factors affecting productivity in Colombian agriculture. It was remarked earlier that Colombian agriculture is in transition. Nowhere is this more true than in productivity: data that will be presented later show tremendous variations in yield per hectare in many crops. If information were available, the differences in yields per man-hour would undoubtedly be shown to be equally great. Agricultural productivity is increasing at an accelerated rate in all advanced countries. There are grounds for believing that it will increase at an even more rapid rate in Colombia, unless prevented by agrarian reform and/or violence, which term includes kidnapping for ransom of well-to-do farmers or members of their families.

It must always be borne in mind that probably 95 percent of budgets and manpower provided for scientific investigation in agriculture have been confined to temperate climates. Very few of the techniques or varieties developed by this research are the ones that would be best adapted for the special conditions of Colombia. The exceedingly limited scientific work there has yielded great results in improved varieties of potatoes, wheat, corn, etc. As this work becomes better organized and financed, we may expect enormous advances. There are whole fields that have not yet been touched not only in varieties and seeds in crops and forages for the great variety of soils and climates, but also in such matters as farm management and farm cost accounting.

Considering how recently the introduction of all agricultural machinery and modern techniques took place, the wonder is not that productivity is low but that it is as high as it is. Already, in crop after crop and in widely differing sections of the country, individuals with relatively little experience or expert help are getting high yields and returns in relation to the average. A rise in the average would mean a tremendous increase in both productivity and production. Data are presented below indicating that already the better agriculture is giving yields above the average in more advanced countries.

It is to be expected that both the government and the various crop associations will devote more time, money, and expert personnel to the scientific study of Colombia's particular agricultural conditions, so that the annual returns of the best farm operators in turn can be further raised. In this way, the country's agriculture will become the recipient of the tremendous amount of research being carried on in more advanced countries, insofar as it yields results adaptable to Colombia, in addition to the results of domestic research. For this reason and because the start is made at a much lower level, the productivity should increase more rapidly. (An increase in average milk production per lactation from 6,000 to 8,000 pounds is 33 percent; from 20,000 to 22,000 pounds is 10 percent.)

Once the country has gained a better mastery of technique, it will be better able to take advantage of a climate that permits two harvests a year from much of its land. The continuous use of a piece of land, when properly carried out, permits various economies over the use of twice as much land which is worked only half the time. This offers the possibility of concentrating agriculture on the lands that can give the highest yields because of climate, soils, or rainfall and that have the lowest relative transport costs to markets.

Another activity as important as the actual cultivation is that of transport and marketing. Considerable progress has been made in the past ten years, but there is still a long way to go. In a study of the state of Meta,[5] the data indicated that of every peso paid by the consumer for meat in Bogotá, only 50 percent was received by the producer in Meta. The division was less favorable in most other products. In too many marketing situations

[5] By Lauchlin Currie, 1961.

there are an excessive number of intermediates. For many crops, properly organized wholesale markets do not exist; nor have grades and classifications been established. The Atlantic Railroad has not yet had its full impact. The possibilities of really low-cost transport with high volume have hardly been visualized.

Against all these factors promoting an increase in productivity (most of them, it will be noted, favoring commercial-type agriculture), some adverse possibilities may be mentioned. Probably the most serious is the threat of a total breakdown of law and order in extensive rural areas. No thoughtful observer of the Colombian scene can dismiss this possibility lightly. The very success of commercial agriculture is creating an army of displaced people with nothing left to lose and whose children are growing up without education, discipline, regular work habits, or respect for law. A dangerous and explosive situation has been in the making for a long time. Already malingering and petty crime, as well as violence, are taking a heavy economic toll in the country.

"Violence" is a general term used constantly in Colombia. It does not cover ordinary crimes of robbery, of which there are many, but has a connotation of crimes against persons, often of a senseless and savage brutality like the killing of a whole busful of humble country people of all ages. In 1965 kidnapping for ransom, partly and apparently by the same gangs, became common. The growth of violence in Colombia is a baffling phenomenon not susceptible of any simple explanation. It is accompanied by increasing robbery and occupation of lands, both rural and urban, by squatters. By all accounts, security of both life and property has declined alarmingly in a single generation. In large areas, religion is not a vital force influencing conduct, and older cultural patterns of behavior have deteriorated. While cultural patterns have, of course, other than purely economic origins, a serious deterioration in personal and property security in a single generation or less cannot be entirely divorced from deteriorating economic levels of large groups of the population, and growing inequality.

Modern commercial-type agriculture, which calls for a heavy capital investment and supervision by the owner, requires a reasonable degree of security of life and property if it is to progress. Since agricultural technification is one of the essential elements in attaining a much higher level of well-being, the extreme gravity of this particular vicious circle can be grasped. But without the availability of other work, agricultural technification, by itself, can only make matters still worse and contribute to the growing insecurity which in turn imposes a brake on further technification. We are driven back to the urgent necessity to find remunerative work for the disguised rural unemployed to increase the effective demand for agricultural products which in turn will encourage technification of agriculture before the growing insecurity makes this solution impossible. Seeing the interaction of agricultural technification, insufficient growth in nonagricultural jobs, growing disguised rural employment, increasing demographic pressure, and growing lawlessness may explain, and I hope excuse, the urgency and occasional vehemence with which I write. There is not much time to find a peaceful and rational solution.

Another brake on agricultural technification may be found in price controls, which are probably not too serious. For some time, the effective demand for food has been probably growing at from 2 to 4 percent per annum. Any increase in production above this rate runs into the familiar inelasticity of demand for agricultural products and results in reduction in prices and lower agricultural incomes. The brunt of this is felt by the poor farmer, but it has its adverse effect also on technification.

The threat of expropriation for land tenancy reform is also a deterrent. How serious it is, is difficult to say as the subject has generated so much emotion. Probably violence and kidnapping are most serious deterrents and, of course, the competition of primitive type farming.

Adequacy of agricultural production. I shall digress at this point for a moment to mention a paradox that has puzzled many observers. How can the admittedly low incomes of the average countryman be reconciled with the fact that the agricultural production is inadequate to cover the dietary needs of the Colombian people? Is not the solution to both problems a generalized increased productivity that would at the same time permit the producer to earn more and the consumer to pay lower prices?

Unfortunately, the matter is more complicated than this. In the first place, most of the dietary deficiencies appear to be among the country people themselves and are the result of ignorance and too low incomes. Inadequate urban consumption is a resultant of individual inadequacy of income rather than generalized inadequacy of urban income or insufficient food production.

Who benefits from increasing agricultural productivity? It is generally agreed that the elasticity of demand for all food is low. Suppose elasticity is unity for a fall in price, that is, the same amount will be spent as the price falls, so that, say, doubled production would sell for half the price. In these circumstances, since transport and marketing costs would be a higher percentage of the total, the countryman's per unit costs would have to decline by more than half for him to realize the same return. In this extreme example, increased money return from the introduction of a new variety of seed, for example, could never be as high as formerly, even if yields more than doubled.

Even if elasticity is slightly greater than unity, we would have to resort to extreme and implausible sources of generalized increased productivity for the countryman to maintain his income. Generally, the process appears to be somewhat as follows: An increase in productivity occurs as a result of some technical development. This permits some of the producers to increase production with no increase in costs. This in turn leads to a reduction in price, which brings returns back to the point where they were but leaves all producers who have not reduced per unit costs worse off than before. If they retire from the production of this particular crop, the price may recover, which will permit the innovators to reap a higher money return than before. Generally, however, one would assume that the innovation will lead to increased production and a permanently lower price.

This example fails to account for the experience in some countries where over considerable periods, food prices in general have remained stable in relation to other prices. Curiously enough, despite government support prices, agricultural prices have declined relatively in recent years in the United States. It could be argued that without price support and the much greater relative fall in prices, the number of farmers and hence agricultural production would have declined, so that there would have been a tendency for food prices in general to return to their previous position relative to other prices. In this case, the benefits of increasing agricultural productivity would, through the mechanism of labor mobility, have been gained by the community, not in terms of lower prices or increased consumption of agricultural goods, but rather in terms of the increased production of other goods and services produced by displaced farmers. The ability to consume this increased production would come about through higher money incomes, in which the remaining farmers would have shared.

In opposition to the view presented here, people have occasionally argued that with technification one would expect food prices to fall relative to other prices. That they have not, and even on occasion have risen slightly in relative terms, is pointed to as evidence that agricultural productivity cannot have grown.

In the first place, we may note that in a poor country like Colombia, foodstuffs are weighted heavily in the cost-of-living indexes, and hence it is unreasonable to expect much diversion between food prices and the cost-of-living indexes. Secondly, there is no index of the prices received by farmers. Thirdly, presumably technical advances and growth in physical productivity are also occurring in the production of the nonfood items in the cost of living. Fourthly, at least part of the adjustment to technical advances lies in the rise of factor incomes in nonagricultural activities and in the fall in average incomes of the growing number of subsistence farmers. (A few mechanized potato-growing operations may supply the market formerly shared by thousands of peasant operators, who lose a cash crop. The mechanism may not show in persistently lower potato prices but in wider gyrations of these prices, which ruin the small grower and force his retirement because he cannot secure more credit after a disastrous harvest.)

Classical economics laid major stress on a freely functioning price mechanism as a means of equating supply and demand at points that would keep incomes at the "going rate" and ensure that above-average advances in productivity would be passed on to consumers. We would today probably place more stress on mobility in the factors of production, so that in a dynamic situation and over a period of time, we would expect the benefits of increasing productivity in individual fields to be diffused through factor mobility rather than through relative price changes. Even apparent exceptions like the relative rise in domestic wages in the United States in the absence of any increase in efficiency turn out, on closer inspection, to fit the rule. The movement of labor to domestic service is impeded by non-monetary factors, so that the higher returns here are due to a scarcity factor.

Thus, over a period of time, the most important factor in the *general* level of real incomes is productivity, which permits money incomes in general to rise relative to prices; the most important factor explaining *differences* in incomes over time is the lack of mobility of factors of production (abuse of a monopoly situation could be interpreted as a reduction in mobility). A conclusion of enormous practical importance follows. The tremendous advances in productivity that have occurred and will continue in Colombian agriculture will benefit the nation only if labor is sufficiently mobile that more and more displaced countrymen come to produce things other than agricultural goods. In this case relative prices will probably not change much, but both urban and remaining agricultural money incomes will rise relative to prices.

In the absence of sufficient factor mobility, and assuming continued advances in productivity, adjustments would have to take place through a relative fall in agricultural prices and/or a progressive withdrawal of marginal producers into a subsistence economy. The outcome would depend on whether increasing productivity and falling relative prices balanced at a point that would make it worthwhile for a much smaller number of farmers to produce all the food required. If it were not worthwhile, production would fall further and relative prices would rise; if it were too profitable and so resulted in excessive production, relative prices would fall. If relative food prices should happen to stabilize at a point lower than before, one could say that urban consumers did benefit to this extent from the increased productivity, but that their benefits were offset by the fact that the displaced farmers had lower real incomes than before.

So we return to the same point. To reap the benefits of increasing agricultural productivity, there must be sufficient mobility in labor and capital to ensure remunerative employment for displaced farmers. At the moment, however, it is not so urgent to reap the benefits as it is to avoid the crisis that is building up. One of the essential functioning parts of the economic machine, factor mobility, is not functioning at all adequately.

Agrarian reform. In an agriculture which is in rapid transition and an economy which is malfunctioning, a new factor has been introduced—the reform in land tenancy. This is still an emotional subject which is difficult to discuss dispassionately. And yet reasoned discussion is most important, because the possibilities for further damaging the functioning of the economy are great if the reform is not carried out in full awareness of its impact on agricultural prices, production, and income.

Myrdal's dictum, "Land reforms have their significance in the national plan not only as a precondition for raising productivity in agriculture, but primarily as a means of shattering the foundations of the old class structure of a stagnating society,"[6] certainly does not apply to Colombia, where the progressive farmers are generally large, and the small farmers are stagnating or retrogressing.

There is evidence that productivity is increasing rapidly in commercial farming with the introduction of improved techniques and the use of more and more capital. This increase in productivity, in conjunction with the relatively slow growth in demand, has made it difficult for colonial-type farmers to survive on their small, hilly holdings, or even on their somewhat larger holdings in the flatland of the hot country. If we take as our model the development of agriculture in all economically advanced countries, we must look forward to the time when a small percentage of the working force will provide all the food and fibers for which there is effective demand. These few farmers will work not family-sized but machine-sized holdings and will have a high level of technical knowledge and a considerable amount of capital. If the displaced farmers find jobs in the cities, and if it is possible to develop more agricultural exports, the number of remaining farmers can be somewhat larger than otherwise, but not much so (even Canada has only 15 percent of its labor force in agriculture).

A mere statement of this prospect serves to pose the problem. If we try to settle a *significant* number of colonial-type farmers on economic-sized units, providing them with capital and modern techniques, the increase in production will far outrun the demand. If we seek to escape this outcome by settling many on small holdings without modern techniques or capital, they cannot compete with the economic-sized commercial farm. By no amount of juggling with words can this dilemma be escaped or solved. Agricultural production in commercial farming is increasing rapidly enough to meet the current growth in demand. There are *now* many too many people trying to make a living off the soil. Any measure that will increase production faster or hinder the provision of alternative employment will only intensify the present difficult position of most countrymen. The agrarian reform, by itself, *cannot* be the solution of the agrarian problem or of the national economic problem.

If it is argued that eventually all the projects of land reclamation, as well as the present number of small farmers, will be justified by the growth

[6] *Economic Theory and Underdeveloped Regions,* Methuen & Co., Ltd., London, 1957, p. 81.

in population and the consequent increase in food requirements, we are in effect saying that the economic vicious circle is unbreakable and there is no solution to the problem of mass poverty.

The appraisal of the long-term impact of the agrarian reform is made more difficult by its possible immediate impact. Thus, in the beginning (1961–1962), there was widespread belief on the part of large proprietors that if they could show their land was in use, they would be left alone. Consequently, enormous areas were cleared, planted to artificial pastures, and stocked with animals. When later it became evident that the agrarian reform organization was going to acquire some of the better lands, the reaction was reversed. Land prices fell, and in 1963 the land that had been cleared and planted to pasture along the Magdalena River two or three years previously could be acquired at considerably below the current cost of clearing and preparation. Relative to 1962, imports of agricultural tractors and equipment in the first ten months of 1963 fell by 34 percent. Since these are mobile forms of wealth, it is to be assumed that more permanent investments in agriculture fell much more.

Thus technification received a severe, if temporary, set back, and urban construction became a more favored investment. For the time being, it could be argued, the reform created the very conditions which were cited as reasons for its necessity. The effect was reinforced by the occupation of land by impatient and desperate small farmers, and their squatting in turn was pointed to as another reason for speeding up the agrarian reform. We seem constantly in this field to encounter vicious circles—as Benjamin Higgins once remarked, the road to development is paved with them.

At the time of writing, the agrarian reform appeared to be accepted by many as the only solution to the agrarian problem, though at the same time the fact was becoming more obvious that it could not be the solution. The country was committed to a relatively large and costly program of land reclamation and resettlement of thousands of small farmers. The long-range impact on the progress of agricultural technification in efficient-sized units is uncertain. It is probable that the forces of technification are now too strong to be arrested, but they may proceed more slowly than otherwise. Much will depend on the administration of the reform and the temper of the peasants.

Another type of agricultural reform has to do with the diversification of coffee farming in the richest coffee-growing state, Caldas. This resulted from the recommendations of an international mission. It is a substantial program designed to diversify the production and increase the incomes of a group of middle-sized coffee growers who own between 3 and 20 hectares. The program is enabling them to add cows, chickens, sugar cane, *plátano,* yuca, cacao, fish, and bee culture. While it should improve the position of the individual farmers involved, it does represent increased competition for farmers who are now producing these products. Thus without a parallel program of job creation for displaced farmers, it is to be feared that the benefits can be pointed to, while the persons harmed will never be identified. The diversification program is called a "pilot operation," but its generalization on a national scale could result in disaster for the smallest and poorest farmers. All such well-intentioned efforts emphasize the need for greater labor mobility.

They also serve to emphasize the importance of supplementing "common sense" and visual observation by theory. No one questions the possibility of aiding an individual farmer or of demonstrating in a pilot operation that he has been benefited. Thousands of visiting experts will visit his farm and satisfy themselves that agrarian reform or crop diversification is successful. Such visits, however, cannot possibly throw light on the impact in general the reform or diversification has had on production, prices, and farm incomes. In this field, as in many others, we must beware of the fallacy of composition. If billions of pesos are diverted to agriculture, we can see the actual projects but we have to make an intellectual effort to visualize the other farmers driven into subsistence farming or the urban jobs that were *not* created because of the diversion of funds.

Employment in agriculture. It is a convenient fiction that anybody living in the country is gainfully employed in agriculture. It is, however, only a fiction. For a variety of reasons, most countrymen are at work only part of the time. It may be that their holdings are too small to justify much work, or that they have intestinal parasites or amoebas, or that they have become demoralized from years of occasional employment.

Only in a country blessed with Colombia's climate could so many people stay alive while doing so little work. In Colombia, Nature is so bountiful, especially with perennial crops like *plátano,* and with the fish of the rivers and lakes, that is possible to keep alive with practically no serious or sustained work. This may be the reason why, particularly in the hot country, one encounters so many complaints over the high turnover of hired labor. It is probable that the obligation and the opportunity of a full day's work day after day exist only in the commercial-type farm. Even in such farms, the very numerous holidays, vacations, and periods of sickness cut deeply into the working year.

A rough estimate of the surplus or unneeded rural labor—the disguised unemployed—is presented below in Tables 9 to 11. It was arrived at indirectly by calculating how many workers would be needed to produce the 1960 crops. Two conditions were assumed: where appropriate, a conversion to mechanization of the type then existing, and a conversion of small holdings in coffee growing to an average site of 5 hectares. On this basis, the "displaceable" population amounted to 70 percent of the estimated "active" rural population. This method may overstate the immediate worker surplus.

A quite different approach to this problem for India is that elaborated by Ashok Mathur,[7] where an attempt is made to determine "the standard man-land ratio" for different-sized farms in three areas and to compare this with the actual ratios. With this method the author arrived at estimates of disguised unemployment of 33.1 percent for West Bengal, 4.8 percent for the Punjab, and 8.8 percent for Uttar Pradesh.[8]

In terms of the productive potentialities of modern commercial-type farming, these estimates are incredible, because they correspond to man-acre ratios of 1.7, 2.9, and 1.6 for the three areas respectively.[9] Granting that there may be some crops where highly intensive hand labor is economically justifiable, the results are still unacceptable. The difficulty doubtless rises from the concept of full employment based on the size of farm rather than on efficient farming techniques.

One of the unknown problems in connection with providing opportunities for remunerative work in cities is the extent to which it would be possible to attract subsistence-type farmers. The problem is twofold: both lack of training and demoralization may keep underemployed farmers from emigrating. Something could be done about the training, particularly for the younger men, but it is admittedly difficult to repair the damages of demoralization. Fortunately, there are extensive regions where the countrymen are serious and ambitious and ask only for the opportunity to obtain steady and well-paying work. Their number will probably be in excess of the new jobs that can be created and the housing that can be provided for some time to come. It is important, however, that efforts be made to reach the younger squatters and subsistence farmers, for among their ranks are the potential ruffian country gangs of the future.

Use of capital in agriculture. It seems to be the general impression that "investment" in agricultural production is "good" and that there cannot be too much of it. To an economist, any real investment represents a sacrifice of current consumption and is, therefore, a cost. The less investment necessary *to achieve a given result,* the better. Clearly commercial farming entails more investment in the farm than colonial, and every effort should be made to achieve the desired expansion in commercial output with the minimum investment.

This, in turn, suggests the desirability of preparing a better inventory of land resources and encouraging a better pattern of land use. In general,

[7] *The Anatomy of Disguised Unemployment,* Oxford Economic Papers, Clarendon Press, Oxford, 1964, pp. 161–193.

[8] *Ibid.,* p. 186.

[9] These figures were arrived at by dividing the number of rural workers into the acres of land in cultivation.

good lands which are near existing main lines of communication, which have a good climate, and which do not require costly reclamation, should be given preference. In this way, investment in transport can be minimized to offset the necessary investment in machinery. Too often a person is attracted by the lure of cheap land, buys in a remote spot, and then expects the national or state governments to construct a costly road to his place. The attractive phrase "developing our national resources" has been often used to justify waste and dispersion of efforts, when what is really required is abandonment of extensive regions and concentration of effort on others. As will be shown in the next section, amazingly little land would be required if cultivation were converted to a commercial type. If development takes the form of developing limited areas of the best and most accessible land for cultivation, the total capital requirements may be kept quite low to finance a major expansion in output. This, of course, will be most unpopular advice to many people, but in economics it is frequently necessary to say unpopular things.

Another piece of unpopular advice is that the prevalent attitude toward extension of credit to agriculture and cattle raising is unwise and should be changed. An extension of credit is part of the mechanism by means of which resources, internal and external, are diverted to certain channels rather than others, since the total amount that may be invested without creating inflation is limited by "real" saving, i.e., the difference between production and consumption.[10] Credit directed toward agriculture permits certain individuals to buy machines, fertilizers, etc., and improve their competitive position in relation to those who cannot borrow. It does not increase the total receipts in agriculture, since that depends on demand. Loans for cattle raising likewise affect the relative competitive positions of individuals, but over a period of time do not affect the number or quality of cattle, because presumably these factors have reached a point where any further change must wait on demand.

The common assumption that there cannot be too much credit diverted to agriculture or cattle raising needs closer examination. The benefits of large extensions of credit to agriculture, and particularly to cattle raising, may actually be experienced by certain producers and consumers at the expense of others. Here, again, a national agricultural policy would ensure that while the most efficient (or fortunate) producers were being aided, alternative employment was being created for the marginal producers being forced out of production.

Summary. Colombian agriculture is in transition—almost, it might be said, in turmoil. Age-old patterns are breaking up and new ones are forming. Most labor is low in productivity, and in addition there is a great deal

[10] Always assuming that otherwise idle factors are not drawn into use.

of idleness, voluntary and involuntary. The impact of the agricultural and transport revolution has resulted, in a few years, in the necessity of massive changes that were spread over many years in more advanced countries. The mobility of labor to cities has not proved equal to the calls made upon it. The result has been great hardship for most of the people in agriculture, who have not been able to compete with the machine or secure alternative employment. A by-product is growing lawlessness.

Agricultural policy appears to have been devised by urban people for urban people. All emphasis has been on increased agricultural productivity and production. Little study has been given to the maintenance of agricultural income or the provision of alternative employment. Agrarian reform is incapable of resolving the problem of excess manpower and idleness in agriculture. If not pushed, it will cause disillusionment; if pushed, a crisis. A new policy of creating alternative employment is needed if the benefits of the agricultural revolution are to be gained and its hardships avoided.

B. Quantitative Aspects of the Agrarian Problem[11]

As has been pointed out repeatedly, the accuracy and comprehensiveness of the statistical data vary as widely as other aspects of Colombian agriculture. Figures on some crops such as cotton are believed to be relatively accurate; on others, such as *plátano,* corn, and yucca, they are very approximate indeed. In some cases we must resort to the results of questionnaries on consumption to obtain global estimates on production. Fortunately, for the purposes of this study great accuracy is not necessary to establish the main points at issue. However, if a rational agricultural policy should be adopted, it would be of the utmost importance to improve the basic statistical data. For example, only with such data could the probable impact on production, prices, and incomes of a new large land reclamation project be determined. Again, in the absence of current production data, the stabilizing operations of the government can have only limited success. The cost of one error in forecasting, to both the government and the producers, can be very many times the cost of collecting current and accurate data.

Area, production, and average yields. Table 1 summarizes the overall picture of agriculture in Colombia for 1960 so far as production, area, and average yields are concerned. Since the same land was frequently cropped twice a year, the area cropped was naturally greater than the area under cultivation.

As can be seen, coffee is estimated to have been the most important crop as far as area is concerned. It occupied nearly a third of the area under cultivation, though very little of this land was flat or permitted machine

[11] The quantitative data in this section were compiled or calculated by Dr. Santiago Rueda, under the direction of the author.

Table 1

Principal Agricultural Products: Production, Yields, and Area, 1960

Type of crop	Production (thousands of tons) *	Area harvested (thousands of ha)	Average yields kg/ha	Crops per year	Cultivated area (thousands of ha)
Perennial crops					
Coffee	562.8	833.1 †	675	1.0	889.1 ‡
Sugar cane	3,270.0	40.0	81,750	1.0	40.0
Panela cane	9,075.0	216.0	42,000	1.0	216.0
Cacao	13.0	35.0	386	1.0	35.0
Fique (fiber)	18.0	30.0	600	1.0	30.0
Fruit	500.0	100.0	5,000	1.0	100.0
Plátano and banana	1,250.0	271.7	4,600	1.0	271.7
Banana for export	197.1	19.8	9,995	1.0	19.8
Subtotal without coffee		712.5			712.5
Subtotal with coffee		1,545.6			1,601.6
Annual crops					
Hot climate					
Sesame	20.0	24.5	816	1.3	18.8
Cotton	193.6	165.5	1,170	1.0	165.5
Rice	430.7	227.3	1,895	1.4	162.4
Beans	40.8	86.3	473	1.5	57.5
Soybean	15.0	10.0	1,500	2.0	5.0
Corn	865.7	729.6	1,186	1.1	663.3
Tobacco	24.9	14.0	1,780	1.0	14.0
Tomato	36.0	3.0	12,000	2.0	1.5
Yuca	740.0	148.0	5,000	1.0	148.0
Arracacha	100.0	16.0	6,250	1.0	16.0
Subtotal		1,424.2			1,252.0
Cold climate					
Barley	109.2	54.5	2,000	1.3	41.9
Wheat	145.2	118.1	1,230	1.3	90.8
Potato	653.3	46.1	14,173	1.0	46.1
Onions, garlic	27.0	18.0	1,500	2.0	9.0
Vegetables	150.0	50.0	3,000	2.0	25.0
Subtotal		326.7			212.8
Total without coffee		2,463.4			2,177.3
Total with coffee		3,296.5			3,066.4

* Source: National Accounts, Bank of the Republic.

† Only plantations of 3 years and up, which include 93.7% of the area ("El Café en la América Latina," CEPAL-FAO).

‡ Includes only the area cultivated with coffee in the most productive states.

cultivation. Of the remaining cultivated land, 30 percent was guessed to be devoted to corn, with extremely low average yields. This leaves us with only 1½ million hectares (ha) for all other crops. Of these, 700,000 ha were in perennial crops, 600,000 ha in hot-country crops,[12] and only 200,000 ha in cold-country crops.

By bulk, sugar cane was far the most important, which clearly brings out why it was most economically grown near sugar refineries or mills that make coarse brown-sugar cakes. It is interesting to note that the area estimated to be devoted to sugar cane for panela was still over five times that devoted to sugar cane for sugar in 1960, though the average yields for the latter purpose are double those for the former. The contrast between commercial- and colonial-type agriculture is clearly brought out in this crop, as in others. The next most bulky crops were *plátano,* corn, yuca, and potato, in descending order.

One might hazard the guess that the same table for later years would show little more area under cultivation as a whole but higher yields per hectare in most of the hot- and cold-country crops. Probably it would also show extensions in areas devoted to sugar cane for sugar, barley, wheat, and probably cotton.

Value of production. Table 2 serves two purposes: one is to indicate the approximate values of the leading agricultural products; the other is to illustrate the unreliability of the statistical data by presenting different estimates of the Caja Agraria (Agricultural Bank) and the Banco de la República (Central Bank). On closer inspection, it will be noted that the more commercial the crop, the closer are the estimates, and that the widest variations are in estimates of the production and value of such crops as yuca and potato. Global figures of the value of these crops vary by over 500 million pesos for 1960 and show widely differing percentage changes from 1959. No attempt is made here to estimate the value of tobacco, fruits, and vegetables, and there are other omissions as well.

It will be noted that on the basis of this incomplete list, the value of coffee in 1960 was equal to that of the combined total of all other crops listed. Sugar cane, rice, cotton, and corn in the Bank of the Republic's compilation were about equal in importance, but all were far below coffee. In both compilations hot-country products were far in excess of cold, and thanks to coffee, the value of intermediate-climate products outstripped them both.

Variations in yields. One of the aspects of major significance for the future is the great variation in yields which is characteristic of an agriculture

[12] Actually, the area may be less, because generally soya and sesame occupy the same land as do cotton. Likewise, *plátano,* coffee, and cacao are frequently grown together.

Table 2

Comparative Value of Certain Agricultural Products in 1960, from Two Sources

	National Accounts, Bank of the Republic			Caja Agraria		
Type of crop	Production (thousands of tons)	Price/ton (pesos of 1958)	Value (millions of pesos)	Production (thousands of tons)	Value (millions of pesos)	Percent of difference between the two sources
Perennial crops						
Coffee	562.8	3,500.7	1,970.2	578.0	2,023.4	
Cane	12,345.0	27.0	333.3	15,419.9	416.3	
Cacao	13.5	4,000.0	54.0	19.3	77.2	
Subtotal			2,357.5		2,516.9	
Annual crops						
Hot climate						
Sesame	20.0	1,323.0	26.5	30.1	39.8	
Cotton	193.6	1,550.0	300.1	197.6	306.3	
Rice	430.7	750.0	323.0	458.1	343.6	
Beans	40.8	1,440.0	58.8	58.3	84.0	
Corn	865.7	370.0	320.3	983.6	364.0	
Yuca	740.0	231.0	170.9	1,445.5	333.9	
Subtotal			1,199.6		1,471.6	
Cold climate						
Barley	109.2	580.0	63.3	137.5	79.8	
Wheat	145.2	870.0	126.3	153.2	133.3	
Potato	653.3	230.0	150.3	988.1	227.2	
Subtotal			339.9		440.4	
General total			3,897.0		4,428.9	13.6%
Without coffee			1,926.8		2,405.5	24.8%
Growth rate of total between 1959 and 1960			3.2%		3.6%	
Growth rate without coffee			3.7%		2.5%	

NOTE: The prices are the same used in the National Accounts compiled by the Bank of the Republic.

in transition. Quantitative information on this aspect is scattered. Yields in different crops by states and even by municipalities, while indicating great variations, conceal even greater variations between individual farms.

In the case of tobacco, for example, yields varied from 1,066 kg/ha in Huila to 4,669 kg/ha in Cauca (*Censo Tabacalero de Colombia,* 1960). In the case of cotton, yields by *regions* in 1960 varied from 500 kg/ha in Socorro and Riohacha to 2,056 kg/ha in Buga. The national average, after stabilizing between 900 and 1,000 kg/ha between 1954–1958, rose to 1,272 kg/ha in 1960, owing mainly to shifts to higher-yielding areas.

Experimental plantings of rice have yielded over 4,000 kg/ha, as contrasted with a national average of 1,900 kg/ha. Yields of potatoes have varied from 4–5 tons/ha to 30–35 tons; of barley, from 1,000 kg/ha and lower to 3,433 kg/ha; and of wheat, from 1,000 kg/ha to 3,619 kg/ha. In the competition sponsored by the Agricultural Bank in 1961, yields of wheat of 5,115 kg/ha were obtained, contrasted with national averages of 1,230 kg/ha. Experimental plantings in corn have yielded over 5½ tons/ha as contrasted with common yields of 1 or 1½ tons.

In milk production, the variation was even greater, ranging from farms with almost nothing to farms with averages per cow per lactation terminated of 12,613 lb in 1960. Individual cows have yielded over 19,000 lb. (Data supplied by Holstein Association.)

Table 3 shows some comparative data on yields obtainable in commercial agriculture in Colombia contrasted with average yields in certain crops in other countries. It must be kept in mind that we are here comparing the

Table 3

Average Yields in Various Countries and Yields on Colombian Commercial Farms

(Kilos/ha)

Type of crop	France	Canada	U.S.A.	Argentina	Brazil	Colombia
Perennial crops						
Coffee					637	1,308
Sugar cane			51,465	36,151		100,000
Cacao					394	450
Banana for export*					28,400	10,000
Annual crops						
Hot climate						
Cotton in seed			890	330	330	1,188
Cotton fiber			520	180	170	612
Rice	4,100		3,750	3,390	1,620	3,000
Soybeans		1,830	1,610	970	1,260	1,600
Corn	3,200	3,280	3,240	1,700	1,280	4,000
Tobacco†	2,000	1,480	1,750	1,060	760	3,500
Cold climate						
Barley	2,480	1,460	1,500	1,230	1,040	3,000
Wheat	2,370	1,210	1,430	1,330	630	3,000
Potato	13,600	13,800	19,600	8,600	5,500	30,000

* The banana for export has such low yields because the banana zone frequently suffers from hurricanes.

† Tobacco yields vary enormously with the varieties. The comparison presented may be misleading on this score.

Source: Anuario de Producción, 1960, FAO, with the exception of the data for Colombia, which are derived from questionnaires of the Ministry of Agriculture and estimates of the Foundation for the Progress of Colombia.

best Colombian performance with *average* performance abroad. The table is inserted to show what could be done in Colombia after a few years of technical effort.

It would be interesting to complete the data on physical yields with cost estimates. In the absence of these, Table 4 presents a comparison of wholesale prices in the United States and Colombia for certain agricultural products. The tremendous relative efficiency of farmers in the United States in the cultivation of cereals such as wheat, barley, and corn, in great extensions, is clearly shown in this table. However, it is encouraging to see that the relative difference of prices for rice and potatoes in April, 1962, was not wide and that Colombia had a relative advantage in cotton, which still required much hand work. The fall in the international prices of cacao reflected the rapidly rising production in Ecuador, Brazil, and some African countries.

Degree of mechanization. Table 5 presents estimates on the degree to which various crops were mechanized by 1960. These estimates were naturally tentative and were built up from various sources and various assumptions. It must be appreciated that no actual census had ever been made of the extent of mechanization. The term "mechanized" itself is not precise, since an operation may be more or less mechanized. Thus, around this time, it was common in the Sabana of Bogotá to see the preparation of the soil and planting of potatoes by machine but the cultivation, fumigation, and harvesting by hand. Again, an example of transition.

Table 4

Comparative Prices of Certain Agricultural Products

Product	Wholesale prices in U.S.A.*		Dollars/kg U.S.A. value in Colombian pesos at 8.90	Wholesale prices in Bogotá market	
	U.S. cents/kg	Date		Pesos/kg	Date
Wheat	7.3	July, 1961	0.65	1.24†	April, 1962
Barley	6.3	Dec., 1961	0.56	1.44†	April, 1962
Corn	4.3	Dec., 1961	0.38	1.06†	April, 1962
Rice	19.1	Aug., 1961	1.70	2.04†	April, 1962
Cacao	78.0	1959	6.94	8.01‡	1960
Cacao	59.1	1960	5.26	8.01	1960
Cacao	49.2	Oct., 1961	4.38	8.01	1960
Cotton	74.0	Sep., 1961	6.59	4.42§	1960
Potato	7.8	1959	0.69	0.89†	April, 1962

Sources: * *Anuario de Producción, FAO, 1960,*
† *Boletín Mensual de Estadística (DANE) No. 134.*
‡ *Boletín Mensual de Estadística (DANE) No. 134.*
§ *IFA. The price of potatoes varies greatly, being at times below the American price.*

Table 5

Estimates of Area Cultivated and Days Worked in Principal Agricultural Crops, 1960

Type of crop	Mechanized area (thousands of ha)	Nonmechanized area* (thousands of ha)	Days worked in mechanized crops		Days worked in nonmechanized crops	
			Per ha	Total (millions)	Per ha	Total (millions)
Perennial crops						
Coffee		889.1			100	88.9
Sugar cane	40.0		40	1.6		
Panela cane		216.0			118	25.5
Cacao		35.0			54	1.9
Fique (fiber)		30.0			48	1.4
Fruit	5.0	95.0	50	0.3	65	6.2
Plátano and banana		271.7			50	13.6
Banana for export	19.8		32	0.6		
Subtotal without coffee	64.8	647.7		2.5		48.6
Subtotal with coffee		1,536.8				137.5
Annual crops						
Hot climate						
Sesame	4.9	19.6	30	0.1	100	2.0
Cotton	132.4	33.1	76	10.1	76	2.5
Rice	100.0	127.3	25	2.5	57	7.3
Beans	8.6	77.7	50	0.4	78	6.1
Soybeans	10.0		50	0.5	78	
Corn	73.0	656.6	15	1.1	47	34.3
Tobacco		14.0			490	6.9
Tomato		3.0			280	0.8
Yuca		148.0			77	11.4
Arracacha		16.0			77	1.2
Subtotal	328.9	1,095.3		14.7		72.5
Cold climate						
Barley	38.2	16.3	10	0.4	33	0.5
Wheat	59.1	59.0	10	0.6	33	1.9
Potato	4.6	41.5	66	0.3	133	5.5
Onions, garlic		18.0			180	3.2
Vegetables		50.0			360	18.0
Green peas		40.0			360	14.4
Subtotal	101.9	224.8		1.3		43.5
Total without coffee	495.6	1,967.8		18.5		164.6
Total with coffee		2,856.9				253.5

* For coffee, the area in cultivation is larger than the area harvested.

With these various caveats, therefore, the estimate is hazarded that of the perennial crops, only sugar cane for sugar and banana for export were fully mechanized, or about 10 percent of the total area excluding coffee devoted to perennial crops, or with coffee, 4 percent. In terms of days of work, it is estimated that the mechanized provided 2 million contrasted with 137 million for the unmechanized.

In hot-country crops it is believed that mechanization in 1960 amounted to 23 percent of the total by area, ranging from cotton and soybeans, which with the exception of harvesting were almost completely mechanized, down to yuca, which as yet was completely unmechanized. Days of employment were estimated at 15 million for mechanized crops to 72 million for the unmechanized. It is in this category that rapid advances in mechanization in all crops, even yuca, may be expected to occur.

In the cold-country crops it is perhaps surprising to note that by 1960 it was estimated that only 30 percent of the area had been mechanized, though this percentage of the area produced a very much higher percentage of the production. What is truly startling is the low estimate of employment in the mechanized section, 1.3 million days, compared with the unmechanized, 42 million.

It is urgent that accurate and detailed information on the degree and characteristics of mechanization in various crops be gathered, analyzed, and kept up to date.

Employment. Table 6 presents estimates on employment, based on questionnaires and assumptions of the average number of days' employment per year per agricultural worker. It may be noted that the total of 1,240,000 persons falls far short of the estimate of the gainfully employed in agriculture of 2,550,000 prepared by the Center of Studies on Economic Development. The difference may be found in cattle raising (440,000?), in small towns, and in the squatters and subsistence farmers, whose activities and production escape tabulation or even estimates (870,000?). It may be added that the Center of Studies estimated the total rural population in 1960 at 8,215,000 or 54.5 percent of the total population, and the gainfully employed at 52 percent of the total.

According to Table 6, persons believed to be active in mechanized agriculture amounted only to 84,000, of which over half were in cotton, which requires much hand labor in collection. The 6,000 workers estimated to be in cold-country mechanized cultivation may be contrasted with the 200,000 in nonmechanized.

Value of output per worker. In Table 7 the estimated values of the different crops are divided by the estimated number of persons employed in producing each crop. It must be kept in mind that this is a gross, not

Table 6

Estimates of Number Employed in Principal Crops, 1960
(Thousands of persons)

Type of crop	Persons active in mechanized crops	Persons active in nonmechanized crops	Families in mechanized crops	Families in nonmechanized crops
Perennial crops				
Coffee		404.1		224.5
Sugar cane	7.3		4.1	
Panela cane		115.9		64.4
Cacao		8.6		4.8
Fique (fiber)		6.4		3.6
Fruit	1.4	28.2	0.8	15.7
Plátano and banana		61.8		34.3
Banana for export	2.7		1.5	
Subtotal without coffee	11.4	220.9	6.4	122.8
Subtotal with coffee		625.0		347.3
Annual crops				
Hot climate				
Sesame	0.5	9.1	0.3	5.1
Cotton	45.9	11.4	25.5	6.3
Rice	11.4	33.2	6.3	18.4
Beans	1.8	27.7	1.0	15.4
Soybeans	2.3		1.3	
Corn	5.0	155.9	2.8	86.6
Tobacco		31.4		17.4
Tomato		3.6		2.0
Yuca		51.8		28.8
Arracacha		5.4		3.0
Subtotal	66.9	329.5	37.2	183.0
Cold climate				
Barley	1.8	2.3	1.0	1.3
Wheat	2.7	8.6	1.5	4.8
Potato	1.4	25.0	0.8	13.9
Onions, garlic		14.5		8.1
Vegetables		81.8		45.4
Green peas		65.5		36.4
Subtotal	5.9	197.7	3.3	109.9
Total without coffee	84.2	748.1	46.9	415.7
Total with coffee		1,152.2		640.2

NOTE: It is assumed that every family, on the average, contains 1.8 persons active.

net, value figure, and that the greater the degree of mechanization, the higher the figure.

The table serves in general to confirm our estimates on mechanization, since the value per person of banana for export and sugar cane for refined sugar is so high. So also are barley and, to a lesser degree, wheat. The figure

Table 7

Value of Production per Harvest per Worker, 1960

Type of crop	Active persons (thousands)	Value of production* (millions of pesos)	Value of production per active person (pesos)
Coffee	408.2	1,747.5	4,281
Sugar cane	7.3	94.4	12,931
Panela cane	115.9	238.9	2,061
Cacao	8.6	77.7	9,035
Fique (fiber)	6.4	33.6	5,250
Fruit	29.6	131.7	4,449
Plátano and banana	61.8	391.4	6,333
Banana for export	2.7	86.7	32,111
Sesame	9.6	30.4	3,167
Cotton	57.3	334.3	5,834
Rice	44.6	380.3	8,527
Beans	29.5	79.6	2,698
Soybeans	2.3	12.0	5,217
Corn	160.9	410.3	2,550
Tobacco	31.4	49.5	1,576
Tomato	3.6	17.8	4,944
Yuca	51.8	224.6	4,336
Arracacha	5.4	32.3	5,981
Barley	4.1	78.2	19,073
Wheat	11.3	127.8	11,310
Potato	26.4	228.7	8,663
Vegetables	81.8	65.4	779
Green peas	65.5	34.6	528
Onions, garlic	14.5	65.0	4,483

* Source: National Accounts, Bank of the Republic.

for cotton is low because of the inclusion of a large number of laborers for the thinning and harvesting.

The figures for *plátano,* yuca, and arracacha appear too high. The explanation may possibly be the fact that they are frequently grown in conjunction with other crops, so that employment may have been underestimated in these crops. In the case of coffee and rice, it should be borne in mind that these figures are averages of a number of larger operations, with much higher incomes per capita, and many smaller ones, with much lower incomes.

Yields in commercial-type farming. Table 8 shows yields easily obtainable in commercial-type farming, with a calculation for each crop of what area would be necessary with such yields to produce the harvests of 1960. The yields selected are not believed to be exceptionable for an economic-sized farm with good management (and luck). The reader may check the yields against estimated actual average yields shown in Table 1.

Table 8

Yields in Commercial-type Farming and Estimates of the Area Necessary to Arrive at Actual Production with These Yields

(Comparison with areas in cultivation, 1960)

Type of crop	Yields, commercial farms (kg/ha)	Necessary area: Harvested (thousands of ha)	Necessary area: Probable crops/year	Necessary area: In cultivation (thousands of ha)	Cultivated area, 1960 (thousands of ha)
Perennial crops					
Coffee	1,300	432.9	1.0	462.0	889.1
Sugar cane	100,000	32.7	1.0	32.7	40
Panela cane	90,000	100.8	1.0	100.8	216
Cacao	450	30.0	1.0	30.0	35
Fique (fiber)	1,000	18.0	1.0	18.0	30
Fruit	10,000	50.0	1.0	50.0	100
Plátano and banana	6,000	208.3	1.0	208.3	271.7
Banana for exportation	10,000	19.7	1.0	19.7	19.8
Subtotal without coffee		459.5		459.5	712.5
Subtotal with coffee		892.4		921.5	1,601.6
Annual crops					
Hot climate					
Sesame	1,100	18.2	1.8	10.1	18.8
Cotton	1,800	107.6	1.0	107.6	165.5
Rice	3,000	143.6	1.8	79.8	162.4
Beans	1,000	40.8	1.8	122.7	57.5
Soybeans	1,600	9.4	2.0	4.7	5.0
Corn	4,000	216.4	2.0	108.2	663.0
Tobacco	3,500	7.1	1.0	7.1	14.0
Tomato	12,000	3.0	2.0	1.5	1.5
Yuca	10,000	74.0	1.0	74.0	148.0
Arracacha	10,000	10.0	1.0	10.0	16.0
Subtotal		630.1		425.7	1,252.0
Cold climate					
Barley	3,000	36.4	1.8	20.2	41.9
Wheat	3,000	48.4	1.6	30.3	90.8
Potato	30,000	21.8	1.8	12.1	46.1
Onions, garlic	1,800	15.0	2.0	7.5	9.0
Vegetables	4,000	37.5	2.0	18.8	25.0
Green peas	1,600	16.3	2.0	8.2	—
Subtotal		175.4		97.1	213.0
Total without coffee		1,265.0		982.3	2,177.0
Total with coffee		1,697.9		1,444.3	3,066.0*

* The difference between this figure and that of 2,856,900 hectares given in Table 5 arises from the difference in areas harvested and cultivated. The first includes the net area utilized. In the second the same area is counted twice if it yields two harvests a year.

The point of this table is to indicate the greatly reduced area that would be necessary to produce the 1960 harvest with a rise in average yields to the levels of the more technical farm operations of that time in Colombia. Area under cultivation in coffee could have declined from 890,000 ha to 460,000—or by 430,000 ha; in other perennials, by 250,000 ha; in hot-country crops, from 1,250,000 ha to 426,000, which is indeed startling; and in cold-country crops, from 213,000 to 97,000 ha—a reduction in the grand total from 3,000,000 ha to 1,400,000, or less than half. Needless to say, this reduction will not occur, since by the time average yields reach these figures, internal and, in certain cases, external demand will have grown, and there are still some imports that can be substituted. They do suggest, however, that for many years Colombia has passed the point of optimum extension of land under cultivation and that new extensions should be balanced by greater abandonments of land elsewhere.

With reference to the total area that would be necessary for hot-country crops of 425,000 ha, it may be noted that there are 3,700,000 ha of alluvial soils in the region of the Regional Corporation of the Valleys of the Magdalena and the Sinú, most of which is or could be made cultivable, to say nothing of the 800,000 ha in the state of Meta west of the River Meta and the extensions in Tolima and the Valle. It appears that land use should be subjected to closer study before we undertake to bring all the land available under cultivation.

Further evidence on mechanization. Perhaps the most conclusive evidence on the reality of the technical revolution that has occurred in agriculture is afforded by the growth from 1951 to 1960 of total agricultural production (the gross product in terms of pesos of constant value). The index rose from 78 to 105, or by 4 percent a year. When it is considered that the rural working force rose only 1 percent a year in this period, and that these indexes are derived from figures that include large sectors which experienced little technical progress, such as coffee, cattle raising, *plátano,* and yuca, the conclusion appears inescapable that the growth in productivity in some sectors must have been substantial. This can be accounted for only by the progress of commercial farming. Without this progress, agricultural prices would have risen relative to other prices, and the colonial-type farmers would have been much better off and urban consumers worse off. Hence, contrary to popular belief, increasing agricultural productivity in a few sectors worsened the conditions of the great majority of countrymen.

Implications of extension of commercial farming. Table 9 shows the number of units necessary to produce the harvest of 1960 under the previous assumptions of yields, and assuming economic-sized units. (Actually, the most economic-sized coffee unit could well be larger than the 5 hectares here postulated.)

Table 9

Actual Production, Economic-sized Holdings, and Number Required to Produce the Harvests of 1960

Type of crop	Production* (thousands of tons)	Optimum-sized holdings (ha)	Number necessary
Perennial crops			
Coffee	562.8	5	92,400
Sugar cane	3,270.0	100	327
Panela cane	9,075.0	100	1,008
Cacao	13.5	20	1,500
Fique (fiber)	18.0	20	900
Fruit	500.0	50	1,000
Plátano and banana	1,250.0	80	2,604
Banana for export	197.1	80	246
Subtotal with coffee			99,985
Subtotal without coffee			7,585
Annual crops			
Hot climate			
Sesame	20.0	80	126
Cotton	193.6	50	2,152
Rice	430.7	80	998
Beans	40.8	50	454
Soybeans	15.0	50	94
Corn	865.7	80	1,353
Tobacco	24.9	20	355
Tomato	36.0	10	150
Yuca	740.0	50	1,480
Arracacha	100.0	50	200
			7,362
Cold climate			
Barley	109.2	100	202
Wheat	145.2	100	303
Potato	653.3	50	242
Onion, garlic	27.0	10	750
Vegetables	150.0	10	1,880
Green peas	26.0	10	820
Subtotal			4,197
Total without coffee			19,144
Total with coffee			111,544

* Source: National Accounts, Bank of the Republic.

Under these assumptions, then, the 1960 harvest of perennial crops could have been produced by 93,000 farms instead of 450,000; hot-country crops by 7,300 instead of 220,000; and cold-country crops by 4,200 instead of 113,000; or the total by 105,000 instead of 786,000! It will be remembered that these families do not include all families in small towns and rural areas. On the other hand, some new-type units will require more than one family.

Table 10 attempts to bring out the same point by approaching the matter from a slightly different angle—that of days' work necessary per hectare for different crops, efficiently produced.[13] By this method it is estimated that 250,000 workers could have been displaced in coffee growing and 175,000 in other perennial crops, 350,000 in hot-country crops, and 165,000 in cold-country crops, or a total of 940,000.

The purpose of these calculations is to call forcibly to the attention of the reader the magnitude of the shifts desirable if the benefits of modern technology in agriculture are to be obtained. They also serve to demonstrate that (1) any diversification of agriculture within coffee farms that serves to reduce the owners' previous demand for food or add to the commercial supply for sale, or (2) any shifting of coffee growers into other forms of agriculture, can only serve to intensify the agrarian problem in general and cannot provide a solution to the problem raised by an excess working force in coffee growing.

In fact, it becomes clear, when we study these tables, that *any* policy of restraining movement out of agriculture is self-defeating. This does not mean that agrarian reform may not be able to do a worthwhile job of changing land tenure on a small scale, or even that no new land should be brought into cultivation. It does mean, however, that such actions tending to increase production should be studied in relation to the whole picture and should be accompanied by measures to provide alternative employment for displaced people on marginal land.[14]

Cattle raising. This is such a large and specialized subject that I shall not enter upon it here. A comprehensive study by Professor Harold Riley, prepared for the U.S. Department of Agriculture, is available. It would have been useful in connection with this study to present some figures on employment in cattle raising, but there are literally none available. In any attempt to derive an estimate by assuming a certain number of head per worker, the difficulty is that in the great ranches there may be hundreds per worker, while many small ranchers may have no more than, say, 3 to 10 beef and milk animals. Since it is generally agreed that the animal population was around 16,000,000 in 1960 and that the majority of these were probably on the larger individual holdings, the number of persons gainfully employed full time was probably not over 380,000. It may even have been less, with, say, 40,000 workers for other types of livestock.

[13] Assuming an average possible work year of 300 days in place of the 220 actually estimated.

[14] As pointed out in Part One, the head of the Agrarian Reform Institute, Dr. Enrique Peñalosa, has stated that today there is need for 1 million new jobs for surplus rural workers, and that this figure will rise to 2 million by 1970.

Table 10

Workdays and Workers Necessary to Produce Harvests of 1960, and Numbers of Superfluous Workers

	Necessary work				Superfluous work	
Type of crop	Workdays necessary per ha in efficient sized holdings	Total days worked (millions)	Persons active (thousands)	Families active* (thousands)	Persons active (thousands)	Families (thousands)
Perennial crops						
Coffee	100	46.2	154.0	85.6	250.1	138.9
Sugar cane	40	1.3	4.3	2.4	3.0	1.7
Panela cane	40	4.0	13.3	7.4	102.6	57.0
Cacao	35	1.1	3.7	2.1	4.9	2.7
Fique (fiber)	48	0.9	3.0	1.7	3.4	1.9
Fruit	50	2.5	8.3	4.6	21.3	11.9
Plátano and banana	32	6.7	22.3	12.4	39.5	21.9
Banana for export	32	0.6	2.0	1.1	0.7	0.4
Subtotal			210.9	117.3	425.5	263.4
Annual crops						
Hot climate						
Sesame	25	0.3	1.0	0.6	8.6	4.8
Cotton	76	8.2	27.3	15.2	30.0	16.6
Rice	25	2.0	6.7	3.7	37.9	21.0
Beans	6	0.1	0.3	0.2	29.2	16.2
Soybeans	6	0.03	0.1	0.06	2.2	1.24
Corn	4	0.4	1.3	0.7	159.6	88.7
Tobacco	150	1.1	3.7	2.0	27.7	15.4
Tomato	280	0.4	1.3	0.7	2.3	1.3
Yuca	21	1.6	5.3	2.9	46.5	25.9
Arracacha	21	0.2	0.7	0.4	4.7	2.6
Subtotal			47.7	26.5	348.7	193.7
Cold climate						
Barley	2	0.04	0.1	0.06	4.0	2.24
Wheat	2	0.1	0.3	0.2	11.0	6.1
Potato	21	0.3	1.0	0.6	25.4	14.1
Onions, garlic	180	1.4	4.7	2.6	9.8	5.5
Vegetables	360	6.8	22.7	12.6	59.1	32.8
Green peas	360	3.0	10.0	5.6	55.5	30.8
Total without coffee			38.8	21.7	164.8	91.5
Total with coffee			297.4	165.5	939.0	521.6

* 1.8 workers per family.

Sources: Caja Agraria; Ministry of Labor; Statistical Bulletin No. 144, USDA, 1954; Analysis and Projections of Economic Development in Colombia, CEPAL; Estimates of the Foundation for the Progress of Colombia.

In any case, any substantial possibility of additional employment in this field, in the absence of the development of large exports, appears remote.

Totals. Table 11 summarizes the estimates on active population necessary under our assumptions of complete convertibility to a feasible technical operation. Hence it is a rough guide to the active population which is displaceable, or for which alternative nonagricultural employment should be found. The total of the latter came to nearly 2,000,000 in 1960. The figure is mentioned not with any idea that this number of jobs and accompanying public services could have been provided in the immediate future, but rather to indicate the magnitude of the problem or, from another point of view, the opportunity. Moreover, the annual addition of 120,000 or more to the working population should not be overlooked.

In this work, the phrases "disguised" and "unemployment" or "underemployment" have been used as synonymous with low productivity of the colonial-type agriculture. With his usual clarity, Viner examined the concept of disguised unemployment and concluded, tentatively, "that there is little or nothing in all the phenomena designated as 'disguised employment,' as 'hidden unemployment,' or as 'underemployment' which in so far as they constitute genuine social problems would not be adequately taken into account by competent, informed and comprehensive analysis of the phenomenon of low productivity of *employed* labor, its causes, its true extent and

Table 11

Estimates of Active Rural Population Necessary and Displaceable, 1960

Sector	Actual (1960)	Necessary	Displaceable	Total rural active in Colombia (percent)	Total rural active necessary (percent)
	(Thousands of persons)				
Coffee	400	150	250	8	3
Agriculture (without coffee)	830	140	690	17	3
Cattle	440	280	160	9	6
Coffee, agriculture, and cattle	1,670	570	1,100	34	12
Other rural activities*	880	90†	790	18	2
Total rural active	2,550	660	1,890	52	14
Total active (Colombia)	4,930‡				

* Includes subsistence-type agriculture, artisans, rural commerce, and forestry workers.

† It is assumed that the occupation necessary in "other rural activities" is 10% of the actual.

‡ Estimated by CEDE for 1961.

Source: Population Projections, Centro de Estudios de Desarrollo Economico. "Necessary" and "Displaceable" derived from previous tables (Foundation for the Progress of Colombia).

its possible remedies."[15] I would concur with this statement and would agree that the terms are ambiguous. But so is the term "productivity." "Unemployment" and "underemployment" have at least the expository virtue of suggesting the remedies for unemployment, whereas "low productivity" is more likely to lead to proposals to improve agricultural "productivity" by more investment, better techniques, and so forth—blind alleys when applied to 50 percent of the working force. The necessity of the redistribution of the working force is so vital to the argument of this book that I have been at pains to show that most rural workers could be spared with no loss of production, that their presence in agriculture slows up the process of technification and thus is indeed harmful, and that in this sense they are truly underemployed or unemployed.

Viner assumes that the phrase applies only to the self-employed and raises the query, "Should there not be a tendency for equalization of the marginal productivity of labor in all agrarian uses where labor can fairly readily move from one type of use to another?"[16] The answer is that there may be a "tendency," but that there are also effective obstacles to mobility and competition in wage rates imposed by the state in the form of minimum wages and fringe benefits, as well as in the demoralization that follows long-continued casual labor. The persistence even in the United States of enclaves of marginal farmers earning far less than hired men is a case in point. Counter to expectations in developing countries, therefore, the number of the marginal farmers is growing, and the gap between their remuneration and that of wage earners, either urban or rural, also is growing.

Finally, Viner complains that the only extensive empirical evidence he has found which bears on the concept of rural underemployment is that of John Lossing Buck's study of 16,000 Chinese farms in 1937. It is hoped that the very different quantitative approach presented in this chapter may at least suggest the existence and magnitude of the problem in one developing country.

Haberler rejects the possibility of long-continued mass unemployment in disguised form in underdeveloped countries because he assumes that such unemployment could arise only from (1) an unchanging relation of employment to capital and (2) insufficient capital to provide full employment. He calls such theories "extreme examples of the modern propensity to overemphasize real factors and to look for real, in this case, literally physical, rigidities, instead of for monetary factors, price and wage rigidities and the like." He would be right in rejecting a necessary or rigid relation of employment to capital. However, other rigidities may result in such a relationship. He did not consider this possibility and concluded unguardedly that "now, as far as employment is concerned, there is probably little chance anyway

[15] "Some Reflections on the Concept of Disguised Unemployment," *The Indian Journal of Economics,* July, 1957, p. 23.

[16] *Ibid.,* p. 19.

of prolonged mass unemployment caused by deficiency of effective demand."[17] If half the working force is eking out a miserable existence in subsistence agriculture, is this not mass, though disguised, unemployment resulting from deficiency of effective demand, caused in turn by various rigidities? To class all such rigidities as "monetary" is hardly playing fair with the reader, because the implication is that deficient effective demand can be remedied by pumping in more money, which of course is not the case. The possibility of the continued existence of mass unemployment, or as Viner would prefer to say, mass employment of very low productivity, coexistent with employment of high productivity, is one of the principal arguments of this book.

Ability of agriculture to meet increased demand. There remains, however, the question whether, with this loss of manpower, agricultural production could increase sufficiently to take care of the additional urban demand. I shall anticipate very briefly the discussion in the quantitative section of this program.

It has been calculated[18] that an expansion of 5,800,000,000 pesos (of 1958 purchasing power) in the GNP consequent upon the employment of 550,000 additional workers would result in an increase in the annual demand for agricultural products (other than coffee) of about 1,000,000,000 pesos or roughly 17 percent. An increase of this magnitude, spread over three years, should not occasion any difficulty, although it would have to be carefully planned and assisted. Except for perennials like cacao and palm oil, there is hardly a crop that could not easily increase its harvests by 5 to 10 percent from one year to another if the demand existed and it paid to do so. If, of course, low price controls were maintained, problems would be encountered.

We have calculated that if the entire increased demand of 17 percent were met by efficient, economic-sized units, and assuming there was no increase in average yields of all existing units, the demand, evenly spread over all crops except coffee, could be met by 3,000 additional units utilizing 150,000 additional hectares. Actually, increased yields would make even these additions completely or partly unnecessary. It is interesting to note that 2,248 farm tractors were imported in 1960.

There have been few studies bearing on the elasticity of supply of agricultural products. With the recent mechanization of potato growing and improvement in varieties, both production and prices have been subject to violent fluctuations. On the other hand, the yearly support price for barley has been so skillfully set by the beer companies that the production has

[17] Gottfried Haberler, *Stability and Progress in the World Economy,* The Macmillan Company, New York, 1958, p. 170.

[18] By Jorge Ruiz Lara, in an unpublished study prepared for the Foundation for the Progress of Colombia, 1963.

shown a steady, orderly rise sufficient to meet the needs of the companies and no more.

On this point I may refer to my study of the cotton industry, in which the price of raw cotton and cotton seed is fixed by the government in a highly untechnical fashion.[19] There are two crops of cotton a year, one in the interior and one in the coast. The study proceeded on the assumptions that (1) the movements in the index of the cost of living would serve as a rough measure of movements in the cost of growing cotton, (2) the relationship in 1954–1956 was such that it led to no change in area planted (the decline in area planted in 1955 on the coast had a special explanation), and (3) the relationship between the cost and value of the crop per ton in one section of the country would have its effect, if any, on the area sown in the other section of the country six months later. It was found that variations in the spread between cotton prices and the cost of living were in general followed by expected variations in the area planted. While weather clearly had some influence, the cotton experience would appear to indicate that the Colombian farmer is motivated by economic considerations and will react, like his kind everywhere, to price stimuli.

In 1963–1964 bad weather prevailed throughout the country, and for the first time in the history of the cost-of-living index, food prices rose relative to others. This rise was followed by large plantings in 1964 and thus by generally large harvests that returned the price of the food component back to its customary relation to the index.

Conclusion. I have devoted much attention in the diagnosis to agriculture, because it appears that the agrarian problem is the most pressing with which Colombia is confronted and that its solution is the key to the solution of many related problems. Another reason for dealing with it in detail is that the agrarian problem has been confused with farm tenancy and with low productivity in the physical sense.

In Colombia's colonial-type agriculture and rural villages, therefore, may be found, in a truly economic sense of the word, the country's tremendous army of unemployed—an army that cannot be employed *efficiently* in growing more foods and fibers, except to the very modest extent to which effective internal and external demand can be increased.

Deterioration in condition of rural classes and consequences. The larger cities have been growing at a rate of 5 percent in the past decade. It seems a reasonable assumption that the very modest increase of 1.3 percent per capita of gross product, or less per capita of consumption, was fully accounted for, and probably more than accounted for, by the rise in the production and income of (1) existing workers in the larger cities, (2) new

[19] Lauchlin Currie, *El Algodón en Colombia* (Cotton in Colombia), Foundation for the Progress of Colombia, Bogotá, 1963.

workers in these same more prosperous cities, and (3) the entrepreneurial class. This, again, would imply a deterioration in the incomes of the colonial-type farmer. Such a deterioration is consistent with the evidence on the growth in the subdivision of coffee and other holdings and the enormous increase in squatters in the Magdalena Valley.

If this hypothesis in turn is correct, it provides an explanation of two other phenomena that have troubled thoughtful Colombians—the steady growth in rural violence up to 1963, and the increasing destruction of natural resources. Violence has doubtless many roots, but unquestionably deep poverty and ignorance are among them. The connection between these and destruction of natural resources is even more obvious.

At a later point I shall have occasion to point out the connection between rural poverty, increasing ignorance, ill health, and increasing lawlessness.

C. Relatively Unproductive Urban Labor

Colombia abounds in towns and even small cities that have no industrial base and subsist either because they are government centers or serve as distributing points for surrounding farms. In most of such towns and cities, the employment is casual and sporadic, many people are engaged in most inefficient selling and distributing operations, and the standard of living is in general much lower than that in the larger or more industrialized cities. Doubtless some of these towns will attract industries and grow. Others probably are as doomed as the colonial-type agriculture on which they live. In Venezuela, it is stated that in towns situated in relatively depressed agricultural areas, the average income is well under half that in Caracas.[20]

It is difficult to estimate the gainfully employed in such unindustrialized, low-standard towns and cities. If we deduct the population of the fifteen more prosperous and industrialized cities as projected by DANE (National Department of Statistics) from the estimated total by CEDE (Center of Studies and Economic Development) of 47 percent in towns over 1,500, we are left with a figure of 20 percent of the population in what we may call low-income towns and cities. Assuming that the percentage of gainfully employed in such places corresponds to the estimated percentage population, we arrive at a figure of approximately 1,000,000 workers who have relatively low employment and income and whose prospects of steady, productive employment are not too bright. To find such employment, it is probable that some of the workers may move to more favorably situated centers. In any case, for present purposes, we may list an unknown but probably large portion of the "urban" workers in unindustrialized cities and smaller towns as being only partially employed at relatively unremunerative work. This,

[20] Carl S. Shoup et al., *The Fiscal System of Venezuela,* The Johns Hopkins Press, Baltimore, 1959, p. 23.

then, is another important element in the diagnosis of the economic problem of Colombia.

D. Productivity of Labor in the Fifteen Largest or Industrialized Cities

The population of such cities may be estimated at 4,500,000, or 28 percent of the total. The percentage of gainfully employed is probably a little higher, say 30 percent, or 1,500,000. These are the people who enjoy the most remunerative work and the highest and most rapidly rising standard of living. This broad generalization, of course, does not apply to all; there are great differences within the total, ranging from the elite of the higher-income self-employed, the salaried worker, and the organized industrial workers, down to the casual day laborer and servants. The latter two constitute very large groups. Nevertheless, their real incomes are in general much higher than those of the average self-employed worker in rural regions and smaller towns or cities which lack any industry. To this must be added the true urban unemployed and another group of the unemployables.

E. The Short Work Year

A distressingly small percentage of the "economically active" have regular full-time work. This group, the most productive, have a very short work year after the deduction of Sundays, holidays, days between holidays and Sundays, and vacations. A calculation made for me by the Planning Office of Bogotá and applying to municipal workers placed nonwork days at 38 percent of the total, giving a work year of 226 days. The small-town and rural workers generally work much less.

This extremely short work year has a most important implication for the use of capital goods. When a single shift prevails (which is general except in cotton textiles and where furnaces must be kept going), industrial capital and machinery, much of it imported at great expense, is in use only 20 percent of the hours of the year. The Labor Code discourages the use of a second or third shift by requiring that rates for night work be 35 percent more than those for day work. Another factor discouraging a 5 to 12 P.M. shift is the shortage of power at evening peak hours. In certain industries mergers have created excess capacity on a single-shift basis. In others, custom and apathy have influenced decisions.

II. *Balance of Payments*

There are, in reality, two balances of payments at two different sets of exchange rates. One is the coffee rate of exchange at which coffee is sold. In addition is the higher certificate rate at which most imports are purchased with the proceeds from the sale of coffee. The other is the higher "free"[21] rate at which other exports are made and at which exchange is purchased for a variety of purposes, including remittances of capital.

Receipts from the sale of coffee rose from US$305 million in 1950 to $589 million in 1954 and declined thereafter to $305 million again in 1961, with total exports rising from $400 million to $700 million and falling back to $485 million in the same years. The absolute advantage of growing and exporting coffee is so great that it is difficult to export any other product at the same rate, or to initiate domestic production of other articles without substantial protection. Since the sales and receipts from coffee are inadequate, however, some protection for domestic production and special stimulus to other exports are justified.

For the purpose of the present diagnosis there are two important observations to be made on the balance of payments. In the first place, receipts from exports of goods and services have not kept pace with the growing requirements of the country, given the present structure and practices. Secondly, part of the receipts have been used for relatively unimportant ends, such as luxury traveling, purchases of consumer goods, exports of capital, and so forth. Even the import of capital goods has on occasion been uneconomic, since it has been for the production of luxury articles or the production of capital goods long before the economies of scale justified such production.

The export of goods other than coffee at the free rate has not yielded maximum benefit to the country, and the wide fluctuations, interspersed by periods of control in the rates, have made the orderly development of new exports difficult. That some progress has been made, however, is shown by the growth in the gross product relative to imports and the increase in the percentage of capital goods to total goods imported. Unquestionably much more could have been done to stimulate exports and to increase domestic production relative to imports. The tendency to seek to pay for more imports through borrowing instead of through current exports of goods and services is a disturbing one, as is also the tendency to give any amount of protection necessary for the establishment of any type of new industry.

Colombians are inclined to overlook the process of repayment of debt and to exaggerate the benefits received from foreign borrowing. For example, in the period 1952–1960 the highway network was largely constructed or reconstructed, with 3,000 kilometers paved, at an approximate cost of $200 million. Loan proceeds of the World Bank spent for this purpose in this period amounted to $19 million. In other words, Colombia paid over 90 percent of the cost and at the same time repaid over $5 million.

During the period 1952–1960, $113 million was spent on the construction of a railroad connecting the interior railroad system with the Caribbean coast (peso expenditures converted at the prevailing rate of exchange).

[21] Actually pegged throughout 1963 and most of 1964 at 10 pesos to $1.

Dollar loans outstanding for this project on December 31, 1960, amountec to $34,438,000, or 30 percent of the total. The figure would be 28.7 percen if interest of over $6,665,000 paid during this period were added to the cost.

Another way of illustrating relative magnitudes is to point out that the net increase in outstanding foreign debt in the decade from December 31 1952, to December 31, 1960, including the increase necessary to refinance commercial debts, amounted to only 2 percent of the value of imports ir the period. Of the total outstanding on December 31, 1959, 60 percen was repayable within the short term of ten years.

Of the total public borrowing from 1945 to June 30, 1961, of $820 million, $585 million had been disbursed, $261 million had been repaid and $324 million was outstanding. The tempo stepped up in 1961. Credits authorized during that year were $249 million, credits in negotiation as of the end of the year were $105 million, and other credits requested as of the end of the year were $173 million, for a grand total of $528 million.[22]

Surveying the record as a whole, it can be seen that Colombia receivec on balance little assistance from foreign loans in the decade 1950–1960 A new trend of accelerated borrowing was started in 1961.

While some of the individual loans have been excellent, what has beer lacking are solidly based criteria, derived from a carefully worked out na- tional program, on the use of export receipts, the stimulation of exports versus the stimulation of import substitutes, and the economic justificatior of borrowings.

III. *Tax System*

It was not possible to make an intensive study of the tax system from the point of view of equity and its impact on savings, investment, anc economic activity.[23] The following comments are more in the nature of impressions and hypotheses.

With respect to equity, the weight of taxation falls more heavily on the salaried middle class, the working classes (in indirect taxes), and certair

[22] *Public International Development Financing in Colombia,* Columbia University School of Law and Institute of International Studies of the University of Oregon New York, 1963, pp. 6, 9.

[23] However, after long neglect of the subject, two comprehensive studies have appeared. One, entitled a *Fiscal Survey of Colombia,* is by Milton Taylor anc Raymond Richmond, with the collaboration of a number of Colombian economists and published for the Joint Tax Program by the Johns Hopkins Press, Baltimore 1965. It is analytical and contains many recommendations. The other is by George Jackson Eder, John Chommie, and Hector Julio Becerra, entitled *Taxation in Colom- bia.* It is of the Harvard Law School World Tax Series, 1965, and is the resul of a prodigious amount of research on a very complicated subject.

companies, both incorporated and unincorporated, that cannot avail themselves of the numerous exemptions, pass the burden along to their customers, or evade taxes.

In other words, the combination of progressive income tax rates, taxes on patrimony, and forced investments makes for relatively high nominal rates. On the other hand, the possibilities of evasion open to certain classes of activity, and the numerous exemptions open to other classes, make these rates actually applicable to a relatively small economic class and to a limited proportion of the higher incomes that would otherwise be subject to such rates.

The large sums raised by the states on articles of mass consumption such as beer, tobacco, and liquor; the amounts raised by the nation on customs duties and by stamp taxes which are finally paid by consumers; the proceeds of gasoline and diesel taxes and others; and the exchange differential retained by the government, are passed on in a large though unknown part to the working classes and middle-income groups in the prices of articles bought. The opportunities for illegal evasion and legal avoidance of taxes open to the very wealthy are numerous. Exemptions are also numerous. Thus the productivity, progressivity, and equity of the tax system have been gravely impaired, especially since 1960. This, to repeat, is a statement based on general observation and would need a careful study to substantiate it. However, there is some evidence to support the inference.

With high and progressive rates applying to both income and property, one would naturally expect that, under conditions of inflation and a rapid rise in the GNP in current money terms, the yield of the income and property taxes would rise more rapidly than the national income, as more income moved into the higher tax brackets. According to Table 12, where the yields are expressed as a percentage of national income, the opposite occurred. Even when the additional surcharge of 20 percent on the income tax in 1963 and 1964 is included, the percentage still falls. Since no discrimination is made in the published figures between company and individual tax returns, the presumption is that income and property taxes paid *by individuals* must be very low indeed. Since the rates are actually high, the conclusion appears inescapable that evasion and exemptions have in large part ruined the productivity and progressivity of the tax system. Of the increase of 27 billion pesos in national income from 1959 to 1964, some 350 million, on a constant tax base, accrued to the state from progressive taxes. The 20 percent surcharge was due to lapse in 1965. Clearly the tax system was becoming more and more regressive, and nothing was being done to hold in check the natural tendency for inequality to grow.

It could be argued that the impact on economic development has not been unfavorable. Since probably a large part of the saving comes from the wealthy, since tax avoidance mostly benefits this class, and since private saving and investment are probably in general more productive than public

Table 12

Yield of Income and Wealth Taxes as Percentage of Colombian National Income, 1959–1964

Year	(1) National income*	(2) Income and wealth tax yields*	(3) Percentage of (2) of (1)	(4) 20% surcharge on income taxes*	(5) Percentage (2) + (4) of (1)
1959	19,080	1,032	5.4		
1960	21,822	1,045	4.8		
1961	25,102	1,049	4.2		
1962	28,241	1,258	4.5		
1963	37,209	1,226	3.3	223	3.9
1964	45,968	1,387	3.0	252	3.6

* Millions of current pesos.

Sources: Income 1959–1962, Banco de la República; 1963–64 derived by raising 1962 figures by cost of living plus 3.5% in 1963 and 5.5% in 1964. The latter estimate may be too high. Tax yields 1959–1963, Informes Financieros; 1964 estimated.

saving and investment, at least in Colombia, the present tax system may be said to favor private expansion. However, exemptions and avoidance also encourage extravagance, luxury building, and foreign travel, and the loss of revenue leads to borrowings from the central bank. The subsequent inflation may be harmful to saving, rather than the reverse. Moreover, the type of private investment particularly favored—importing, office building, high-class suburban developments, and similar activities carried out generally by unincorporated business—may not be the most useful in raising the standard of living, or in achieving the economies of scale possible in the mass consumer goods industries. The subject is obviously complex and should be accorded careful and objective analysis.

The hypotheses set forth above may provide a partial explanation of what otherwise is a puzzling phenomenon—the relative apparent prosperity throughout much of 1962 at a time when the Ten-Year Plan of Development was in complete collapse. The decline in tax yields as a result of exemptions and evasions (1) made more private savings available (2) forced curtailment of what in many cases were public expenditures of probably low productivity, and (3) caused recourse to borrowing. Thus the level of private domestic investment may have risen while public investment in real terms was falling. A contributory factor was the heavy increase in foreign indebtedness in 1961–1962. Hence a completely unplanned program may have yielded, for a time, apparently good results in terms of the GNP. These results, however, could not be continued without an excessive curtailment in public spending, excessive internal and external borrowing, or a rise in taxes. So the possible course of events in 1962 could hardly be commended as a long-term program, though it is suggestive. Toward the close of that year, exchange was being severely rationed, borrowings from the central bank were being resorted to to meet the budget deficit, and the cost of living and the free exchange rate were rising. In 1963 and 1964 there was evidence that the rise in prices had at least temporarily outrun consumer buying power: sales of textiles declined, and industrial employment failed to grow, despite heavy foreign borrowing.

IV. *Imperfect Competition*

In Part One reference was made to elements in the economic and cultural environment that have led to large areas of imperfect competition in the industrial sectors of developing countries. This is particularly true of Colombia. One company dominates the tobacco industry. Directly and through stock ownership, one company dominates the beer industry. Three financial groups control the cement industry. Three companies consume 84 percent of all raw cotton produced and are entering the synthetic fiber field. One company dominates aviation, and one has a favored position in maritime transport. Two companies supply all the domestically produced steel. A few large branch banking systems control most of the banking resources, and recently financial corporations have been playing an increasingly important role in directing the flow of investment funds. The list could be greatly extended. The workers and employees of most, if not all, of these entities are organized and secure a host of fringe benefits in excess of those guaranteed by the voluminous and complex Labor Code.

Although "monopoly" is never a nice word, the climate of opinion is really not hostile to it. Protection is granted to any extent necessary to encourage a new industry. On the other hand, the government generally takes a benign attitude toward the demands of organized labor (unless Communist influence is alleged), and the larger and wealthier the companies, the more they are expected to do for their workers. It is accepted as a matter of course that the companies will pass along any increase in labor costs to the consumer, or alternatively, will retain any gains from increased efficiency for their workers and stockholders.

There is a complete lack of any awareness that the high per unit cost-price attitude may impede demand and slow up industrialization and the creation of urban employment. Thus at the time of the devaluation of 35 percent at the close of 1962, which should in itself not have resulted in a rise of the cost of living by more than 4 percent, an across-the-board increase of 3 pesos a day (the minimum wage varied from 9 to 11 pesos a day) was decreed. This increase was generally considered to have been the principal factor in the rise of 30 percent in the cost of living in 1963.

In the important and exceptionally efficient cotton textile industry, the three largest companies (that consumed 84 percent of the raw cotton) experienced a rise in production per man-hour from 1957 to 1962 of 28 percent or 5.07 percent annually. In the same period, reported profits increased by 80 percent and dividends by 73 percent. Average earnings per worker increased by 106 percent. The price of cotton increased by 42 percent and of cloth at the factory by 47 percent, which was the same as the rise in the cost of living.[24] In other words, all the benefits of increasing productivity, cost reductions, and intensive use of equipment (80 percent of the hours of the year) in this industry were distributed among the workers and stockholders. In addition to the salaries, wages, and dividends paid in this period, the consumers supplied 56 percent of the increase in the working and fixed capital requirements.[25] There was, doubtless, a causal relationship between this record and the decline in consumption of cotton per capita. Consumption exhibited a strong upward trend from 1952 to 1960 of almost 8 percent. From 1960 to 1962 it fell to a rate equivalent to the growth in population, 3 percent. It is believed that it fell still further in later years. The official index of employment in textiles generally showed no growth from May, 1962, to the end of 1964.

It is believed that a study of other mass consumer goods industries would indicate that cotton is not an exceptional case. This suggests again that a problem in developed economies which has recently been given much attention—wage and cost inflation—is even more serious in its implications for the industrialization of developing countries. In developed countries the phenomenon contributes to continuing unemployment and threatens the balance of payments situation of first one and then another country. The British government in particular has been working on an incomes policy applicable to wage negotiations. It is expected to be extended to certain prices and profits. In Colombia the annual addition to the labor force is so large and the need to create urban jobs for surplus agricultural labor is so urgent that industrial incomes inflation has much more serious implications, and an incomes policy is more urgently needed. In 1962, factory employment provided jobs for less than 6 percent of the working force (312,000 out of 5,434,000).

This discussion serves also to illustrate the earlier remarks on the growing inequality between organized labor and the self-employed. It was argued earlier in this chapter that agricultural technification in conjunction with a continued growth of agricultural workers was probably resulting in lower real incomes for many marginal agriculturalists. On the other hand, the real incomes of textile workers rose 40 percent in the short space of five years. In addition, the companies helped to provide housing for their workers and education for the workers' children. In 1963 the index of factory hourly wages in industry generally rose 4 percent in relation to the cost of living (and there was probably an even greater rise in fringe bene-

[24] Lauchlin Currie, *El Algodón en Colombia,* pp. 100–109.
[25] *Ibid.,* p. 93.

fits)[26] at a time when the index of factory employment failed to show any rise.

Albert Berry of Yale has kindly let me see and quote some studies he has made on the movement of real wages in Colombia for an as yet unpublished study. Although his series show some puzzling year-to-year variations, perhaps because of the deflator used or because of defects in the data, they do suggest that over the twenty-five-year period up to 1963, there was virtually no growth in real agricultural wages, which indicates an actual decline in the real income of the growing number of subsistence farmers whose incomes are lower than those of rural wage earners. For industrial workers during the period from 1955 to 1962, he was able to add fringe benefits to nominal wages and showed a rise in real income in the seven-year period of 65 percent, at a time when the per capital real income of the country was rising little more than 1 percent per annum. These are highly important findings supporting the thesis advanced here.

V. *Public Administration*

This was one important sector in which no improvement was discernible in the past decade. Conditions described in the *Public Administration Report*[27] of 1951 on ministerial management remained applicable in 1965. The flight from these conditions had resulted in an unbelievable proliferation of government functions in numberless agencies and had made executive direction and responsibility impossible. The Planning Office itself illustrated in its organization a characteristic confusion of ideas about its place and function, mixing administrative and executive with planning responsibilities at all levels of government. The inevitable results were plainly shown in the lack of good current advice to the President on general planning, fiscal, monetary, and exchange matters.

The growing discrepancy in salaries between government and business made it increasingly difficult for the former to attract and hold the better-trained and more competent people. As the quality of administration declined in the ministries, more and more functions were farmed out to semi-autonomous agencies. Gradually the functions of ministers like the Ministers of Agriculture and Development became more than anything else those of serving on boards of nonministerial agencies.

The whole public administration called for thoroughgoing reform, but political conditions made this impracticable. Virtually all agencies of govern-

[26] The rise in real factory wages was 7.4 percent in the first two months of the year, but part was lost in the subsequent rise in the cost of living.

[27] *Reorganización de la Rama Ejecutiva del Gobierno de Colombia* (Reorganization of the Executive Arm of the Colombian Government), a report of a mission directed by Lauchlin Currie, National Press, Bogotá, submitted in 1951, published in 1952.

ment at all levels had functions and responsibilities that they were unable to discharge efficiently. Considering the range and importance of the functions and the volume of money involved, this is a very grave matter and cannot be omitted from a serious diagnosis of the Colombian economic problem.

VI. *Sectionalism*

Sectionalism is very strong and doubtless results in large part from the topography of the country, which led to virtual isolation of many states throughout most of Colombian history. The economic consequences have been a very heavy burden in the construction of roads and cost of transport. In addition, the sectionalism has undoubtedly led to a waste of public funds in order that all states might share in public projects.

> An analysis of the detailed budgets also indicates that large sums are being allocated by the National Government to highways, national and departmental [state], which form no part of the recommended long range plan. . . . In 1961 there were 294 such projects with a total cost of 142,000,000 [pesos] or 51% of the total funds allocated to construction.[28]

The feeling of sectionalism may lessen in the future, since the country now has a good transport system which should (1) stimulate movement from less to better favored lands and (2) reduce the demand for national funds for local projects. As cities grow in importance, it may be anticipated that the national government, on the one hand, and urban governments, on the other, will grow in importance relative to state governments. For the present, however, sectionalism is one of the important elements in any diagnosis.

VII. *Lack of a National Urban Policy*

Growth is proceeding most rapidly—at a rate of 5 to 6 percent—in a few cities. The North American pattern of low-density single-family suburbs is being followed, with single-family units comprising workers' sections also. Congestion, with all its costs, is already appearing, along with the deterioration of zones surrounding the center. A continuation of this pattern will result in increasing diversion of national savings into luxury homes and transport facilities for private transit—with, naturally, less money available for expenditures that raise the minimum standard of living of the many.

A continuation of the present rate and type of growth of Bogotá would

[28] Parsons et al., *Plan for Improvements in National Transport,* Bogotá, 1961, vol. II, p. 70.

result in a metropolitan area of over 4 million within eighteen years, the disappearance of the rural character of the surrounding Sabana, horrible congestion, high public service and transit charges, and very heavy expenditures in these fields.

VIII. *Education*

The rural population is so diffused and so poor, debilitating diseases are so widespread, the annual output of trained teachers is so low, and life in rural regions is generally so unattractive to teachers, that secondary rural education is virtually nonexistent, and primary is confined to a year of generally very poor instruction. Even in the capital city of Bogotá, almost all secondary schools are private and nearly half the children receiving primary instruction were, in 1962, in private schools. Very few pupils in public primary schools complete the five-year course. The lack of instruction is not as serious as the lack of discipline, regular hours, character formation, and training in good working habits.

The economic deterioration in rural regions, accompanied by restless migrations of squatters, the breakup of family life, and the increase of lawlessness, constitute an atmosphere for hundreds of thousands of children which is frightening to contemplate. Certain cultural institutions such as the family and religion, which in a way compensated for lack of formal education, are losing their hold. With poverty, disease, and migration, family ties have weakened greatly. The present generation of rural children is growing up in poor physical and mental health and, naturally, with poor social and cultural values. The comfortable upper-class picture of the Colombian peasant as a deeply religious, moral, hardworking family man, clinging to his traditional cultural values and passing them on to his children, while perhaps still true in certain areas, is a travesty of the facts in large sections of the country.

On the other hand, it is also true that the type of primary education offered, even in the cities, is humanistic, formalistic, and not well adapted for fitting poor children into their environment. The curriculum for each grade for the whole country is uniform and is prescribed by the National Ministry of Education and is doubtless in large part responsible for the large percentage of children who fail to gain promotion, are repeating courses, or who drop out of school. In Bogotá, in 1961, 27 percent of the children in the first grade of public schools failed to pass the final examination. Of 18,181 who entered the first grade in 1955 only 3,040 finished their fifth year. Of 32,189 who were accepted in the first grade in 1960, 19,908 were over 7 years of age, probably meaning they were repeating the course. In Barranquilla in 1964, 29 percent of first grade pupils in the public schools failed of promotion. In a smaller town in the state of

Atlántico 43 percent failed in the first year.[29] Obviously, a drastic revision in educational philosophy is called for.

IX. *Transport*

In the past decade or so the revolution in transport has been nearly as dramatic as in agriculture. By and large, the main cities and best-producing areas are now connected by good highways and the railroad. There are still some urgent investments needed, such as a good road from Medellín to connect at Honda for Bogotá; the completion of paving on the Bogotá-Villavicencio road; a good link with Venezuela at Maracaibo and the coastal cities; additional rolling stock and improvement for the national railroads, and so on. However, in general, the capacity of the transport facilities is far in excess of current use. This means, again in general, that it would be more economic to secure more intensive utilization of existing means than to duplicate them. In particular, every effort should be made to utilize more intensively the great low-cost transport facilities of the Atlantic Railroad and so reduce per unit costs per ton-kilometer.

The implication of the agricultural section earlier in this chapter is that, at least for the time being, the level and most accessible lands should be exploited. The value to the economy of penetration roads and roads to far-distant colonization projects is doubtful.

X. *Monetary Policy*

In Colombia there is a chronic tendency toward an excessive expansion in the means of payment, as indicated by the more or less steady rise in the cost of living and the necessity of periodic devaluations. The only period of relative stability in the past decade or so was in the years 1951 to 1952, despite the devaluation of 25 percent carried out at the beginning of 1951. During this period the budget remained balanced, and the Comité de Desarrollo Económico, and later the newly formed Comité de Planeación, were keenly aware of the importance of moderation in the expansion of means of payment and kept closely in touch with the central monetary authorities and the President on the matter. This interlude ended in 1953.

In seeking for the cause of this chronic bias, account must be taken of (1) the cultural factor (inflation is common throughout Latin America);[30] (2) of the fact that, largely owing to chronic inflation, there is no capital market worthy of the name, and emergency borrowing at conventional rates

[29] Data for Bogotá derived from *Una Política Urbana para los Países en Desarrollo* (An Urban Policy for Developing Countries), Ediciónes Tercer Mundo, Bogotá, 1965, pp. 133–134. For Barranquilla and Atlántico, from an unpublished socioeconomic study of the state of Atlántico, contracted by Governor Francisco Posada de la Peña with the Foundation for the Progress of Colombia, 1965. Both studies were directed by Lauchlin Currie.

[30] Venezuela has been an outstanding exception.

of interest takes place from the Central Bank; and (3) of the constant pressure arising from cost-push inflation, discussed above under the section Imperfect Competition. It should be noted that up to 1963 the responsibility for monetary policy was diffused among the government and the largest borrowing groups who comprise the board of the Bank of the Republic (the central bank). The consumer as such is not represented. There is an unquestioned feeling that every lending institution, including the Corporaciónes Financieras (industrial finance companies) and the government, has a right to a borrowing quota; and people do not appreciate that it is high-powered money or reserve funds that are being borrowed. The chronic inflation has naturally led to high current rates of interest, so that borrowing from the central bank is extraordinarily profitable.

The inability of the bank to resist the multiple demands for rediscounts, together with the awareness that multiple expansion of the means of payment can take place as a consequence, have led to the development of a series of complicated and devious offsetting factors, such as high reserve requirements—frequently 100 percent on deposits above a certain figure—and the maintenance of private deposits in the Bank of the Republic in connection with importations.

Considerable faith is placed in the channeling of credit (selective credit control) into allegedly "productive" uses, presumably with the vague idea that if production is stimulated and speculation is discouraged, the danger of inflation is reduced. These "common sense" views die hard. Each important branch of economic activity tries to have its own bank, such as the Coffee Bank, the Cattle Bank, etc. Practically no analysis of any kind has been made of the theory, success, and consequences of selective credit policies. This is a field where "common sense" reigns supreme. The fact that more loans to cattle raisers do not increase by one cent the demand for meat or its prices does not reduce the spread in price between the producer and the consumer, and does not lead to an increase in quality or the introduction of more technical methods, was noted earlier. They may increase competition among cattle raisers, though this is not certain as loans may be offset by withdrawal of other capital from the industry.

Generally the income velocity of money has remained fairly stable. This is another way of saying that if means of payment rose more rapidly than production, prices rose so that the relation between money and gross product in pesos remained relatively steady. The enormous expansion of the means of payment in 1961 (25 percent) and 1962 (20 percent), however, was not reflected in anything like a corresponding rise in prices at the time. Drs. Jorge Ruiz Lara and Marta Fernández speculated that it might be explained in terms of increased real production and drawing down of stocks.[31] Some of this may have occurred; on the other hand, the impact

[31] *La Expansión Monetaria de Enero de 1960 a Marzo de 1962* (The Monetary Expansion from January of 1960 to March of 1962), CEDE, University de los Andes, Bogotá, Agosto 1962.

on prices was in part delayed until the devaluation of 1962, to which the expansion of money in 1961 and 1962 was a contributing factor. The increased liquidity preference (an increased demand for money to hold as command over goods, in the Marshallian sense) of these years may, on the other hand, have been a reflection of a growing crisis in confidence caused by political as well as economic developments. The growing concomitant yield on stocks (the failure of stock prices to rise with growing earnings and dividends) may have been another reflection of this crisis in confidence.

Toward the close of 1963, responsibility for monetary policy was centered in a monetary board dominated by government members. Excessive monetary expansion continued, however, in the first three-quarters of 1964 (15 percent in the means of payment).

XI. *The Allocation of Resources*

It was noted in Part One how extreme inequality in income results in an allocation of new capital and the distribution of labor in the private sector in a pattern that makes little sense from the rational point of view of satisfying the community's most urgent wants. In these circumstances, investment based on the most expert cost-benefit analyses and marketing surveys can do little to enhance national well-being. It is a natural impulse to look to the public sector to correct deficiencies. But here sectionalism, the low level of public administration, and the proliferation of governmental entities and international and foreign lending agencies again militate against a rational allocation of resources. How do the claims of primary education weigh against those of the army and police, of raising the salaries of government employees against the construction of new roads, of urban public services against land reclamation projects?

The truth is that in Colombia, as is probably true in other developing countries, there is little possibility of establishing a rational system of priorities. Money goes to projects or activities for which there is the strongest political support or to entities which are the best organized or who have detailed plans for projects that offer the better chances of receiving foreign financial support or to public entities that have been able to secure earmarked sources of revenue outside the national budget, of which there are now a considerable number. Another favored device is to start a large number of projects with small allocations in the hope that additional funds will somehow become available. This not only results in the selection of projects of low priority but also in the existence at any given time of a large proportion of unfinished work and dead capital.

Underlying the organizational deficiencies are conceptual defects. In the first place, in the absence of an overriding national plan, there are no criteria for determining priorities—for determining what are the primary and most urgent problems to be solved and what are the secondary or derivative ones. This applies not only to individual projects and activities but also to the determination of the proportion of national income that should be allotted to the public sector. The concept of real or opportunity costs is completely absent.

It is quite common to turn to engineering firms for preliminary feasibility studies and I know of only one case where such a firm made an adverse recommendation. In the private sector a client usually wants the best advice he can get from technicians. In the public sector the client usually wants a favorable finding from the technician. In one case I was asked to make a feasibility study of a proposed costly irrigation works after technical studies had already been made. I found that much of the region had 80 inches of rain a year and that the small area that could benefit from irrigation could be served at small cost by employing existing canals and brooks. My recommendation was rejected and work on the original costly lines is proceeding. The contracting engineers indignantly said that to adopt my primitive solution, the public entity in question would not need engineers! The last review of the transport situation in Colombia in 1961 was contracted with an American engineering firm, although the problems it had to deal with were mostly economic.

I am not being jurisdictionally minded about this. In all the missions I have headed, I have insisted on including specialists from other fields. But just as I would not entrust the construction of a dam to an economist, so I would not ask an engineer to do the work of an economist. It so happens that an economist's training comes closer to enabling him to determine priorities in public spending than that of most other disciplines. One reason why an economist's work is frequently disappointing is that the clients have not asked him to consider alternatives. A project by itself may appear to be viable. In relation to alternative investments, however, it might be given very low priority. Without the consideration of alternative uses of funds, misallocation of resources cannot be avoided.

There is, however, no one person or entity in the public sector concerned with making a given sum of money go as far as possible and yield the highest possible return to the economy in terms of well-being. Original cost estimates are invariably exceeded, partly because of original excessive optimism and partly because of mistakes, unforeseen expenses, and inflation. Generally a large project seems to capture the imagination and receives preference over a number of smaller ones, regardless of their merits. A spectacular example of this was the favorable preliminary feasibility report, again by a large American engineering firm, of the proposed 5,600-kilometer highway along the Eastern Andes from Venezuela to Brazil to cost $500 million. Similarly slogans like "opening up the country," "bringing new land into cultivation," and "eliminating the middlemen" are worth volumes of arguments and statistics.

In developed countries, spectacular mistakes or instances of waste in public spending are frequently the subject of subsequent government investigation, and awareness of this possibility is presumably a salutary influence in preventing them. In Colombia this is rarely the case, partly because of lack of interest and means to make such an investigation and partly because chronic inflation in time covers up a multitude of mistakes.

One of my reasons for proposing in 1961 a consortium of foreign lenders for Colombia was to establish priorities in accordance with a general plan of development. Something was accomplished in a small sector by the consulting group of foreign lenders, and the U.S. Agency for International Development has tightened up its control of the use of counterpart funds resulting from dollar loans and the use of proceeds from the sale of surplus foods. On the whole, however, there is still much lack of coordination and, worse, lack of any agreement on a basic plan of development which would provide criteria for lending.

This whole theme merits much more study but perhaps enough has been suggested here to indicate why the substantial yearly investment of national savings and foreign borrowings in both the private and public sectors and the other expenditures of public bodies can have only limited effect in raising the standard of well-being of the poorest classes. To say that the whole apparatus for allocating the annual volume of funds available for investment and other public spending is in need of drastic revision is only to say that the country needs a plan carefully thought out to accelerate its development.

XII. *Favorable Factors*

In this diagnosis we have naturally concentrated on problems and difficulties, which may have conveyed an impression of hopelessness. Actually, there are many bright spots.

Colombia is still, despite much destruction of them, tremendously rich in natural resources relative to population. It has an excellent industrial base, is rapidly mastering agricultural technification, and has strong and active entrepreneurial and professional classes—all great assets. The varying climate permits a great variety in crops, although this must be offset against the high transport costs resulting from the topography. Other assets are the abundance of hydroelectric power, affording some of the cheapest electric energy in the world, and relatively abundant oil reserves. Even in crops that do not lend themselves to machine cultivation, such as coffee, the consolidation of holdings and technification would permit the country to compete on favorable terms with any other country.

The variety and richness of resources and the strong industrial base have made the country much less dependent on imports than it otherwise would have been.

XIII. *Synthesis of the Problem*

Many factors, obviously, enter into the explanation of the low standard of living and the slow rise in that standard. If this diagnosis is correct, however, the problem centers on lack of remunerative work, particularly in rural regions and small towns, or underutilization of human and material resources. Associated with this phenomenon are widespread and dire rural poverty, ill health, ignorance, very high birthrates, destruction of natural resources, and violence and lack of security in rural regions. The atmosphere for the new generation is very bad and getting worse. Technification of agriculture is proceeding faster than jobs are being provided for those no longer needed in rural areas. On the other hand, the surplus of rural manpower is slowing up technification. The problem has invaded what was formerly the most profitable branch of agriculture—coffee growing—which is suffering from increasing subdivision of holdings and limited growth in demand.

Production in urban areas is much lower than it could be with existing equipment because of the very short work year and the general practice of working only single shifts. The distribution of the limited national production is characterized by two different forms of inequality—that between the rich and the poor, intensified recently by tax evasion and exemptions favoring the rich, and that between organized workers and self-employed rural and small town dwellers. With over half the population on or near a subsistence basis, demand is limited for the products of industry, and the economies of scale are difficult to obtain outside the mass consumption industries.

Foreign-exchange resources have not grown with the growth in national product. A substantial, though unknown, part is utilized in the purchase of luxury goods, travel, and capital remittances. A rapid rise in national product would require more exchange and/or better utilization. Looking ahead, it would be desirable if additional exchange could, in large part, be earned rather than borrowed.

To be realistic, a program at the present time should not be dependent upon skilled public administration. The more it relies upon the private sector, the greater the chances of success. Until a thoroughgoing reform in ministerial management is carried out, reliance will have to continue to be on semiautonomous agencies that can pay and attract more competent people.

A national urban policy is lacking. The rapid growth of large cities is proceeding in a form prejudicial to a more widely diffused national well-being. On the other hand, with some exceptions, the country is relatively well provided with highways and railroads. The main area in which more skilled public administration is indispensable is urban education. Other public services and housing can be largely decentralized in agencies that can command better talent than is available to ministries and state and municipal governments.

Technically and materially, Colombia has all that it requires to ensure a high and rapidly rising standard of well-being. The two things that it most needs are a soundly conceived economic program and leadership strong enough and wise enough to secure its adoption and execution.

XIV. *The Need for a Breakthrough Program*

A. Growing Poverty in Rural Areas

An important element in the diagnosis is the growth in inequality. There are no comprehensive statistics bearing on this point, but a comparison of the growth of income and consumption per capita of the country as a whole with that of organized and urban activities seems to leave no doubt that inequality is growing. It is stated that the growth in real per capita gross product in the decade 1950–1960 was 1.6 percent per annum and in real consumption less than 1 percent per annum.[32] On the other hand, the growth in per capita real income of the employees and workers in the main cotton textile companies from 1957 to 1962 inclusive was at a rate of nearly 8 percent per annum.[33] Similarly, average remuneration in petroleum, sugar growing and refining, metalworking, and various other well-organized industries far outstripped the average for the country. There are no trustworthy data on the distribution of income, but the combination of chronic inflation and what is in reality a regressive tax system suggests that the propertied and professional classes are improving their positions. This inference receives some confirmation from the large volume of luxury-type building in the leading cities.

B. Population Growth

Although the returns are not available from the census of 1964, various samplings suggest that the rate of population growth is one of the highest in the world, around 3 percent per annum, and that with the decline in the death rate, the rate of growth has increased from 2.3 percent per annum in the past twenty years, or by 30 percent. The total population is believed to be over 17 million, and if the present rate of growth continues, it could reach 75 million in less than fifty years. If this should occur, it would make the attainment of a high per capita income very difficult. Colombia appears to be a country, therefore, that badly needs a breakthrough program of accelerated development. It must be admitted that initially the program might have the result of raising the rate of growth in population because of a further decline in infant mortality. But this would soon be counteracted

[32] Four-Year Plan of Public Investment, National Planning Office, Bogotá, 1961, p. 10.

[33] *El Algodón en Colombia.*

by the lower urban birthrate. A consequence of the rapid increase of population is the existence, so often noted in developing countries, of an unfavorable ratio between the people of working age and their dependents.

The vicious circle of widespread and growing poverty, a high and growing rate of population increase, and still more poverty, appears to demand a program designed to obtain a period of accelerated development, or what I have characterized as a breakthrough program. At least, the programs followed to date do not appear to have placed Colombia safely in the self-generating-development class of countries. The heavy foreign borrowing program mostly serves to support a portion of the rapidly growing population. On the other hand, its cessation, in the absence of other offsetting measures, would bring on an economic crisis.

The gravity of the problem may be grasped by a study of Table 13, showing calculated, estimated, and projected birth and death rates in Colombia from 1912 to 1971. The gross birthrate declined very little from 1912 to 1961.

Table 13

Gross Birth and Death Rates, Colombia, 1912–1971

Year	Gross birth rate	Gross death rate	Rate of growth in population
1912–1938	48	27	2.1
1938–1944	47	25	2.2
1944–1951	46	18	2.8
1951–1956	44	17	2.9
1956–1961 (est.)	43	15	2.8
1971 (projection)	41	11	3.0

Source: J. V. Grauman, Some Aspects of Population Growth in Colombia, ECLA, Santiago, 1962. Reproduced from Albert Berry, Breve Estudio de los Determinantes del Crecimiento de la Población en Colombia, CEDE, Bogotá, 1965, p. 3.

CHAPTER 13

Trial and Error—But Mostly Error

As noted in Chapters 5 and 8, Colombia has been the testing ground for various approaches. Through a series of unrelated events, the country was in the forefront of economic programming in 1961, with a Planning Office, a Four-Year Plan of Public Investment, and a Ten-Year Plan of Development, both plans prepared with the help of ECLA technicians. It had enacted agrarian reform legislation and had joined the Latin American Free Trade Area (LAFTA).

Chapter 5 discussed the ECLA approach and pointed out its deficiencies in terms of objectives, diagnosis, and program. It is possibly unjust to attribute the Colombian Plan in all its aspects to ECLA, since its technicians worked anonymously and the plan has certain inconsistencies that may have resulted from an attempt to combine features of different origins. It apparently began merely as a program of increased public spending in various fields. By a trick in semantics whereby this program was called "public investment," and because the assumption was that it constituted a net increase in "investment," the transition was made to a general program of development. It was not noticed that the proposed increased investment came not from true savings or increased taxes, but from monetary expansion and foreign borrowing. Even so, to be arithmetically consistent with a goal of a 5.6 percent rate of growth in the GNP, a further assumption was made of an increase in the ratio of output to all existing capital.

That somebody had misgivings about this procedure is indicated by a strange discussion of the low productivity of social expenditures, the improbability that the long-range benefits would be felt during the life of the program, and the gloomy conclusion that "the betterment in social conditions implies, in short, a certain sacrifice by the present generation in the field of welfare in favor of the future."[1] Yet the program was largely in these social expenditures!

[1] Ten-Year Plan, National Planning Office, Bogotá, 1961, p. 221.

As remarked before, the lack of provision for adequate financing of the increased public expenditures, together with tax exemptions and evasions, led to a budget deficit in 1962, expansion in 1962 of 21 percent in the means of payment (on top of a 25 percent expansion in 1961), the decision to devaluate at the end of 1962, a subsequent 36 percent rise in the cost of living, and the struggle throughout 1963 and 1964 to recover budgetary and monetary stability. That the struggle was not too successful is suggested by a continued, though modest, budget deficit; the growth in the means of payment of 12 percent in 1963, with indications of an additional 15 percent expansion in 1964; and the continued rise in prices.

Dr. Samuel Hoyos, an able Colombian economist, commented wryly on the manner in which the devaluation of 1962 was made: "At least we must have the unique distinction of carrying out a devaluation that made it more difficult to export and increased the pressure to import." Actually, the rise in revenues was so sluggish and the rise in prices so rapid that, as indicated in Table 14, national government expenditures (other than debt service), as a percentage of estimated national income, declined from 13.2 percent in 1961 to 9.2 percent in 1964. This must constitute almost a record for divergence of plans and actualities.

It appears that contrary to the plan, real investment in the public sector declined. The combination of inflation, tax evasion, and exemptions increased inequality and possibly private saving. Because of the threat of rural land expropriation and/or occupation, agriculture lost its favored and traditional attraction for investment, and this was taken by urban apartment and office construction and by dollars. Mechanization of agriculture, as shown by imports of agricultural equipment, received a bad setback. This development, accompanied by one of the worst droughts on record, led for the first time to a rise in agricultural prices in 1963 relative to others. The growth in industrial employment flattened out in 1962–1964, the factory employment index for workers showing virtually no change from May, 1962, to the end of 1964. Since this is the most dynamic sector, we should have hoped that the increase would have been at a much higher rate than the

Table 14

Colombian Government Expenditures as Percentage of GNP and National Income

(Millions of pesos)

Year	Expenditures*	GNP†	%	Nat. income†	%
1961	3,316	28,306	11.7	25,102	13.2
1962	3,726	31,830	11.7	28,241	13.2
1963	4,198	41,937	10.0	37,209	11.3
1964	4,214	51,810	8.1	45,968	9.2

* 1961–1963 derived from Informes Financieros, 1964 estimated.

† See note Table 12.

rate of growth in the working force. The inpouring of foreign aid and the 25 percent rise in the price of coffee appear to have been unable to make headway against internal developments and policies, at least in the vital field of employment.

Concomitantly, hourly wages rose in 14 out of 19 groups of manufactures in 1963 in relation to the rise in the cost of living.[2] The relative rises ranged from 3 up to 48 percent, with the overall index rising 4 points relative to the rise in the cost of living. This does not include the more than proportional growth in fringe benefits. This indicated a worsening of the condition of various other nonunionized and nonfactory workers, since the per capita production probably increased very slowly in that year. The gap I stressed earlier undoubtedly widened. On the other hand, monthly salaries of industrial white-collar workers did not keep pace with the cost of living of this class.

In short, it appears that all developments were contrary to the plan except inflation and foreign borrowing, although the GNP, for reasons mostly unforeseen by the planners, continued to grow slowly. The key series of cement production, which increased by 150 percent in the decade 1950–1960, slackened to 19 percent from 1960 to 1962 and declined to 3 percent from 1962 to 1963.

The Ten Year Plan would doubtless have been mercifully forgotten if it had not become a sort of a basis for aid under the Alliance for Progress program and a reason for the International Bank to organize a loan program of a so-called consulting group. In a curious way, the fiction of a Plan had to be maintained to justify the continuance of that group. It had initially been badly oversold. The missions, one by the International Bank and one by the Committee of Nine, while critical of certain features and suggesting certain changes, had nevertheless approved of the goal and the general idea of obtaining the goal by an increase in general investment. Thus the Planning Office could maintain with some reason that the plan had been "approved" by the highest authorities. Actually, the International Bank has always taken the position that the responsibility for mission recommendations is borne by the head of the mission. Nevertheless, the fact that it continued with the consulting group was interpreted as giving tacit approval to the plan. Spokesmen of the United States administration, either because they did not know better or because they wanted to encourage other countries to "plan" and have an "agrarian reform," praised the Colombian initiative in extravagant terms and referred to Colombia as a showpiece of the Alliance. All this effectively spelled the doom of the type of approach that I had advocated and made it difficult to convince people that the emperor had no clothes on when so many authorities insisted that he was lavishly attired.

[2] *Boletín Mensual de Estadística,* Bogotá, Marzo, 1964, pp. 132–134.

The Bank approach differed from the ECLA approach only in being more rigorous in the application of the arithmetic in recommending more internal taxes (675 million pesos a year), less internal borrowing, and a greatly increased foreign borrowing program (from $125 million to $190 million). The 1961 figure was $40 million. In fact, the foreign borrowing program was so large that the report stated that the debt burden would rise by 1965 to $1,235,000,000, which would be "unsafe" if supplied on "conventional" terms.

On objectives, the Bank mission report accepted the ECLA–Alliance for Progress rate of growth in the GNP. It had little apparent interest in welfare or in the distribution of income and consumption. It stated: "The resources allocated for social investment in the General Plan appear to represent a reasonable compromise between the desire to accelerate social advance and the necessity to support continued economic expansion." The distinction found between "social advance" and "economic expansion" is revealing.

The diagnosis is implicit rather than explicit. It is low productivity, especially in agriculture, due to low savings and investment. "Colombia cannot achieve self-sustaining progress on its own resources. . . . there are severe limitations on what the Government can do, particularly in its ability to increase savings, to further restrain imports and to expand exports." In agriculture, "the essential task at the moment is to create circumstances which will induce commercial farmers to expand output at an increased rate and by the most economic means. Quick-yielding action must be emphasized." Fixed investment in agriculture should be increased from 458 million (1958 pesos) in 1959 to 813 million in 1964, and manpower from 2,245,000 to 2,662,000. Agricultural credit should be increased from an annual rate of 5 percent to 8 percent. Even the Institute for Agrarian Reform is exhorted "to direct its effort into situations which promise prompt and self-augmenting yields," whatever the latter may be. Returns to coffee growers, it is stated, should fall with the anticipated fall in the price of coffee. (Fortunately, in early 1964 world coffee prices rose.)

No statistical or other evidence is offered as a basis for these recommendations. If adopted, they would have resulted in a fall in average rural incomes, so it is difficult to see how even the large foreign lending program could be expected to result in a 5.6 percent growth in the GNP unless an even greater growth in inequality was expected.

In manufacturing, emphasis was to be shifted from consumer goods to capital goods and to "new" industries. Tax exemptions, promotional effort by the Instituto de Fomento Industrial, an increase in custom tariffs or "a general rise in import costs," and a $40-million-a-year external loan fund were counted upon to stimulate the growth of industry.

In short, on the objective, diagnosis, and programming, there could hardly be a greater difference between the Bank mission's views and mine, which is a most depressing commentary on the state of planning as applied to the problems of development. If Colombia, so richly endowed, cannot achieve self-sustaining progress on its own resources, the prospect is indeed gloomy for all developing countries.

In agrarian reform the program has been pushed energetically, but by its very nature not much could be done in three years. However, many land reclamation projects have been launched. These should have the effect of increasing agricultural production and investment considerably in the next few years, thus intensifying the competition for the colonial-type farmer on his tiny holding of marginal land, while improving the lot of the fortunate few. (An offsetting development would be a check to the growth of commercial-type farming.)

For a contrary view in which the enactment of land reform in Colombia is characterized rather extravagantly as "surely one of its finest hours," see Albert Hirschman.[3] Hirschman noted well along in his essay that the agricultural problem was becoming a problem of continued low rural income rather than of inadequate production. "Nevertheless, the next phase of policy-making, from 1958 to mid 1960, was marked by a somewhat hectic attempt to avoid facing this problem or dealing directly with it." The statement might with equal justice be applied to Hirschman's own treatment. Taking me to task for accepting the implications of the above statement of the problem and for attempting "to face and deal directly with it," he said, "The problem of the idle or underutilized latifundia [large estates] was still a long way from being solved."[4] Is the implication that all the land in large holdings has to be "utilized" before the problem is solved? And what problem is this: the problem of low income, or that of low production?

In LAFTA, Colombia slightly increased its imports from other Latin American countries, but sold no more to them. Up to 1964 the contribution of LAFTA to the industrialization of Colombia was nil. In fact, exports other than coffee to the world in general actually decreased in 1963 as internal costs rose relative to the export rate of exchange. A standby loan from the Monetary Fund was employed to stabilize the "free rate" of exchange.

Throughout 1963 and part of 1964, imports of American surplus goods under P.L. 480 were financed by dollar loans instead of pesos, as in the past. The reason was that the bookkeeping profits of the importing agency were in this way larger, since the government contracted the debt and the importing agency secured nearly 100 percent profits. This is an example of how complicated economics can become in developing countries. A new Minister of Agriculture, Dr. Virgilio Barco, stopped this by negotiating a new agreement providing for repayment in pesos.

In summary, the bright hopes and expectations of 1961 dimmed. Progress

[3] *Journeys toward Progress,* Twentieth Century Fund, New York, 1963, p. 131.
[4] *Ibid.*, p. 131.

continued slow and lopsided, with inequality undoubtedly growing. What progress there was, was supported by heavy foreign borrowing estimated to have reached a total of $700 to $800 million by the end of 1963, up from $350 million at the beginning of 1961. Despite the steady rise in internal costs throughout 1963 and 1964, the rate available for exports other than coffee was pegged. Exports consequently were increasingly difficult until near the end of 1964, when a heavy run forced the authorities to abandon the pegging, at least for the time being, and the free rate rose sharply with a favorable but rather disorderly effect on minor exports. As a testing ground, Colombia can offer a rare assortment of monetary, fiscal, and exchange experiments, but it is to be feared that there is little which is original in these experiments and that the results have been strictly in accordance with informed economic expectations.

In short, by 1965, in comparison with 1961, the situation had sensibly deteriorated. Despite the Alliance and growing debt, production did little more than keep pace with population and was most unevenly distributed; despite LAFTA, exports to other member countries remained insignificant; with the collapse of the much touted Ten Year Development Plan shortly after it was announced, the country remained in reality without a plan; despite Agrarian Reform and the army, into both of which large sums were channeled, rural violence continued and was more recently accompanied by widespread kidnapping of wealthier farmers. It began to be doubtful whether the great potentialities of commercial type farming, herein stressed, could be realized.

As was perhaps inevitable in a country of little economic understanding and widespread poverty, increasing uncoordinated intervention and proposals to nationalize this or that or freeze this or that appeared. A new vicious circle of slow growth—impatience—recriminations—radical proposals—declining confidence—slow growth began to appear. The solution to the economic problem became daily more difficult with the interaction of cultural, political, and economic factors inimicable to rapid progress.

No forecast is offered here because it is hoped that policy will be reoriented. However, it is obviously possible that if present trends continue, in a relatively short time the level of foreign borrowing will be near the Bank mission's "safe" limit; but despite this rapid increase in debt, no corresponding significant rise in the condition of the poorer half of the people will have taken place. Moreover, industrial expansion will be characterized by a spectacular growth in petrochemical plants, auto assembly plants, and synthetic fiber plants, duplicating Venezuelan capacity in these fields, rather than in wage goods; building activity will continue in luxury homes, slums, and apartment and office building, with growing traffic congestion and continued large and increasing expenditures on urban roads and transport; a few show pieces in agrarian reform will have been completed, providing a solution, at considerable expense, for a few thousand farmers. In short, it is probable that the country will have used up most of its borrowing capacity on conventional terms with no breakthrough having been achieved.

This pessimistic outlook need not materialize, but unless a drastic change takes place, it can very well be the consequence of present policies. If so, foreign lenders cannot escape their share of responsibility. It may serve a purpose in demonstrating that aid taking the form of mere additions to capital formation, even when substantial, is not enough; but it seems hardly necessary to provide yet another demonstration of this fact. The uninspiring prospect can always be changed by extraneous events, such as a drastic change in the world coffee market, or great oil discoveries within the country, or by the continuance of the extravagantly high exchange rate for minor exports that a flight of capital brought about in 1965, but such developments could not be credited to any national plan of development.

There is a further danger that should be kept in mind. The acceleration principle appears to apply to a foreign borrowing program. At first there is a lack of suitable, well-prepared projects, and much time is spent on ironing out legal and technical difficulties. As these are overcome, actual commitments and disbursements tend to accelerate. Thus the year preceding the outbreak of alarm over the volume of total foreign debt could be a prosperous year with a buoyant trend in the indexes commonly used to indicate growth. Such a possible development would be an additional obstacle to the adoption of any basic change in policy. The possibility places even greater responsibility on the foreign lenders. Insofar as the growth in the GNP is dependent on foreign borrowing, even a slowing up in the rate of growth, to say nothing of its cessation, can have profound reactions on the borrowing country. The acceleration principle can work in reverse.

A similar danger is that if there are abundant exchange resources and imports financed by loans, the "free" or export rate of exchange may be held too low for too long a time, with consequent prejudice to the development of exports, as happened in 1963–1964.

In view of the complete failure of the plans and reforms of 1961 in the immediately succeeding years, one may perhaps be forgiven for pointing out that the burden of proof now rests on the national and international authorities. Will they continue to rely on the General Plan of Development, the Alliance for Progress, the agrarian reform, and the Free Trade Association? Or will they make a basic reappraisal of the problem? A third possibility, of course, would be to try out a new approach in an easier and more receptive country.

CHAPTER 14

Application of Breakthrough Plan to Colombia

THE BREAKTHROUGH PROGRAM of accelerated development sketched in Part One would appear to apply admirably to Colombia. The requisite technical conditions of (1) an industrial base, with most plants working on a single shift, (2) mastery of the beginnings of technification in agriculture, (3) relatively large numbers of subsistence farmers and low-income casual laborers, (4) great possibilities of augmenting exports, (5) rich resources in relation to population, although the population is increasing very rapidly, (6) great inequality of income, with consequent distortions in the production-consumption pattern, (7) insufficient mobility of labor, (8) lack of an incomes policy and a national urban development policy, (9) excellent credit standing to facilitate foreign borrowing—all these elements suggest the need and the applicability of an accelerated development program.

The obstacles to application of the breakthrough program might be listed as:

1. Parts of the important cotton textile industry, and certain others as well, are already on a three-shift basis.
2. Urban public services are generally already overloaded, and housing is deficient.
3. The government and international agencies have shown themselves disinclined to depart from a conventional approach—a very severe obstacle indeed.

Rather than repeat in more detail all the elements of the breakthrough approach presented in Part One, I shall assume that the reader is now familiar with that plan and the diagnosis as applied to Colombia. The discussion in this chapter will be confined to special aspects of the situation in Colombia.

First Steps

1. It is obvious that the international and national lending agencies must first reach agreement on some basic principles, viz., that they will pool their resources and act in concert in furthering the type of approach presented here.

2. Agreement must then, of course, be reached with the government on the nature of the program. (It is conceivable, though unlikely, that the initiative might be taken by Colombia and later agreement be reached with the associated lenders.)

3. Next would come the creation of the new administrative agencies required—chiefly the development fund and the home loan authority—and the planning of the program in qualitative and quantitative terms by foreign and national technicians. In a program of this nature, one would naturally prefer to have all details planned and programmed in advance—the way a general would like to wage a war, and with various alternatives at hand. But, as in war, this is expecting too much. All we can reasonably ask is that as large a portion as possible of the internal and external resources of the community be mobilized and allocated to the program; that we strive for concentration of effort and consistency of aims; that while pushing ahead as fast as we can, we are alert to bypass obstacles and break bottlenecks. Again, the analogy of a war would help.

4. In the process of determining magnitudes, goals, investment requirements, probable bottlenecks, and so on, criteria could be developed for internal and external loans, rationing of imports, the granting of building licenses, and accelerated depreciation allowances.

5. As soon as tentative overall objectives were determined (the number of additional nonagricultural jobs, their localization, and housing requirements) they could be translated into projected effective demand and production by sectors, the feasibility of the goals could be assessed, and limiting factors requiring special action could be singled out.

6. At this stage it might prove desirable to organize a number of industry or economic activity committees (including, of course, trade-union representatives) to work with the central planning office and development fund on bottleneck problems, recruitment problems, incomes policies, and so on. This is not as formidable as it probably sounds, because much of Colombian industry is in relatively few units and is well organized, and some branches of agriculture are also well organized.

7. Concurrently with the economic programming should be a somewhat differently constituted group working on the first stage of a long-range master urban development plan for the country. This plan would have to be reconciled with the economic program.

8. Still another group of technicians could be working on possible steps

in an integration program with Venezuela and a coordination of such steps with the economic and urban development programs.

9. Another field requiring careful study would be that of exports, both in general terms and product by product. This study would be separate from but coordinated with the joint Venezuelan-Colombian study.

10. At an early stage it would be desirable to improve and expand the necessary basic statistical series, so that the whole program could be followed closely and currently.

11. As considerable resistance and skepticism would undoubtedly be encountered, it would be prudent to set modest goals for the first full-year operation, and after easing into the program, to accelerate it as fast as bottlenecks and the elasticity of supply in critical areas (food production, for example) permitted.

12. Even before the programs were worked out, it would probably be desirable through informal administrative action to prevent anticipatory action inconsistent with the program, such as starting construction of a large number of luxury-type homes, office and apartment buildings, etc.

13. The central planning office, working closely with the development fund, would be charged with keeping the President informed and advising on the coordination of fiscal, monetary, and exchange policies and general economic programming.

14. Close study of the tax system and collection methods, as well as study of government management methods in general, should be started at an early date.

Sundry Reflections

In short, although the breakthrough program involves a minimum of direct government operation and relies in its working out on the profit motive and the desire of people to improve their condition, accelerating development does require an intense planning effort. It would be a great mistake for the foreign group not to provide as strong a team of economists as possible, since Colombia as yet has few highly trained economists with experience in the field of imaginative overall programming. It has been pointed out that in the process of a country's development, the highly skilled and specialized workers are increasingly engaged in designing the new machines and programming work, while the actual operation demands fewer skills. The analogy applies in part to the planning and execution of an accelerated development program.

It was remarked in Part One that the program abounds in paradoxes. It is, therefore, essential that the President, ministers, and other important members of the government and Congress be thoroughly briefed and in a position to explain and defend the program in all its aspects. This in turn requires that a close liaison be maintained between the planning group and the government.

In addition to the creation and organization of the development fund and the home loan authority, it would be desirable to secure legislative authority to create urban renovation authorities in the main cities, with wide powers for acquiring land by the issuance of bonds with cost-of-living escalator clauses and for the planning and development of large urban areas. (There is a renovation authority for Bogotá, but its powers and financing are limited.) Changes in tax legislation which eliminate further grants of exemption for "basic" industries, for exports and other purposes would be desirable. The suggestion made in Part One to apply accelerated depreciation allowances to industries where intensive use of equipment and rapid additional expansion in productive capacity are desired would be a helpful instrument in ensuring cooperation, in increasing savings and facilitating financing, and in conjunction with an incomes policy, in avoiding price and cost advances instead of additional employment and production.

Authority to alter the provisions of the Labor Code insofar as it relates to extra pay for night work, to convert certain holidays into work days with double pay, and to exempt certain industries and firms from application of the general provisions of the Code *at the request of the union* would be desirable. General authority to change and regulate exchange rates and conduct foreign trade should be conferred on the government by Congress, since these are generally not suitable subjects for specific legislation.

By its nature the breakthrough program introduces an element of discontinuity in the economy and makes projections on the basis of past experience somewhat hazardous. In fact, the success of the program depends on a change in past relationships of investment to production, investment to employment, and imports to production, as well as a change in the composition of production and consumption. However, we are probably safe in assuming that the bulk of the demand in the first instance will be concentrated on housing, public services, foodstuffs, beer and soft drinks, cotton textiles, shoes, commerce, transport (both urban and long distance), and other miscellaneous goods and services (furniture, toys, school supplies, movies, etc.).

The initial pump-priming operation would be in a large expansion in housing and public services. The actual additional employment in this field, however, would be by private contractors, who presumably would do their own recruiting. The increased employment in all the other fields would also, in very large part, be by private firms and individuals. The only additional public employment would be in municipal services of all kinds.

A point to be studied is how far the recruitment should be left entirely in private hands and how far the state should seek to influence the location and kind of recruiting. If the matter were left entirely to private companies, there would probably be some competitive bidding for actual trained workers, thus raising costs and decreasing employment. Thereafter, the preference would doubtless be for artisans from smaller towns and workers from mechanized farms. Small farmers and squatters, without savings, references, connections, or training, might have difficulty securing urban employment, though of course they would benefit indirectly from the increased demand for food, and from employment opportunities in small towns and on mechanized farms. An argument could be made for a special program to take young people from isolated areas with no future and give them special SENA[1] training and help in securing jobs. This would involve recruitment, loans, and dormitories. In such cases the gain in productivity would be almost 100 percent. The dangers are the usual ones of inefficiency in public bodies and of political pressures.

In Colombia, it would appear on balance advisable to take special measures to recruit younger men from rural areas that are overcrowded or manifestly have no economic future because of erosion, unfavorable terrain or climate, or distance from markets.

Organization of Housing Program

The previous section discussed the nature of the housing program and the administrative devices to carry it out. Attention will be devoted here to the problem of mobilizing the capital, physical resources, and demand necessary to carry out a great effort in this field. It is assumed that the major part of the construction, by value, will be (1) in high-rise apartment buildings in which the individual apartments will be for rent or for purchase, and (2) in single-family dwellings or low apartment buildings away from the centers and near factories. It is hoped that all this housing will be constructed by private builders. Certain changes are desirable, however, to ensure a much larger supply and demand for this type of construction.

The common assumption is that the poor record in the private provision of low- and medium-cost housing has its basis in the shortage of capital. Certainly it has its basis in the relative unattractiveness of housing as an investment for private capital. In this case, as in others, an attempt was made to adapt Northern institutions and procedures to the peculiar conditions of Colombia, with indifferent results. Long-term borrowing up to 80 to 90 percent of the cost of a home at fixed low rates of interest is possible only where the value of money is relatively stable and there are large amounts of savings available for investment in this form. Under conditions where the value of money customarily and normally falls more than any fixed acceptable rate of return can compensate for, reliance on fixed-rate mortgages for home financing in effect restricts the amount of capital available to that provided by the government and by institutions whose obligations are likewise fixed. This, of course, is an inadequate amount.

[1] A government apprentice training institute.

Actually, potential homeowners do not require the prospect of valorization and fixity in repayment of borrowings and interest as inducements. They are content merely with the opportunity of acquiring ownership by a small down payment, and with remaining payments spread over a period of years so that the cost of shelter bears a reasonable relation to income. The present system, therefore, penalizes would-be lenders and confers unnecessary benefits on those fortunate enough to secure fixed loans. The outcome of this inequitable system is high down payments, short-term loans, and an inadequate volume of building. Acquiring a home, instead of being the normal prerogative of all citizens, partakes more of the nature of a lottery.

While the country has managed to get by, after a fashion, under the present system, it obviously would be unable to cope with the housing requirements envisaged under the breakthrough plan. For this, the provision of housing *must* be made attractive to private capital. The method proposed is briefly as follows:

1. Private, bank and insurance company, and government funds would be pooled in a single home mortgage institution.
2. This institution would be permitted to issue obligations to private nonbank, noninsurance company lenders whose interest and amortization are linked with the cost-of-living index, and to collect from mortgagees an adjustment to compensate for the fall in the purchasing power of money. Lenders will thus be guaranteed against any loss of purchasing power of their loans and interest receipts, and in addition will receive a good rate of return.
3. Variable payments would be required only on the proportion of the total funds represented by private funds.
4. Mortgages could be granted up to 85–90 percent of the cost of new homes and for 15 years for the purchase of houses that meet certain specifications, whether for occupancy or for renting.
5. Loans from individuals and banks could be repayable over a 10-year period. The difference resulting from amortization of these 10-year loans and the 15-year mortgages will be supplied by the government out of income from its loans to the home mortgage institution—or if this proves insufficient, out of new loans. There will also be a difference arising from the cost-of-living bonuses being paid by homeowners on amortization payments on a 15-year basis and being received by lenders on a 10-year basis.
6. Any losses resulting from foreclosures could be borne by the government, if the reserves of the mortgage institution prove insufficient.
7. Short-term construction loans up to 80 percent of the cost of construction, and 2-year land acquisition loans up to 80 percent of the cost, would likewise be available to developers who undertake to build homes to the required specifications and prices.
8. Home construction to be initially financed under this program would

be of two types—low-cost single- or two-family homes near factories and other working places in the suburbs, and apartment buildings in large-scale developments in the accessible but blighted areas of large cities.

9. The above measures should be accompanied by other measures to reduce the cost of homes. These would include a rise in the property tax on unimproved land within city limits, combined with a reduction on housing built in accordance with the program. Also, committees would be formed to study and recommend measures to reduce legal costs and unnecessary delays in administrative procedures.

This program may appear a little drastic, but it is considered the minimum necessary to accomplish the purpose. For the first time it would make lending for housing attractive to private savers. It would resolve the problem of the down payment and length of time for repayment, and it would make development operations for low-cost homes feasible. Government funds would be used as leverage to secure private participation instead of being the main source of funds.

As opposed to these advantages, the prospective homeowner would face the possibility that the interest and principal repayment on a portion of his borrowing would rise with the cost of living. But in that case, it is presumed that both his income and the total value of his home also are rising, and it is not believed that this will be a deterrent to buying houses. Provision could even be made at small cost to set up a fund for the rare hard-luck cases where incomes do not rise proportionaly to the cost of living.

This is a tentative approach to medium-cost home financing. The essential ideas of escalator clauses in private loans, and the use of government funds as a means of giving somewhat different terms to private and institutional lenders on the one hand and borrowers on the other, are believed to be sound. Exactly what form the subsidy should take and what amount it would be, however, require more study. The advantages of a flat combined interest-amortization rate of repayment would have to be weighed against the greater subsidy required and the higher cost-of-living adjustment to be paid by borrowers in the later years. The possibilities of utilizing a greater proportion of industry balances by offering one-year notes each year would have to be studied, as well as other alternatives.

Foreign Economic Policy

This section will treat exchange rate policy, foreign borrowing, and export and import substitution policies. In Colombia two circumstances are of paramount importance in this general field. One is the dominant position of coffee in the country's exportations. The other is the great inequality of incomes. The significance of the latter is that if imports were controlled only by the rate of exchange, the demand for luxury consumer goods, foreign travel, remittances of capital, etc., would be so strong that the rate would be very high, which in turn would encourage consumption by the coffee growers, decrease national saving, and result in a high cost of imported capital and intermediate goods. Purists may reply that in that case we should secure a better income distribution, but up to now Colombians have preferred other controls on imports.

Foreign-exchange specialists have always been somewhat criticial, impatient, or irritated with Colombian exchange policy, and undoubtedly it has on occasion been ill-advised or unnecessarily complicated. But it is most important that foreign specialists understand the underlying nature of the problem and be more sympathetic in helping to work out solutions.

After having risen greatly, dollar receipts from sales of coffee returned by 1963 to where they had started in 1951.[2] And yet, despite the fall in the price of coffee and the relatively low coffee rate of exchange of 7.30 pesos to a dollar, the coffee grower on a holding of 5 to 6 hectares in the better areas of the country could still make a better living than he could in other forms of agriculture. The low returns of most producers were a consequence of excessively small holdings that did not provide sufficient work or income.

On the other hand, the absolute advantage of coffee is such that at a rate adequate to call forth permitted production, the country cannot export anything else. And yet the progress of the country and the necessary imports require more foreign exchange. It is not perversity that explains the existence of another rate of exchange for other exports, but necessity. For import substitution, the low coffee rate can be offset by high customs protection. For other exports, however, there must be a higher rate or, what seems to be much worse, concealed subsidies in barter deals or in other ways. What are urgently needed are different conversion rates for coffee and for other exports to secure the volume of exchange needed. The higher rate is *not* a subsidy rate or dumping rate, but rather a rate at which it is barely possible to export things other than coffee.

We may now consider the second characteristic that gives rise to criticism—the system of rationing or licensing exchange. Clearly, such a system lends itself to abuse, to arbitrary and even capricious decisions, to weakening the forces of competition and strengthening tendencies to monopoly, and even to bribery and favoritism. On the other hand, given the pattern of distribution of incomes and the income elasticity of demand, as well as the prevailing political and economic insecurity, it would appear uneconomic and unrealistic to imagine that any rate of exchange would be a self-equilibrating rate or would ensure a good allocation of exchange. All we can hope to do is to reduce the extent of individual official decisions, improve the

[2] Coffee prices rose 25% in the first two months of 1964 and the bulk of the rise was retained through 1964 and 1965.

theoretical basis of allocation, discourage excessive imports of luxury goods by higher customs duties, and discourage foreign travel, contraband, and capital remittances in other ways. At the present time, the licensing authorities lack clear, soundly based criteria on which to make decisions.

It is suggested, therefore, that the criterion for the determination of the rate of exchange to apply to coffee receipts should be that rate necessary to evoke Colombia's quota of sales under the world coffee pact. Presumably such a rate would permit the owner of a 5-hectare farm a good livelihood in relation to other types of farming.

It is suggested that a second and higher rate apply to other exports, such as bananas, cotton, sugar, meat, etc., and that the proceeds of such exports be made available by the exchange licensing authorities for specific purposes, such as travel abroad for business or professional reasons, other travel (with a supplementary tax), and capital remittances of clearly specified types. For the remaining exchange, licenses might be granted for certain classes of goods, or probably better, people granted licenses would pay a composite rate determined by the percentage of exchange available for goods imports, payment of interest, etc., derived from each of the rates.

There would clearly be a final rate that could be known as the contraband rate. The supply of foreign funds for this market would come from clandestine exports, import of unregistered capital, overvaluation of imports, and some travelers. In general, foreign governments, representatives, and travelers could be appealed to not to sell dollars at other than the export rate through banks and registered dealers. By making it unpatriotic to use the "contraband rate" and by providing foreign exchange for most purposes at the export rate, the government could keep the supply of foreign exchange at the former rate low and prevent much capital from being exported, except at prohibitive cost.

In the course of time it is to be hoped and expected that proceeds from the export rate would exceed those at the coffee rate. Imports would be made at both the certificate rate and the higher export rate. The composite rate at which foreign exchange would be available for most purposes would be somewhere between the certificate and the export rates. As it is to be expected that the rates would be changed infrequently and in line with changes in the cost of living, and the proportions of exchange available at the two rates would change slowly, importers would generally know what to anticipate, and the element of uncertainty would not be great.

The criteria for licensing exchange would presumably be included in the general unspecified loan agreement with the foreign lending group. It would probably be desirable to leave a large measure of discretion to the development fund in framing its recommendations to the licensing authorities. In general, as much as possible of the exchange available for goods import should be used to permit companies to use their existing equipment as intensively as possible, except where this necessitates heavy imports of raw materials and intermediate goods in fields not considered essential to meet the demands for housing and articles of mass consumption. The closer a company in these former fields approached a full-capacity rate of operations, the higher would become its priority for imports. The more a capital good is shown to be essential for the inauguration, let us say, of a second shift, the higher its priority. Clearly, all equipment for the purchase of which the development fund made loans would have high priority. This field would require continuous and expert analysis and would presumably occupy a good part of the time of the development fund staff.

In addition to assuring the best use of foreign exchange, it is urgent to increase the supply through the development of new exports. The two policies should proceed together, and the suggestions are designed to accomplish this. However, it is important to bear in mind that merely providing a better rate, while essential, is not sufficient. Each possible export has its own peculiar problems and should be accorded individual study.

I gave considerable time to the study of how cattle exports might be initiated.[3] It early appeared that the quality of Colombian meat, particularly because of the age at which it is marketed, was not good enough to compete in world markets, and that under existing conditions, it did not pay to improve the quality. It did not appear practicable to try to carve out an enclave of high-quality cattle specifically for the external market.

The only alternative seemed to be to create a well-financed fund which would, through its investments, enter into domestic *and* external marketing, eliminating the hoard of middlemen, and setting grades of quality. The fund would pay premium prices direct to the producer for young animals of high quality, and it would charge higher prices for premium meat to the well-to-do consumer while maintaining lower prices for the present second- and third-class meat for the poorer customers. This new approach from the side of demand gained many adherents among the various cattle associations and was endorsed by the government. However, it was opposed by the agencies whose business it is to loan to the producers, even though such loans demonstrably were doing nothing to increase demand, improve quality, or lessen the wide spread in prices paid the producer and charged the consumer, and even though higher and better demand would permit a more technical loan operation.

In the case of cotton, a promising export market was at least temporarily lost when internal costs and prices moved up relative to the export rate. If the export rate on the basis of 1961 had been adjusted in accordance

[3] As director of the so-called Currie-Anderson Cattle Study for the National Railroads in 1961 and as director of a study made by the Foundation for the Progress of Colombia for the Cattle Bank and Regional Corporation of the Valley of the Magdalena in 1962. Results were presented in two addresses and an *anteproyecto de ley* (draft of a bill).

with the rise in the cost of living, it would have remained possible to continue the export of cotton without loss in 1964.[4]

In any case, the lessons are that each possible export has its own peculiar problems and that any reform must contend with existing vested interests. As remarked before, the flight from the peso and the repayment of private dollar debts forced the abandonment in October, 1964, of the policy of supporting the free rate of 10 pesos to a dollar. The rate subsequently soared. This gave an enormous stimulus to reported minor exports and there were reports of the renewal of a large clandestine export of all types of goods to Venezuela. I am not advocating anything like this, since the rate gave excessive windfall profits and threatened maladjustments in the domestic market. However, the episode does suggest that the type of policy advocated herein could be used to help secure an orderly and controlled expansion in exports other than coffee.

One approach which has won some support is that of barter deals or tied selling (*compensación*). Its adherents maintain that to sell to certain countries, this is the only practical method. However, the familiar objections to barter deals still hold. In order to sell, one frequently accepts something one does not particularly want or at a higher price than it can be obtained elsewhere. A case comes to mind where, to dispose of an excess of potatoes, the import of very costly sports cars was permitted. Undoubtedly, isolated cases can be found where barter may be justified, but the ideal should be to attempt to have the proceeds of foreign sales available for the most urgent necessities of the country on the best international terms.

The large short-term commercial debt contracted during the Administration of General Rojas was in large part unjustified, insofar as it led to imports of luxury consumer goods and insofar as it was not matched by a growth in the country's ability to repay. The later large short-term borrowings of 1961–1962 probably represented better value. After running up a large debt and repaying most of it in the decade of the fifties, in the process devoting enormous time and energy to the matter, the country ended with about the same capacity to repay, with an average growth in per capita gross product of a little over 1 percent, and with probably growing inequality in income and consumption. It would have been infinitely better if some of this energy had been devoted to the development of more exports rather than to borrowings.

The only aspect of early formulations of the breakthrough program that the International Bank and the Committee of Nine were disposed to accept, at least in part, was the proposal to provide loans to underwrite a program's foreign-exchange requirements, instead of having a host of unrelated specific

[4] Lauchlin Currie, *El Algodón en Colombia* (Cotton in Colombia), Foundation for the Progress of Colombia, Bogotá, 1963.

projects (or of making a fund available for unspecified loans to the private sector). This small triumph, however, was nullified by the nature of the general program with which it was linked. The theory is still sound, but it assumed a carefully worked out plan. In the absence of such a plan, the $40 million of unspecified loans a year that is currently (1965) being made is dissipated in financing an unprogrammed deficit in the current balance of payments, and a diffused program of public investment—another case where a sound idea may be damaged through faulty application.

It is customary to stress worsening terms of trade as an explanation of Colombia's difficulties and to talk of the need for loans, stabilization of coffee prices and markets, and the development of a Latin American Free Trade Association. While I have laid considerable emphasis on the desirability of loans, under certain conditions, and the need for more exports, I have had little to say about coffee and the Free Trade Association. The explanation is that although it is most important that Colombia maintain its percentage in world coffee exports at prices as favorable as possible, and that Colombia explore the possibilities of the Free Trade Association, I have sought to emphasize here the things the country can do for itself in the near future, rather than distant objectives difficult of realization.

The inspiration of the Free Trade Association was, of course, the European Common Market. The great success of the latter should not cause us to underestimate the enormous difficulties and the vastly different conditions confronting Latin American countries, including chronic monetary and exchange instability, differing stages of development, lack of contiguity, and so forth. The technical difficulties of persistently lowering trade barriers and maintaining general equilibrium in the volume of trade among nine or more scattered countries are truly formidable.

For this reason it would appear that we should still devote our major effort to the development of certain primary exports such as meat and cotton and should make a new and well-organized approach to developing the Venezuelan, Colombian, and Ecuadorean trade zone. This offers a truly grand opportunity, and the type of program proposed here offers a means of overcoming the difficulties that have blocked any progress in the past. The economies of Venezuela and Colombia, in particular, are in part complementary. With combined available exchange for imports of $2 billion, a good industrial base, and a market of 25 million people with rapidly rising incomes, great economies of scale could be obtained for industrial expansion.

The secret of the successful formation of a customs union is a rapid expansion in the respective home markets and in the demand for each others' products. This is precisely what the program set forth here is designed to achieve. A reduction in the trade barriers must not throw people out of work. The expansion in effective demand would be so great that there would be abundant demand for equipment and available manpower in the countries concerned.

There is probably no need to persuade Colombia of the tremendous advantages that would flow from the addition of 8 million nearby higher-income customers for the products of Colombian industry and agriculture, and the possibility of earning dollars. The real difficulty would lie in assuring Venezuela that she too would benefit and that her small-scale industry would not be threatened. As part of the overall program, it might be to Colombia's advantage to agree to restrain the growth of its heavy iron and steel and petrochemical industries as a means of regulating the total volume of purchases and sales of all goods from and to Venezuela. As Venezuela could supply only a part of Colombia's requirements for goods now imported, it is to be expected that Venezuela would switch part of her purchases from abroad to Colombia and that her imports from Colombia would exceed her exports, so that dollars would become available to Colombia to supplement those derived from its exports to third countries.

With the adoption by each country of the type of national program proposed here, the trade barriers could be lowered rapidly without occasioning any unemployment, since the overall effective demand would be increasing rapidly. It is estimated that the creation of some 550,000 additional urban jobs in Colombia alone would result in an increase in effective demand for goods and services of some 6 billion pesos (1958). At the present time, any lowering of barriers is thought to threaten some national enterprises or to result in loss of exchange. Thus restrictive, timid policies encourage more restrictions and timidity. It is very fortunate that the Valle del Cauca and the coast did not break away from the rest of Colombia. If they had, there would now be every possible barrier to trade and interchange among the three separate countries. All would be much poorer, and all would present strong arguments why they would be ruined by lowering trade barriers between them.

The European Common Market is one of the outstanding economic achievements of our time. It was possible because of contiguity and skillful policies that geared the lowering of barriers to internal expansion. Owing to the immense number of vested interests and national differences, the achievement of a common market was a task of infinitely greater technical difficulty than that of a common market between Venezuela, Colombia, and Ecuador would be. If this obviously mutually beneficial first step cannot be achieved, it would appear doubtful that much progress with a Latin American Free Trade Association could be made. To put aside this grand opportunity and to proceed cautiously with most of the other Latin American countries at the same time probably means that there will be little to show for a great effort.

Given the common cultural background and similar political and economic institutions, it would seem reasonable that freedom in trade within the "Bolivian association" would in time be accompanied by freedom in the movement of people and capital and by the adoption of certain common policies. Thus Colombia's need for dollars, the Venezuelan need for markets, and the mutual need to raise the well-being of the people could provide the driving force to overcome the ancient fears and suspicions that hold both countries back and have resulted in an incalculable loss in welfare for the people of these countries.

The first steps would be the creation of study groups in both countries (and later Ecuador), the adoption of expansive and complementary national economic programs, and the institution of a permanent inter-country commission which would have powers to undertake, on the basis of sound and agreed-upon criteria, a progressive lowering of exchange and customs barriers and agreements to meet increases in demand for specific products. Further steps in the direction of broadening this union by joining with more countries could await its initial success.

A combination of induced industrial expansion, technification of agriculture, and free trade and movement within the Bolivian Association could result in one of the highest rates of growth in well-being in the world. Unfortunately, its attainment requires vision, understanding, and dedication —qualities in very short supply.

The Agricultural Policy

The reader will recall the lengthy treatment of agriculture in Chapter 12 on the diagnosis for Colombia. The discussion centered on the fact that the greatest pool of underutilized labor is in the agricultural sector. In fact, a major part of the motivation of the breakthrough plan is to provide more remunerative work for as many actual rural workers as possible and to increase the effective demand for the production of the others.

Once this was declared to be the objective and a program was launched to accomplish it, the way would be cleared for an all-out effort to mechanize and technify agriculture. This would imply less land and fewer workers and a concentration of effort in the best and most accessible land. A new land-use pattern would naturally evolve, replacing that which has existed since colonial days. It is hoped that every attempt would be made to enter the world market with more primary products, a move which would supply needed exchange and reduce the amount of labor and land to be retired from agriculture.

As was discussed earlier, we are only on the threshold of the possibilities in this field. Now that the first essentials of mechanization and technification have been grasped, progress can be as rapid as jobs can be found for displaced labor. The urban part of the program would be the limiting factor; not the ability to feed, clothe, and export.

In the case of coffee, there are also great possibilities for increasing yields per hectare and per family. The problems here are those of providing urban employment for most of the coffee growers who are now on the smallest holdings and of assisting others to acquire economic-sized units. If we keep in mind that the acquisition of land, from the national economic point of view, is not a cost, and that the major obstacle up to now has been the lack of alternative employment, it should not be difficult to work out a system of incentives and deterrents which will check the process of subdividing (*minifundia*) and initiate a program of consolidation of holdings in the best areas.

Naturally, the same considerations apply to cattle raising. Since a relatively small area of the best lands, well cultivated, can supply the requirements of the domestic market, Colombia, unlike most other countries, can afford to practice intensive cattle raising on the rich alluvial soils of the Magdalena and Sinu Valleys. With protection from flooding and/or better drainage, these lands can carry a greatly augmented livestock population which will counterbalance the low costs of extensive nontechnical operations on the poorer but cheaper plainlands.

Increasing technification and productivity do not necessarily mean increasing diversion of national savings to agriculture. Concentration of the best lands along existing lines of transport would permit large increases with relatively small investment. As pointed out earlier, England has perhaps the most mechanized and productive agriculture in the world and yet the annual investment is only 3.5 percent of total investment and replacement. In Colombia's Ten-Year Plan the projection for agriculture was 12 percent, not including rural roads, education, and public services in rural towns.

To expedite the conversion to commercial-type farming, much reliance could be placed on the various credit agencies and on the coordination and reorientation of agricultural research. It is urged that the activities of the Agrarian Reform Institute (INCORA) be concentrated on the conversion of renters and sharecroppers into owners with equipment and knowledge of commercial-type farming and on the consolidation of small uneconomic farming units into economic-sized units.

The discussion to this point provides the theoretical basis for the agricultural and agrarian program that should be an integral part of the operation. Specific ways and means of encouraging productivity in commercial farming are too well known and constitute such a large field that it is not proposed to try to discuss them here.

As a general rule, main reliance in hastening the conversion should be placed on the profit motive. The state can, however, do much to lower costs through work on agricultural experimentation and research; on transport costs; on costs of machinery, parts, and diesel fuel; and on marketing and distribution costs. In addition, through the provision of roads and reclamation works it can influence the development of cultivation in the best-suited and -situated lands from the point of view of achieving lowest costs per hectare in relation to yields. For example, through a regional corporation, the successive development of one river valley after another in the western part of Meta can be guided in order to secure the economies of concentration of effort.[5] In such cases, where financing of roads and hydraulic works is necessary, the regional authority is justified in exerting certain pressures and force, if necessary, to secure adequate utilization of land to lower the per hectare cost of public works provided by the state.

A regional authority will, it is to be hoped, properly determine priorities within its region in terms of calculated ratios of benefits and costs. A national body is needed, however, to decide on priorities between the top-priority projects in different regions. In the present circumstances, this could well be the National Planning Office. For lack of such overall decisions, works are being initiated that would assuredly have low priority on a national scale.

Conservation of Natural Resources

In the diagnosis, the current appalling destruction of natural resources was attributed to the overcrowding and poverty of rural dwellers, rather than the absence of adequate laws. It is believed that only when these basic conditions are remedied will it be possible to enforce the laws, permit the regrowth of forests, protect fish, and restore and maintain the fertility of the soil.

Personal and Property Security

The immediate combating of violence in Colombia is outside the scope of this study. It is believed, however, that the root causes can be traced again to poverty and ignorance and that over the long run, measures to provide urban jobs, raise the incomes of those in the country, and concentrate agriculture in the richest sections, will be the most effective ways to achieve a larger measure of security for life and property in rural regions.

Transport Policy

The breakthrough program will be reflected in transport requirements and policy in various ways. The rapid growth of the larger cities will mean both more inward- and more outward-moving freight, to be shared by the various means of transport, depending on the city. The growth of both exports and imports will also mean more traffic, though to a much less degree for trucks and the river transport than for the railroads. The growth

[5] This suggestion was spelled out in my study of the state of Meta, 1960.

of the cities will mean more traffic for the airlines, both in passengers and cargo. Traffic between the large cities in the interior will greatly increase requirements both for railroad rolling stock and trucks and buses. The increased food requirements of the cities will result in both more short-haul truck movements and more long-haul rail traffic.

The economic advantages of concentration and the costs arising from dispersion of population are not generally realized. Transport is one of the important elements in the cost of production, particularly in Colombia, and everything should be done to minimize it. The more the market for the products of industry is concentrated, the lower the per unit cost of transport. The heavier the traffic, say between two cities, the lower again is the transport cost per unit. The fewer the penetration roads it is necessary to build, and the shorter the distances they must cover, the better.

There are, of course, offsetting considerations. Soil and climatic factors may make it less costly to haul agricultural goods greater distances. However, the principle still holds. The fewer the transport routes and the more heavily utilized they are, the lower the transport cost per unit of goods moved. Therefore, the more the population is concentrated in the cities, and the more the exploitation of natural resources is carried on near cities, or near main heavily used lines of transport, the lower will transport costs figure in the final price of goods.

There is a characteristic of a large fixed-capital investment that is not generally appreciated. Before such an investment is made, it is natural to assume that it will be based on studies indicating that it will earn at least the going rate of return. Once the investment is made, however, any returns over and above operating costs constitute a net gain, even if lower rates are set to secure the additional traffic that would be necessary to cover all fixed charges at a given volume of traffic. In reality no attempt is made to cover the going rate of return on the capital invested in highways, and road transport charges need only cover what in the case of a railroad would be called operating costs and depreciation and maintenance of rolling stock.

When these considerations are applied to the case of the Atlantic Railroad, several conclusions of great importance may be drawn. A large investment of some $120 million (converting peso expenditures at the rate of exchange prevailing when they were made) has been made. The capacity of the line for rapid-haul traffic is far in excess of immediately available cargo. In fact, it is likely that because of the initial low volume of cargo and its unbalanced nature, the railroad will not at first be able to earn the going rate of return on investment. On the other hand, the *operating costs* per ton-kilometer will be very low, perhaps 2 centavos per ton-kilometer upward, 1 centavo downward (assuming down-haul traffic is only 25 percent of upward).[6] Therefore, from the point of view of the railroad,

[6] Based on 1958 prices. Lauchlin Currie and Henry Eder, "La Conexión del Ferrocarril del Atlántico con Barranquilla" (The Connection of the Atlantic Railroad

any additional traffic at a tariff that will leave something above these costs is a net gain. The same is true from a national economic point of view. In considering which regions of the country are most economic to develop, this factor should be kept in mind, and the comparison of transport costs should be between railroad *operating* costs and truck transport costs. Such a comparison will go far to offset the generally greater distance of the Magdalena area from the main consuming centers. Moreover, the existence of unbalanced traffic would justify very low rates to encourage down-haul traffic, especially exports. Another conclusion is that, for the lower valley of the Magdalena, considerable emphasis should be placed on the provision of connecting roads to the railroad.

It will be seen that a spurt in production has the added advantage of (1) permitting a higher utilization factor to be obtained by the Atlantic Railroad and the main intercity highways and hence a lower cost of transport, and (2) obviating the necessity of extending penetration roads indefinitely in all parts of the country. Reduced transport costs, in turn, favor industrialization, mechanization, and concentration of agriculture and exports—all elements of the breakthrough program.

Greater Productivity of Urban Labor

The proposed program should increase the productivity of urban labor in various ways by permitting it to share in the economies resulting from more intensive use of existing equipment, in promotions, and in the opportunities for greater specialization. In addition, it would be desirable that as many as possible of the various religious and patriotic holidays be transferred to the nearest Sundays and the former holidays be made Double-Pay Days.

The Apprentice Training Institute (SENA) could well utilize its own buildings, equipment, and staffs more intensively in increased training programs. In general, too much emphasis seems to be given to industry. Actually, only a relatively small percent of the additional jobs would be in manufacturing, and there would be a greatly increased demand for men skilled in trades, building construction labor, chauffeurs, salesmen, artisans, etc. It is just as important that there be more shoemakers as that there be people manning shoemaking machines in factories, and that there be people to transport, sell, and clean things as well as people to make them.

In the future, with the urban tendency toward smaller families and with housewives doing more of their own housework, the great pool of labor represented by domestic servants can be drawn into other occupations before marriage.

---

with Barranquilla). Published in the *Report to Congress of the Minister of Public Works,* 1960.

Education

If, after the first three years of the plan, 60 percent of the children are actually receiving a full six-year primary education and the opportunity to continue with a five-year secondary education, and if they are free from debilitating diseases and are receiving a better-balanced diet, a major accomplishment will have been achieved in this field. If, in the next ten years, this percentage can be raised to 70 or 75 percent and the remaining 25 to 30 percent are receiving at least three to four years of much better training and care than now, the problem will be largely solved, and the country will be well on its way to achieving, through peaceful means, a classless society.

It will be said that we cannot afford the expenditure and that we must first strengthen our economic base, that teachers do not exist, that the program discriminates against rural children, that the government is proceeding as fast as it is financially and physically able to raise the general level in both cities and the country, and so on. In answer to the first objection, it is proposed to provide the necessary additional facilities and manpower not by restricting present consumption levels, but by utilizing the present slack in the system to produce more goods. The discrimination is more nominal than real. Providing a year of schooling by an incompetent teacher to an unhealthy child, which is now the practice in rural areas, may be a sop to one's conscience, but it is little else. At least the program could concentrate on better salaries for rural teachers, better utilization of existing facilities, and school lunch and vermifuge programs. To try at this time to provide adequate, universal, and complete primary training for all rural children, with accompanying health measures, is obviously out of the question and would be proposed only for demagogic reasons.

It is earnestly hoped that the curriculum for public primary schools will be revised and that the present system will be modified so that many more children will remain in school for five years and will have the benefits of passing to higher grades with different teachers. Again, we repeat, the important thing at these ages is not what is formally learned, but the formation of character, discipline, team spirit, and the keeping of regular hours. It is in these latter characteristics that the Colombian primary school system has its worst weakness.

On the matter of teachers for the city program, emergency measures may have to be devised. The first measure would be to raise salaries. Secondly, emergency training programs can be provided for graduates of secondary schools. Thirdly, use can be made of publicity and patriotic appeals to recruit such graduates to bridge the period before a sufficient number of professional teachers can be attracted and trained. The fact that the big expansion will be in the larger cities will greatly facilitate the recruitment of teachers. In this and other problems connected with the carrying out of the program, it must be born in mind that incredible things can be accomplished if there are the will and enthusiasm, as in wartime, and little can be done in their absence.

This is perhaps the place to say a word on economic education, which is a thorny and controversial subject. I can do no more than state my personal conviction that there are too many undergraduate faculties of economics in Colombia, teaching the wrong kind of economics in the wrong way. I would like to have more elementary courses in economic theory available for university students in general, to separate the teaching of business administration from economics, to restrict teaching for students who wish to become professional economists to not more than two graduate schools for the time being, and again, to have the emphasis in these schools on theory. For the present, the further specialization could be more profitably gained abroad, and teaching and research after a student's return would be essential requirements for the final degree. From this point of view, advanced mathematics would not be a universal requirement but an optional specialty. The present need is not so much for numbers as for quality, and for different specialities and types of mind. The trend toward identifying economics with a certain type of quantitative and mathematical economics, and of making this a universal pattern, is, I believe, of serious concern to the country.[7]

Fiscal Policy

The actual fiscal picture can change so rapidly that there is no point in discussing a situation which, it is hoped, is passing (that of 1962–1965). Of longer-term interest, however, is the incidence of the tax burden. Only a careful quantitative study could determine this with any exactitude. But if, as suggested in the diagnosis, it is found that, through a combination of legal exemptions, evasions, the nature of new taxes, and the exchange differential, the tax system has become much more regressive, the obvious policy would be to attempt to restore its progressivity. This would require a thoroughgoing study of the present exemptions and evasions (legal and otherwise) and of the real incidence of the tax burden as a prerequisite for reforms in the system as well as in the enforcement, collection, and liquidation procedures.

The same study should take into account the productivity and elasticity of the tax base of the various levels of government in relation to long-term

[7] Apparently this view is shared by Howard Ellis. See the excellent book by Howard Ellis, Benjamin Cornejo, and Luis Escobar, *The Teaching of Economics in Latin America,* Pan American Union, 1963. My own views are elaborated in *La Enseñanza de la Economía en Colombia* (*The Teaching of Economics in Colombia*), Ediciónes Tercer Mundo, Bogotá, 1965.

trends of requirements. Offhand, contrary to popular belief, it would appear that the requirements of the national government and the larger cities are growing relative to those of the state governments. The ineffectiveness of tax exemptions as a spur to development was discussed earlier.

Naturally, it would be desirable that part, at least, of the sums destined for rural areas be diverted to purposes of the program. The so-called investment expenditures for roads, waterworks, sewers, and schools in rural areas and small towns have never been examined with real care and from the point of view of relative priorities. Frequently, a road that can promise little traffic will be given preference over the widening of a road like that from Bogotá to its suburb Fontibón, which carries 10,000 vehicles a day. The greater the contribution the national government could make to the necessities of the larger urban centers through a national home finance corporation and a national development fund, the faster the overall program could proceed.

Monetary Policy

There is not much to be said about this policy except that every effort should be made to avoid inflation, with all its bad consequences. It would doubtless be helpful if this were solemnly declared to be an essential part of the government's program and the monetary board were charged with carrying out the policy, insofar as inflation was attributable to excessive expansion in the means of payment. Prompt publication of the relevant statistics and discussion of their significance by the board would be helpful. By writing an escalator clause into all home mortgages in the manner proposed in the housing section of this study, popular awareness and interest in the avoidance of inflation would support a firm policy.

To handle emergency financing, such as coffee retention and temporary government deficits, efforts could be made to anticipate the needs and to organize a consortium among the private banks to handle the situation with minimum recourse to the central bank. The importance and significance of the monetary control function of the central bank should be stressed on every occasion, and the concomitant significance of loans of the bank as providing reserve funds, rather than funds for expansion, which has been the dominant view up to now. Reserve requirements and rediscount privileges need a careful review from the standpoint of monetary control.

In Colombia, the avoidance of inflation requires that monetary policy be backed up by a fiscal policy that does not necessitate borrowing from the central bank, and an incomes policy is needed to avoid intolerable pressure on the monetary authority to authorize expansion for supporting a level of costs and prices initiated by nonmonetary factors. Another element that would assist monetary policy would be that of raising depreciation allowances under certain conditions which would increase saving and reduce the pressure to borrow from commercial banks.

It must be admitted that the proposed program would put pressure on prices, especially agricultural prices, to meet the increased demand. Policy should be to try to counteract this pressure by coordinating monetary and fiscal policy with other more direct instruments and policies, particularly in the industrial fields, always provided that sufficient stimuli are left to increase production in essential lines. A small rise in agricultural prices relative to others would be sufficient to supply the stimulus in this field.

Industrialization Policy

By and large, the profit motive is relied upon to meet effective demand when it pays to do so, since Colombia has an alert and able entrepreneur class. However, it is proposed that the state, acting chiefly through the two new administrative organizations, and possibly a new ministry of urban affairs, provide certain incentives and deterrents (1) to secure a more intensive utilization of existing equipment, especially in the consumer goods industries and industries supplying them; (2) by making loans, granting accelerated depreciation allowances, and making foreign exchange available if these are needed to prevent bottlenecks and provide for rapid expansion of industries approaching capacity three-shift operations (3) in influencing the location of new plants in accordance with the master plan of urban development.

In determining priorities and depreciation allowances, preference would be given industries making mass consumer goods, public services, additional industrial capacity necessary for urban housing, agricultural equipment, transport, and any equipment needed for developing exports. In order that the maximum number of jobs can be created quickly, it is suggested that heavy and secondary industries which, though eventually desirable, will need a lot of foreign exchange, heavy protection, and time to get in production, be delayed until the second stage of the program, unless all their exchange requirements can be met by foreign investors.

An analogy that might be of some help in guiding the administrators of the program is that of wartime, where the aim is maximum possible production of war material and the subordination of projects that do not promise a contribution to the war or are too costly in resources or time. The end would be vastly different, however. The program would not entail rationing of consumer goods, but rather the avoidance of rationing. Once the market for basic consumer goods is greatly expanded, the internal production of many intermediate and capital goods will become so profitable that the establishment of industries in these fields may have to be controlled rather than forced, as now.

In certain fields, study might be given to the possibility of avoiding waste by pooling resources. The Colombian market is too small to permit the economies of scale in certain fields where the market must be split among fifteen or twenty separate firms. But it might prove possible for all interested representatives of, say, foreign trucks and jeeps to pool their resources into two assembly plants and secure the license to assemble trucks under neutral names for distribution within the country.[8] The suggestion is offered with a good deal of hesitation, because frequently the wastes caused by excessive competition are much less than the waste resulting from official errors. However, with a little prodding by the government, it might be something that a committee of the National Manufacturers Association, the National Merchants Association, and the Corporaciónes Financieras could profitably give some study to.

Administrative Devices and Public Administration

As has been discussed, the level of public administration, especially in the ministries, is very low. A national economic program must not, if it is to be realistic, rely on a level of administrative competence that is not immediately available. In general, the national program here envisaged does not call for increased activities on the part of the ministries. Rather, it requires (1) planning of a high order and (2) a pooling of financial resources to finance a large housing program as well as to provide international loans and foreign-exchange resources for the public services and private industries essential to the overall program.

For the pooling and allocation of financial resources there do not appear to be any existing agencies adequate for the task. Thought should be given, therefore, to creating a new development fund and a home finance corporation. The fund would be in large part the administrator of the program, channeling both peso and foreign funds to break bottlenecks, to expand the capacity of consumer goods industries that are prepared to work on a two- and, where practicable, three-shift basis, and to provide pesos for the urban services and urban housing program. It is suggested that foreign lenders be accorded minority representation on the board of the fund and that technicians be provided to assist the staff of the fund.

The housing finance corporation would take over parts of the staff of the existing central mortgage bank and the housing institute. Probably it should be restricted to financing the acquisition of new and existing homes, in accordance with the overall program. For large-scale renovation projects, it would probably be desirable that each large city have its own organization which would work closely with the housing finance corporation and, with its approval, issue bonds guaranteed by the nation to acquire property.

[8] This would be especially practical if the Venezuelan and Colombian markets could be combined.

A weakness lies in the public administration of the larger cities, particularly in the fields of planning and education that cannot be decentralized in service companies. It would appear desirable that the national urban policy, to apply to all large cities and to include a master plan for the future urban growth of the nation, be worked out initially by an *ad hoc* Presidential commission with an expert staff. Thereafter the ministry of urban affairs, if it were decided to create one, and the larger cities, might set up advisory boards nominated by the professional societies in this field, whose assent would be necessary for changes in the master plan and who could recommend changes.

A great deal would depend on both the independence of the development fund and the support it receives from the government and international agencies. Otherwise inadequate financing, or contradictory fiscal and monetary policies, could ruin any program. Again, much would depend on the ability and tact of the foreign representatives. In Colombia, ever-present dangers are lack of persistency in carrying out a program, excessive readiness to compromise, and sectionalism—dangers that the foreign representatives could help to combat.

Up to this point I have suggested a coordinated program in various fields as a means of resolving the various problems set forth in an earlier section. There remains, however, the problem of public administration in general. This may appear extraneous and unrelated to our major economic and social problems, but in reality it is vitally connected with them. The country simply cannot hope to achieve the desired economic goals without modernizing its manner of conducting public business and making it much more efficient. The routines have not changed in essentials for forty years, or since the Kemmerer Mission. Methods which even then were archaic and out of date have persisted to this day. The only difference is in the economic role of the state, which has grown tremendously in importance since the 1920s. What was perhaps tolerable then is becoming intolerable now: The objective underlying the conduct of public affairs is not efficiency but rather the safeguarding of public funds.

One cannot deny, of course, the importance of honesty in government. But there are various ways of ensuring this objective without such a sacrifice of efficiency as now occurs. The whole system of multiple responsibility (in which no one is responsible), multiple signatures, endless shuffling about of papers, preaudit and postaudit (Kemmerer's fatal error in not appreciating the difference between auditing and accounting has cost Colombia untold millions), monthly budget allotments, archaic tax enforcement methods, and complete disregard for the convenience of the public, is costing the country heavily in unnecessary bureaucracy, unnecessary delays, and a great waste of time on the part of anyone who has anything to do with government, which includes practically everybody. The other source of inefficiency lies in the lower pay and generally lower quality of personnel as compared with private business.

This indictment and the indicated remedies we set forth in considerable detail in the public administration report of 1951.[9] Unfortunately, no attention was paid to the suggestions, and conditions have since become worse rather than better. Some improvements have been achieved in the organization of the ministries, but the basic methods and routines have remained virtually untouched.

Since few people in Colombia have either the familiarity with modern government methods of conducting business or the requisite prestige to be listened to, only a very strongly headed and staffed foreign mission, drawn from the governments who have made notable progress in this field, and strongly supported by the President, offers hope of instituting basic reforms. Even then, the job will be a difficult and time-consuming one. Sooner or later—sooner, it is devoutly to be hoped—it must be done. The government today is big business, spending large sums a year, and it should not be conducted like a notary's office.

Programming Techniques

Macroeconomics has become so identified with national accounts and sector analysis, and quantitative programmers have become so accustomed to think in terms of the capital-production ratio approach, that the actual programming of the approach suggested here poses peculiar difficulties. It requires not only different emphases—a different slant, as it were—but also data that there has been no interest in collecting yet. Past relationships, while helpful in certain parts of the program, can be definitely misleading in other parts, because it is the very essence of a breakthrough program to break with past relationships, to change radically and quickly the relation of the stock of capital to output, the relation of the annual addition of capital to production, the relation of employment to capital, the productivity of employment, the relation of imports to output, and the composition of investment and indeed of the whole GNP.

Another difficulty that has possibly more theoretical than practical importance is the disentangling of the additional labor and more intensive utilization of capital aspects of the program from the "normal" growth in productivity, capital formation, and "normal" additions to the labor force aspects. Still another would be the forecasting in quantitative terms of the better allocation of the labor force in terms of remuneration. Averaging the return of highly mechanized farm operations with those of subsistence

[9] *Reorganización de la Rama Ejecutiva del Gobierno de Colombia* (Reorganization of the Executive Arm of the Colombian Government), a report of a mission directed by Lauchlin Currie, National Press, Bogotá, 1952.

homesteaders may be more misleading than helpful. What we are interested in is putting idle (in a true economic sense) people to work for a longer work year producing especially articles of mass consumption (including housing and public services) by the more intensive utilization of existing and new equipment. Ideally, for a time practically all the imports and new internal capital formation (with the exception of housing and inventories) would be of the bottleneck-breaking sort permitting more intensive and productive utilization of the existing stock of capital. An exceptionally large proportion of internal capital formation would go not into additional factory construction but into homes, public services, and inventories until the emergency phase of the operation slacked off. Then increasing attention would have to be paid to increasing productive capacity by means other than more intensive use of existing factors. Even then, much of the additional capacity could be planned for two- or three-shift use, thus continuing the break with past relationships.

Under these conditions, there are hazards in projecting the income elasticities of demand for goods in the various sectors on the basis of past relationships, since the heavy emphasis on increasing the buying power of the poorer segments of the population may, and indeed should, change past patterns. Insofar as success was achieved in cutting down the numbers of subsistence farmers, the apparent commercial effective demand for foodstuffs should increase by more than would be suggested by the past income elasticity of demand for food. And so on.

Obviously, programming a crash or breakthrough program that entails profound and induced structural changes in the economy also entails imagination and inventiveness analogous to that required in wartime. One should no more demand complete assurance of accuracy in projections than is demanded in wartime.

Two early pioneering studies on the quantitative side were made in Colombia. One, by Oscar Gómez, was based on a questionnaire to industrial firms on excess capacity. A good sample was obtained on the basis of which it could be affirmed (in 1961) that the great majority of firms operated on a single shift. The main exceptions were the spinning, weaving, and finishing cotton textile plants and certain plants where it was too expensive to suspend the operation of furnaces.

The other study, also contracted by the Foundation for the Progress of Colombia, was made by Jorge Ruiz Lara.[10] This is a pioneering study relying heavily on past relationships and weak statistical data. In reality it is a study of the possible impact in Colombia on demand and the value of production resulting from a given increase in urban jobs in a given period, and as such it is most interesting. It relies on the continuance of a high

[10] Some of the findings were published under the title "Aspectos Cuantitativos de la Operación Colombia" (Quantitative Aspects of Operation Colombia), *Review of the Controller General's Office,* Year Five, vol. 20, 1963, pp. 30–35.

ratio of capital to production and does not attempt to assess the impact of more intensive use of equipment and imports and the effect of a longer work year. It furnishes, however, a basis for future work, and it demonstrates that a combination of past trends in productivity, plus sufficient additional nonagricultural jobs to permit an absorption of the annual addition to the work force, plus a small net shift (120,000 in three years) out of agriculture would in themselves be consistent with a 4.7 percent increase in annual per capita production. When to this are added the various steps proposed herein, the possibilities become truly alluring.

As remarked, the statistical data are not too trustworthy. They suggest a high ratio of capital formation or saving to production (26 percent). On an incremental basis a peso of increase in the GNP is associated with 261 centavos increase in internal capital formation on a constant price basis—a capital coefficient widely different from that of most other countries. In Ruiz's own projections from 1963 to 1966, he has the increase in production double the increase in capital formation.

A finding of much interest is the relation of industrial jobs to other nonagricultural jobs, estimated at 312,000 to 2,617,000 in 1963. Of his projected increase in nonagricultural jobs of 670,000 in three years, he anticipates that only 100,000 of these would be factory jobs, giving a ratio of 1 factory job to 5.7 nonfactory urban jobs.

Another finding of great relevance to the present study is the sharp fall in imports relative to the GNP after 1956, which apparently was associated with a policy of imposing tighter direct controls, giving priority to capital goods, and seeking to substitute for imports.[11] There appear to be even greater possibilities still in this field by utilizing the bottleneck criterion.

For the purposes of the approach set forth here, some insight may be gained from a study of individual firms. Apparently, it was during the Second World War that the few large cotton textile mills decided to go to a three-shift, longer-work-year basis despite the 35 percent surcharge on wages for night work. In any case, it was a momentous decision for the country and raised the hours worked per year to 80 percent of the possible hours, in contrast to 20 percent in most other industries. "In other words, to produce the same yardage . . . would have required nearly four times as many looms and presumably spindles and other equipment in like proportion. The saving is not only measured by the interest or earnings and depreciation that did not have to be paid, earned or charged on this additional equipment but also in the heightened productivity per worker resulting from continuous operation."[12]

Another study, private and unpublished, of an individual capital-intensive company indicates that by building up its operations to a three-shift basis,

[11] *Ibid.*, p. 33.

[12] Lauchlin Currie, *El Algodón en Colombia,* chap. V.

it could increase considerably its profits and reduce its costs and prices, even after paying the labor surcharge. It could triple its production and labor force with a relatively small additional expenditure to permit twenty-four-hour-a-day, six-day-a-week operation in all operating departments. In the case of less captial-intensive companies, the advantage to the individual firm would be less marked, but there would still be savings possible.

The evening peak in consumer demand for electric power would probably pose a problem in some cities. In the case of the textile companies mentioned above, supplementary power facilities are maintained. In Bogotá, rationing of advertising and commercial use has on occasion been resorted to.

In Chapter 8 it was pointed out that a reduction of the rural gainfully employed from 50 percent to 40 percent of the total in three years in a country where the total working force is growing by 3 percent would require an addition to the urban labor force of over 30 percent. This would be a tremendous undertaking but, viewed in the light of wartime achievements, not an impossible one. In Colombia the working force is probably increasing less than the growth in population, which appears to have been rising in the past ten years. If we assume, then, that the natural growth is 2.3 percent (or 367,000 in three years), and in addition jobs are found to permit a decline of 4.6 percent a year in the rural work force (343,000 in three years), the task becomes one of creating a grand total of 710,000 new urban jobs, as well as housing and public services for approximately 500,000 family units.

As remarked earlier, it may well prove impossible (1) to mobilize a sufficiently large portion of the annual saving to permit building enough decent permanent homes and (2) to prevent the increase in total investment from increasing gross product by more than the physical production can be increased in this period, in which case we would have to resort to dormitories for some of the single workers and even to temporary housing. After all, in wartime a sizable portion of the "working force" is customarily so housed. In any case, it is precisely to provide a much larger volume of funds than previously for housing and public services that it was proposed to curtail luxury housing and office construction temporarily and to give inducements to companies in mass consumption industries to pass to two- and three-shift operation. It would be the task of the programming office not to follow past relationships but to break them. It must be remembered that the diversion of factories, labor, and materials in wartime from making passenger cars to producing war matériel had no peacetime precedent. We are, it is true, concerned to create jobs or, better, supply more remunerative employment; but not at any cost. The basic objective is to put the poorer segment of the population to work producing the things it is so desperately in need of.

The only notable exception to this rule is the provision of better housing for actual urban workers and the transfer of their houses to the new arrivals.

With this change of emphasis, the important thing is not that the productivity per worker is far higher in a dacron plant than in a carpenter's shop, but rather that the carpenter is making an article of mass consumption for which there will be far greater demand than there existed before for the product of colonial-type rural agriculture. Simple tools or machines that permit immediate employment in industries producing goods of mass consumption, or in industries producing for such industries, are preferable to complex equipment for industries further removed from mass consumption, even though the latter may be more "productive."

Theoretically, therefore, the increase in the value of goods and services resulting from the absorption of the unemployed into work at urban wage scales can be very large, even if a substantial part of the additional employment is in services and construction. More important than the impact on the GNP, however, would be the gain in welfare through the leveling up in the consumption of the poorer classes. This leveling-up process can result from the imposition of wartime types of controls and the natural pursuit of self-interest. But it can be helped along by the state, which can provide special assistance for training and placement to enable people to leave the most depressed and overpopulated areas that offer the poorest economic prospects. Otherwise, people in such areas may be entangled so hopelessly in their vicious circles that the breakthrough may not reach them, and their numbers and misery can in time defeat our best efforts.

It seems clear that a program of taking up slack by creating more better-paying jobs will have the effect of increasing saving in absolute terms. Whether it will increase saving relative to income (i.e., reduce the propensity to consume) is less certain. It would appear reasonable to assume that the nature of the program here proposed would have that result, since it would mean a sudden and large increase in all incomes, restraints on luxury expenditures, and a new and marked increase in saving to pay for the new housing. Should this be the case, the multiplier would decline and the investment program could be stepped up without danger of an excessively large total demand emerging in relation to the physical ability to meet it.

Government tax revenues would naturally increase and with them government expenditures. Dernburg and McDougall have argued that this development in itself would lead to a further increase in disposable private income.[13] To the extent that this point is valid, it would complicate our problem. I shall, therefore, consider it briefly. In the illustration used by these authors, a 20-billion increase in taxes-government expenditure leads to a 20-billion increase in disposable private income.[14] This surprising result

[13] T. F. Dernburg and D. M. McDougall, *Macro-Economics,* McGraw-Hill Book Company, New York, 1960, pp. 84–85. Also Paul A. Samuelson, *Economics,* 5th ed., McGraw-Hill Book Company, New York, 1958, p. 279.

[14] This is quite apart from the increase in national income that results from

arises by assuming an unchanging propensity to consume and from the fact that a multiplier of 4 (marginal propensity to consume of 0.75) is applied to the increase in government expenditure to give a total increase of 80 billion whereas the additional taxes reduce consumption by only 15 billion (and saving by 5 billion). Applying the same multiplier to the reduction in consumer expenditures gives a total reduction of 60 billion. Therefore total disposable private income has been increased by 80 billion minus 60 billion, or by 20 billion.

But if we change our assumption to one that envisages a decrease in the propensity to consume as income increases, we arrive at a different result. Let us assume it declines to 0.68. The multiplier then becomes 3.1. The net increase in disposable private income is reduced to 62–60, or 2 billion. Considering that earlier the authors postulated a point of zero saving (at 100 billion income), it would seem reasonable to expect that a rise from 180 billion to 260 billion would be accompanied by a decrease in the propensity to consume.

The theoretical point we have just considered calls attention to the danger of too easy reliance on the saving-investment approach in quantitative planning and the continuing necessity to "feel one's way." Not only is it impossible to predict with any certainty the movement in the propensity to consume in a rapidly developing situation, but also a relatively small variation in the propensity (from 0.75 to 0.68 in the example above) can result in such a relatively large change in the multiplier (from 4 to 3.1). Actually, more reliance on controls and less on quantitative forecasting does not appear to be too serious an objection to undertaking a breakthrough in development.

We may summarize the technical task that would confront the programmers, if this approach were adopted, as follows:

1. Determination of the goal in terms of nonagricultural employment. This should be high enough to provide not only for the addition to the work force but also for a net movement from rural to urban areas.
2. Determinations of first approximations of the distribution and localization of the additional jobs and in terms of value of additional demand, production, investment, and consumption.
3. Appraisal of the reasonableness of the first approximations (time and resources to break emerging bottlenecks, time and stimuli required to reach goals in production of goods of mass consumption, synchronization of housing programs with job programs by cities, etc.).
4. Revision of overall and individual sector goals and working out of overall and industry programs to achieve goals. (At this stage problems of timing

---

the inclusion of additional government expenditure not offset by the deduction of additional taxes from private income.

would become most important, especially in rate of increasing housing and public service construction, rate of cutting back luxury and other types of construction, application of bottleneck criteria to exchange rationing, time required to increase agricultural and textile production, and so forth.)

5. Organization of sector and regional committees to revise goals, enforce price and incomes policies, work on capital goods and financial requirements, and reconcile urban planning to program.

6. Reconciliation of financial with physical aspects of overall program.

7. For Colombia, the pioneer studies of Jorge Ruiz Lara and Oscar Gómez offer a convenient point of departure and would permit an acceleration of the programming stage. What has not yet been begun is both a rigorous and an imaginative study of the possibilities of economic integration of the contiguous and partly complementary, partly competitive economies of Venezuela and Colombia.

8. A properly weighted cost-of-living index for the working class would be a valuable aid in determining the criteria for utilizing various controls and in forecasting income demand elasticities. The pioneer index for Colombia, constructed by Jacob Perloff in 1953, may need revision.

Economists who have been concerned with the theory of growth would probably be inclined to emphasize in the proposed approach the dangers and problems raised by the acceleration principle (induced investment), both in the upward surge and in the deceleration phase. If, however, we are aware of the nature of the problems and have in our arsenal a combination of indirect inducements and restraints, as well as an assortment of direct controls, the job of taking up slack and later maintaining intensive and maximum use of existing and new capital should not be insuperable. The fact that mistakes would undoubtedly be made and that demand in various sectors would probably outstrip supply elasticities, thus resulting in exhaustion of inventories and pressure on prices, is not in itself a valid reason for not making the attempt. It would be most unreasonable to be asked to guarantee a smooth, efficient operation before consideration is given to the adoption of a general policy which has already been worked out successfully by one important sector of one important industry.

While every effort should be directed toward the stimulation of goods and services of mass consumption, undoubtedly problems will arise both in the domestic and foreign markets from the growing incomes of the well-to-do classes—problems similar to those that arose from the same phenomenon in wartime. Through taxation and the provision of attractive investment instruments, effort must be made to channel this buying power to the financing of housing and the other purposes of the program, and to prevent it from diverting internal factors and foreign exchange in undesirable ways. Again, full awareness and publicity concerning the nature of the problem and the reason for the means taken to meet it would be essential in securing support to resist the growing pressure for consumption and investment in luxury-type industries.

After the Breakthrough

There does not appear to be much point in programming too far ahead, though more distant targets should be set and kept in mind. As the initial phase approaches termination, the degree of success in the resolution of the agrarian problem, in the continued mechanization of agriculture, and in the attainment of a decent minimum standard of living for the masses may all be better appraised and be weighed against the growing urban stresses and strains and the growing backlog of delayed types of construction. It may very well prove advisable to provide a breathing spell to give the lagging sections in the economy a chance to catch up and to plan for a renewed period of accelerated development. As success is achieved in attaining the initial goals, more attention may be paid to basic reforms such as public administration, tax reform and administration, a national program of balanced urban development, continued export diversification and technification, and so forth.

However, it must be kept in mind that a breakthrough program is not a single short program. The whole point of such a program is that it raises an economy to a point where mechanization and technification in agriculture can proceed rapidly, where jobs are waiting for all the workers released from agriculture, where the diversification and growth in exports can provide the growing capital goods requirements, and where falling birthrates offset falling death rates—where, in short, a benign circle replaces a vicious circle. This means that a breakthrough has not really occurred unless the basic developments just mentioned continue until some 10 percent or less of the gainfully employed are in agriculture, until the rate of population growth falls to 1 percent or less, until the rungs of the educational ladder are available for all, until we have passed beyond the pain economy, until basic equality of income, consumption, and opportunity prevails, and until all people have some protection from the economic insecurity of life.

The magnitudes and the efforts mentioned as appropriate for Colombia undoubtedly will have the effect of making most people think that a breakthrough is not worth the effort. But without this effort it is difficult to see how the vicious circle of poverty, and particularly the high rate of population growth, can be broken in those countries which despite so large a percentage of rural population can afford modern programs of preventive medicine. Perhaps the galvanizing effect can result from new wars or, as in certain regions in Chile, from an earthquake. It would be too bad, however, to wait upon wars and catastrophes to do what we should have the wit and the will to undertake deliberately in order to remold and reshape our environment. It may be that we do not have too much time to make it possible for great numbers in the developing countries to gain meaningful control of their economic destinies.

Surveying developments since the Second World War, I believe that the burden of proof is on those who still believe that a well-intentioned sprinkling of good works and loans is all that the problem requires for its solution. The group of countries under survey desperately need help to break the vicious circles in which they are enmeshed. But that help must be meaningfully and purposefully directed. Consequently the final answer will depend not only on the leaders of those countries but also on the economists of the developed countries. It is to be hoped that they will join with other disciplines in attempting to give guidance first to the harassed leaders of national and international organizations, and secondly to leaders of one or more developing countries, to see if a practical solution is available to the most urgent problem of our time. Economists have never hesitated to drop their academic work when their countries were at war. Surely a situation where two-thirds of the world's population has only one-sixth of its income, *and the proportions are daily worsening,* merits as much concern as a war. Even if some countries, by good fortune, great effort, or both, escape to the ranks of the "haves," "It is hardly an attractive prospect that less than half of the world may be living in a slick, clean, and immensely prosperous industrial civilization, while the majority remain shut in a vast agricultural slum."[15] This is not a hysterical forecast. It is a sober possibility that would result from a continuance of existing trends in large areas of the world.

A final question: Is a breakthrough possible in countries whose conditions differ significantly from those of Colombia? It is difficult to answer this question in the abstract. However, any country that is competent to wage a war, i.e., to mount an effort on top of its existing effort, or to change the composition and distribution of existing production, should theoretically be able to make a much greater effort to break its vicious circles than it is now doing. Matters discussed here then become relevant. Is the labor force badly distributed, as shown by differences in income? Why? How can a better distribution be attained? Is cost-push inflation a factor? Is inequality lessening, or growing? If the latter, are distortions in the pattern of production, consumption, and investment appearing? If so, how can the country secure a more rational pattern (rational, that is, from the point of view of the standard of living of the masses)? How much slack is there in the system? What are the early bottlenecks and how might they be broken? Can a breakthrough be programmed leaving exchange freely convertible? Should the emphasis on more roundabout, heavy projects be reduced while other and perhaps more urgent things are attended to? Are

[15] Raymond Frost, *The Backward Society,* St. Martin's Press, Inc., New York, 1961, p. 14.

there neighboring countries with whom exports and imports can simultaneously be increased? Would agricultural technification be accelerated if returns to farmers were higher?

Once there occurs a reorientation in goals, measures, and techniques, all these and other questions posed in this book become relevant. They can be answered only in the light of the problems and conditions facing each underdeveloped country.

CHAPTER 15

Conclusion: A Checklist of Elements in the Plan

So many topics have been touched upon that it may be useful though dangerous, to present a brief checklist—useful for recalling the highlights, dangerous because a checklist can never do justice to an integrated plan. The topics have been grouped under four major headings: the objective, the diagnosis, the means and the prerequisites. I believe it is helpful and indeed necessary to treat these separately even though together they form a coordinated and, it is hoped, an internally consistent and defensible plan. What is lacking is the quantitative programming. At this stage, however, it seems more important to focus attention on broader issues—on the objectives and strategy as applied to a certain group of developing countries. The development of special programming techniques adapted to meet the peculiar requirements of this type of plan in a particular country must wait acceptance of the plan.

1. **The objective:** To break the vicious circle of poverty (ignorance—low productivity—high rate of population growth—poverty) by a single concentrated effort to raise the standard of living of the poorest half of the people.

2. **The diagnosis:** Disguised mass rural and small town unemployment, excessive competition in agriculture, insufficient labor mobility, monopoly elements in industry and organized labor, urban wage inflation, inequality, distortion of consumption and resource allocation patterns, small market, small degree of utilization of capital equipment, high rate of population growth, high relation of dependents to wage-earners, sectionalism, faulty public administration, economic illiteracy and lack of dedication.

3. **The means:** Creation of additional urban jobs in housing and

public services, an incomes policy, curtailment of luxury building, increase in demand for and production and consumption of goods and services of mass consumption, removal of surcharge for night work, rationing of exchange and accelerated depreciation allowance to secure more intensive utilization of existing equipment, reduction of existing number of holidays, new policies of national urban development and housing, underwriting of part of foreign cost of program by an international lending group, participation of representatives of group in programming through a development fund, means to channel national savings to investment requirements of program, escalator clauses in financing houses, national housing authority, export and exchange policies, programming and data requirements, use of industry committees, tax and public administration reforms, work on second and third stages after initial trial and the setting of new targets.

4. **Prerequisites:** Support of leading economists in developed countries, separation of planning and programming—subordination of latter to former, willingness of international group to make experiment and willingness of suitable country to adopt the plan, development of programming techniques to requirements of new objectives and of the plan, development of criteria for building licensing and exchange licensing, development of criteria for incomes and price policies, development of necessary current statistical series for control and information purposes.

Index